FLORA TRISTAN was born in Paris in 1803, the daughter of a French mother and a Peruvian-Spanish father. Her first publication was a pamphlet, *Nécessité de faire un bon accueil aux femmes étrangères* (1835). This was followed in 1838 by her autobiography, *Pérégrinations d'une paria*, which made her famous, and in the same year she published her only novel, *Méphis*. In 1839 Flora Tristan visited England for the fourth time and wrote her *London Journal* which was published in French in 1840 and 1842 as *Promenades dans Londres* and ran to four editions. Astonishingly, this translation of the popular 1842 edition is its first appearance in English.

In 1843 Flora Tristan published her manifesto, *L'Union ouvrière*, calling for a world-wide Workers' International. Many of the ideas formulated in it were used by Marx in his 1848 *Manifesto*. The following year she travelled through France addressing workers' meetings, making a record of this in her *Tour de France* which remained unpublished until 1973. While on her journey, Flora Tristan contracted typhoid fever and died at Bordeaux at the age of forty-one and was mourned throughout France as 'the worker's saint'. Her last book, *L'Emancipation de la femme*, was completed by Alphonse Constant and published posthumously in 1845.

JEAN HAWKES is a graduate in French from St Anne's College, Oxford. She spent a year in Peking, where she taught English to Chinese students. Married with four children, for the past three years she has been researching and working on the writings of Flora Tristan in Oxford, where she lives.

The London Journal
of
FLORA TRISTAN
1842

 *or*

The Aristocracy and the Working Class of England

A Translation of
Promenades dans Londres
by
JEAN HAWKES

Virago

Published by VIRAGO PRESS Limited 1982
Ely House, 37 Dover Street, London W1X 4HS

First published in French as *Promenades dans Londres* 1840 & 1842
1842 edition first translated into English by Jean Hawkes, 1982

Typeset by Colset Private Limited

Designed by Adrienne Gear

British Library Cataloguing in Publication Data
Tristan, Flora
  The London Journal of Flora Tristan, 1842.
  1. London—Social life and customs
  I. Title   II. Promenades dans Londres. *English*
  942.1′074′0924   DA688

  ISBN 0-86068-214-5

*The emblem on the title page is
a recreated version of one of
Flora Tristan's personal seals.*

Printed in Great Britain by The Anchor Press Ltd
and bound by Wm Brendon & Son Ltd
both of Tiptree, Essex

Flora's dedication

'We must either find an effective remedy for the scourge of poverty or be prepared for a worldwide upheaval, for poverty may have greater power to destroy society today than slavery had in pagan times.'

Eugène Buret, *The Poverty of the Working Classes in England and France (1840)*

Contents

SKETCHES

List of Plates

Translator's Introduction

Flora Tristan is one of the most attractive figures in the history of nineteenth-century socialism. In her and in her books are combined the conflicting qualities of the aristocrat, the revolutionary, the social scientist, the pariah, the feminist and the visionary. She is at the heart of French Romanticism, she inhabits the Paris of *Les Enfants du Paradis*; yet her voice comes through to us today with astonishing clarity, for in her short life she tried to resolve many of the problems that still confront us. Her goal was nothing less than the rapid and peaceful transformation of society. A contradiction in terms perhaps, but Flora was an impatient lady, full of contradictory impulses, inspired with an active love of humanity and a vision of international harmony, yet constantly driven to attack and criticise friend and foe alike.

This book is a translation of the fourth – the popular – edition of Flora Tristan's *Promenades dans Londres*, published in 1842, an idiosyncratic record of her visit to London in the summer of 1839 which also draws upon her three earlier visits to England in 1826, 1831 and 1835. All I have omitted from it is the introduction, a survey of English politics and economics by an unidentified friend of the author which adds nothing to her work. The text used is a photocopy of the one in the British Library. Flora would never agree to alter anything she wrote, but I have taken the minor liberty of pruning the excessive number of dashes and exclamation marks – sometimes three in a row – which she used when her emotions overflowed.

Beneath the deceptive title of the French original, with its suggestion of leisurely rambles, there lies an indictment of English society. Its villains, as the subtitle makes clear, are not the rising class of industrialists, but the aristocrats. Yet the author was herself an aristocrat by birth: she was born in 1803, the daughter of a French *émigrée* and a Spanish-Peruvian nobleman who met and married in Spain, and set up house in Paris. Flora's early childhood there was idyllic, but her father died suddenly in 1807, his property was confiscated by the French government (as France and Spain were by then at war) and she grew up in comparative poverty in the country, returning to Paris with her mother in 1818. By then her first romantic dreams of marriage had been shattered by the discovery that she was technically illegitimate, as her parents had been married by a priest and never obtained any civil record of their marriage. Thereafter Flora saw herself as the pariah, which was how she insisted on being represented in the many portraits she was to commission in later years. But already she felt she was fated never to experience the 'breath of God', as she described her concept of love.

It was to escape from life with her mother in the poverty of the slums that Flora married her employer, the minor artist and engraver André Chazal, in 1821. The marriage was a failure. Flora left her husband in 1825, a few months before the birth of her third child, Aline, and never lived with him again. André persecuted her for years in his attempts to gain custody of their children, because he believed she was leading an immoral life and was unfit to have them in her care. The full weight of the law was on his side, as women had lost most of the rights they won during the French Revolution. Divorce had been abolished in 1816 and in spite of vigorous campaigning for its restoration it was not until 1884 that it was restored, which explains why Flora presented a petition in favour of divorce to the Chamber of Deputies in 1837, and why she makes such frequent and bitter reference to the indissolubility of the marriage bond. The domestic warfare between husband and wife was to continue for the next thirteen years, with only occasional periods of relative calm in which Flora had the opportunity to attend to her neglected education and study the theory and practice of the social reformers Saint-Simon, Fourier and Robert Owen. In this way she grew aware of the forces which had shaped not only her own life, but the lives of all the poor and oppressed, particularly women. Flora had the advantage of the self-educated in that she was free to form her own judgments. She took from every writer just as much as she found relevant, and she never committed herself to any single doctrine – except of course her own!

After Flora had left her husband her most pressing problem was how to maintain herself and her children, so she left the two boys and their baby sister in her mother's care, and spent part of the years 1825 – 1830 as companion to a succession of English ladies with whom she visited Switzerland and Italy, as well as making her first trip to England in 1826. (Her elder son died in 1828, and while she took her daughter with her whenever she could, her surviving son, Ernest, spent his childhood partly with his father, partly with Flora's mother.) It was in these years that she began to accumulate her impressions of England and the English, but as she later destroyed every shred of evidence relating to this part of her life, on the grounds that she found the memory humiliating, it is impossible to trace the development of her gifts as writer and observer. However, it seems safe to infer that her passionate desire to improve the lot of women and the poor dates from this time, and proceeds from her own misfortunes rather than from an abstract sense of her social duty.

In 1829 a chance encounter with a Captain Chabrié, later to play a crucial part in her life, put her in possession of some useful information concerning her father's family, the immensely wealthy and influential Tristans of Peru. Flora immediately wrote to her uncle Don Pio, the head of the family, in hopes of being recognised as one of his legal heirs, but as she made no secret of the circumstances of her parents' marriage, he felt no obligation to acknowledge her as his elder brother's legitimate daughter, and only replied to her letter in affectionate terms, enclosing a gift of 2,500 francs (£100) and a legacy from his aged mother. News of this windfall made Chazal furious and he renewed his persecution, succeeding in gaining custody of the elder child, Ernest; but this was not enough for him, and he demanded Aline as well. His intransigence so terrified Flora that for six months she roamed France with her daughter, under an assumed name. Then in 1833 when she was virtually penniless, she conceived the bold and desperate plan of going to Peru to confront her uncle in person and throw herself upon his mercy.

It was a hazardous journey. The sea voyage alone took four and a half months, and Flora was the only woman on board, alone with nineteen men. In this unlikely setting she resumed her education. The ship's officers and the only French-speaking passenger instructed her with political discussions and readings from Lamartine, Hugo, Walter Scott, Byron and Voltaire – a nice blend of scepticism and faith – and arias from Rossini as light relief! The captain, that same Captain Chabrié who had befriended her in 1829, offered her not only his protection but his love and life-long devotion; Flora was moved and grateful, but some intimation that she was destined for a higher role kept her from repaying his confidence with her own, and she could not bring herself to confess to him that she had a husband as well as a daughter. In any case, her foremost ambition and the sole purpose of her journey was to claim her rights and gain a fortune, so she kept the poor man in suspense while she pressed on overland to Arequipa (where her uncle lived) and after days of agonising resorted to the ruse of killing his love by asking him to connive at forging a document for her – a dishonourable act to which she knew he would never consent.

This quest for gold marks a turning-point in Flora's life. Had she achieved her ambition and returned to France wealthy – and hence respectable – she might never have written another word, and then she would never have established any claim to the respect and gratitude of posterity. It is just as well that her uncle, though captivated by her beauty, courage and vivacity, refused to do any more for her than continue to make her an allowance; so after seriously considering throwing herself into the revolutionary struggles in Peru, Flora returned to France, via England, in 1835, drained of any personal and material aspirations, but carrying in her journals the raw materials for one of her most attractive works, the *Peregrinations of a Pariah*.

It was to be another three years before this tumultuous chronicle of love, war and travel reached the public. In the meantime Flora made her literary début with a modest pamphlet called *The Necessity for making Foreign Women Welcome*, which contains many of the themes she was to reiterate all her life: the welfare of women, international unity, peaceful co-existence. She announced that she was planning a similar little book on England and this is the first mention of the work that was to appear, in so changed and expanded a form, as the *Promenades* of 1840. But for the moment the only record of her visit to London of 1835 – which she insisted was her first, though there is good reason to doubt her – was published in two issues of the *Revue de Paris* in 1837. Written in the form of letters to an English architect, this account of the various buildings and monuments she observed reveals a predictable admiration for the Gothic style, and raises questions on the functions of architecture which William Morris was to take up in very similar terms in 'Gothic Architecture', his famous lecture of 1889.

Flora sent a copy of her pamphlet on women to Fourier and offered her services in the cause of social reform, but at this point she had to deal with a serious domestic crisis. Chazal had abducted Aline. The little girl was now ten years old, and this was the first time in her life she had seen her father. For the next year or two he kept her in a succession of boarding-schools; on one occasion she ran away to rejoin Flora, but André obtained a magistrates' warrant for her return. She had to be removed by force from her mother's elegant apartment to her father's miserable lodgings and later, when he could no longer afford to send her to school, this was where she had to live. She was desperately unhappy, and one of her letters threw Flora into a state of panic and outrage: Aline had described how one night when she was freezing in her makeshift bed, she had crept in to join her father and brother in theirs, whereupon her father had behaved in a way that upset her very much. Flora immediately had her husband arrested on a charge of attempted incest and took Aline back to live with her, while Ernest returned to his grandmother. André had to spend a month in prison before the case was dropped for want of evidence; this gave him the time to write an account of his wife's alleged misdeeds which he had printed and distributed among his friends. Flora retaliated with her own version of events, which had a considerably wider circulation, since she incorporated it into her *Peregrinations of a Pariah*, published in 1838.

This delightful book – really several books in one – richly deserved the warm welcome it received, for it is written in a vigorous natural style and contains a gallery of memorable characters. Flora describes the terrible voyage round Cape Horn to Valparaiso; the love she inspired in the honourable Captain Chabrié; the encounter with her uncle Don Pio and the rest of the Tristan family; the manners and morals of Peruvian society; the factions involved in the revolutionary struggles and the not inconsiderable part she herself played as intermediary between the warring sides. She added interviews with several of the country's leading personalities, including the President himself. But her frankness did not endear her to the Peruvians, especially Don Pio, who was so incensed by the portrayal of himself as a miser that he had all the copies of the book he could lay hands on publicly burned, and gave orders to stop Flora's allowance.

In the same year, 1838, Flora published her only novel, *Méphis*. Here she sets forth her vision of woman's mission in society: to elevate man's soul above the vanity of worldly ambition and make him capable of great deeds; however, ignorant of her destiny, woman cheapens and betrays her divine gifts by sacrificing herself, deforming her body with corsets (which Flora never wore) and risking her own health and that of future generations all to give man a few fleeting moments of gratification. This blend of romantic exaltation and practical commonsense reflects the degree to which Flora was influenced by the current search for a female Messiah, the woman destined to regenerate mankind. This is a central part of the doctrine of Saint-Simon and Fourier, and finds active expression in the adventures of Prosper Enfantin, an eccentric disciple of Saint-Simon, who after setting up a bizarre community in Paris, went off to Egypt, where he combined the vain quest for a mother-figure for his sect with hard-headed research into the possibilities of constructing a canal at Suez. Flora did not subscribe to Enfantin's cult, but she never lost her faith in the power of woman as a regenerating force.

Meanwhile she was acquiring the reputation of an unconventional, not to say notorious, woman. In March 1838, when she applied for a separation from her husband, André's counsel regaled the court with spicy extracts from the *Peregrinations*. Nevertheless, Flora's application was granted. The Tribunal decreed that Ernest was to go with his father, while Aline was to be apprenticed in whatever trade her parents chose for her. But now it was Flora's mother who precipitated events; although in the past she had always maintained relatively cordial relations with André, she refused to surrender Ernest to him.

This was the breaking-point for André. Over the years he had lost his wife, daughter, profession and home, and it seemed that he was now to lose his only son as well. He became obsessed with the idea that Flora must have a powerful protector beyond the reach of the law, and that the only way to rid society of his wife's corrupting influence was to kill her. Accordingly he bought some pistols and began to practise marksmanship. Madame Tristan was warned that he was planning some desperate act of violence and sent

Ernest back, but it was too late to deflect Chazal from his course, and on 10 September 1838, he lay in wait for Flora and shot her in the back. For some days it was uncertain whether she would live, and all Paris waited to read the daily bulletins on her progress, but at last she began to recover. During her convalescence she returned to her writing and earned warm public approval by addressing a petition for the abolition of the death penalty to the Chamber of Deputies. Meanwhile the sales of *Peregrinations* soared.

Early in 1839 André Chazal went on trial for the attempted murder of his wife. His counsel pleaded extenuating circumstances: M Chazal was a respectable citizen whose mind had been temporarily deranged by the charge of incest and the damaging publicity he had suffered from his wife's book. The Prosecutor was obliged to remind the court that this was a clear case of premeditated and attempted murder, but he allowed that there might be grounds for leniency. The jury brought in a verdict of guilty and Chazal was sentenced to twenty years' hard labour, later commuted to imprisonment alone. He served seventeen years and died in 1860, four years after his release.

His removal from the scene marks another turning-point in Flora's life. She was still only thirty-six, and although – as she wrote to her friend, the artist Traviès, later that year – her hair was beginning to turn white, her heart and mind were still young. The writer Jules Janin gives this picture of her:

'She was admirably pretty – if the two words can go together. She had an elegant supple figure, proud expressive features, eyes full of the fire of the East, black hair long enough for a cloak, a beautiful olive complexion quick to reflect her changing mood when youth and idealism combined to suffuse her cheeks with a consuming flame; fine white regular teeth and a bewitching smile; a graceful bearing, a firm step, an austere style of dress. Young as she was, you could see at a glance that she no longer set out to please or attract compliments on her beauty; such feelings she despised or had long since rejected. . . . Only to see her with her eyes shining, curled up in her armchair like a snake in the sun, you would guess that she was of remote origins, the daughter of sunlight and shadow, a child of warmer countries, lost in the lands of the North.'

Flora was now at the height of her fame; she had an established literary reputation, her apartment was a meeting-place for many of the well-known and controversial figures of the day; every year at least one portrait of her was submitted to the Salon by her good friend Jules Laure, and at the popular Paris balls she was surrounded by gentlemen eager to claim the honour of dancing with her. But to Flora these pleasures soon palled, and within a few months she had left her beloved Paris for the country she regarded as a cultural wasteland, England, where she was determined to expose the hypocrisy of a nation which for so long had been upheld as the seat of all the virtues and the haven of constitutional liberties.

England had gained this reputation because, like Holland and Switzerland, it had for centuries suffered marginally less from the abuse of aristocratic and ecclesiastical privilege than the rest of Europe, and a slightly larger proportion of its citizens was permitted to exercise political rights. England had had a constitutional monarchy since 1688, whereas as late as 1830 the French had driven out their king, Charles X, when he attempted to restore the absolute power of the monarchy. On the other hand, in France the Revolution of 1789 had abolished the feudal dominion of king, nobles and clergy at a single stroke, whereas in England the aristocracy and the landed gentry between them still owned four-fifths of all the land in the United Kingdom; and while England looked askance at any attempt to restore absolute monarchies in Europe, professed support for all subject peoples in their struggles for freedom, and granted asylum to thousands of political refugees from the continent (as Flora herself testified), the establishment was still so terrified of the French Revolution that at home every reformer was regarded as a dangerous revolutionary, and the government refused to take any radical measures to alleviate the distress of the working classes.

It was true that the Reform Bill of 1832 had extended the franchise to the prosperous section of the middle class, but the workers were still excluded, and when Flora arrived in London in May 1839, the Chartists were about to submit their political demands to the House of Commons in the form of the first People's Charter. It was rejected by 235 votes to 46, and there were widespread fears – and hopes – that a revolution was imminent – hence Flora's solemn exhortation to the aristocracy to fear the vengeance of the people and appease their wrath. It was her bitter disappointment at the failure of the Chartist uprising at Newport in 1839 that prompted her contemptuous remark that when it came to revolution, the English were amateurs who should take a lesson from the French, a remark typical of the sort of chauvinism that in her calmer moments Flora utterly repudiated, but in which she so frequently indulged.

However, in most respects Flora's strictures on England were entirely justified. The appalling contrast between wealth and poverty excited the horror, anger and compassion of many observers besides herself. England was at that time the most advanced industrial nation in the world, and London, with a population approaching two millions, was the world's largest city, a magnet drawing thousands of visitors from the continent, most of whom were content to admire its splendours or exploit the opportunities it offered to speculators. But some, like Flora, were more concerned to expose the human suffering on which this conspicuous luxury was based. These critics were not nostalgic for an imaginary idyllic past. They welcomed scientific and industrial advance because it heralded a new age of progress and prosperity for mankind; but seeing all around them the evidence of poverty in the midst of plenty, they demanded that the benefits of progress should be more equitably shared. In comparison with some of the detailed surveys produced at this time, Flora's brilliant forays into London life are the merest sketches, as she herself admits, but she has the advantage in the sheer range of her investigations, and the passionate indignation – today no longer considered compatible with serious inquiry – in which they are expressed.

Flora's observations, though clearly based on personal experience, do not constitute a day-by-day record of her visit; in fact, the amount of straight reporting in the book is comparatively small, and in some chapters does not appear at all. The book opens with an impressionistic description of London seen through the eyes of the bewildered newcomer, followed by an essay on the then fashionable topic of the effect of climate upon mental development. But we are soon on the more familiar terrain of modern sociological inquiry with a powerful evocation of the alienation of the city-dweller, which recalls countless pages from Dickens. Then come first-hand accounts of visits to political meetings, factories, prisons, schools, slums, a brothel, an asylum and the races, all used as a base from which to investigate the functions of institutions in a repressive society, and the evils they both perpetuate and engender. The only omission is a scene of life in the workhouse, surprising when one considers how its shadow darkened the existence of so many workers confronted with the stark choice between it and starvation, which was all the new Poor Law of 1834 allowed them.

The chapter on English women is particularly interesting. It adds a new dimension to our appreciation of the great Victorian women novelists and their frustrated heroines, as well as opening up to the general reader a vast forgotten field of lesser talents. Flora rounds off her book with a series of sketches, uneven in quality, illustrating aspects of English manners and morals.

It is the combination of eye-witness account and authoritative documentation that makes the book so convincing a record of English society in the 1830s, enhanced rather than invalidated by Flora's frequent outbursts of pity and rage. She must be unique among her contemporaries for her instant acceptance of all the pathetic human wrecks she saw in London's slums as her brothers and sisters in the eyes of God, with as much right as she had to food, clothes, shelter and work. Marx, of course, had no use for this early manifestation of socialism with a human face, and dismissed it in the *Communist Manifesto* of 1848 as bourgeois and Utopian. While he praised other social reformers for their attacks on existing institutions, he condemned their failure to recognise the significance of class antagonisms and their refusal to support revolutionary class action.

However tame Flora's views may have seemed to Marx, they were considered sufficiently subversive to preclude any mention of *Promenades dans Londres* in the fashionable, influential periodicals of 1840, though the book was favourably reviewed in the French working-class journals and established her as a serious writer. In England, where it was published in French by W Jeffs of 15 Burlington Arcade, Piccadilly, not a word was ever printed about it save in the Owenist journal *The New Moral World*, and it was not translated into English. Of course, the book sold well in France. Considering Flora's colourful reputation, it could hardly have done otherwise, but she was dismayed to find that it was almost universally interpreted as nothing more than an attack upon England. Flora wanted her readers to learn a lesson from her book, not to gloat over the hypocrisy of their traditional enemy. For her, the key sentence in her preface was: 'I have pointed out the evils of the English system so that we on the continent may make a deliberate effort to avoid them.' So when she revised the book for a new edition at a price the workers could afford, she wrote them a dedication outstanding for its clarity and admirable for its warmth, and she added a foreword to stress her international outlook. She omitted everything which was unlikely to appeal to the workers, like the chapter on the English theatre and the gossipy anecdotes about French *émigrés* in London. But she did not want new generations of workers to be deceived by the myths which had grown up since the death of Napoleon in 1821 and reached a peak following the return of his ashes to France in 1840, so she included a new chapter on Napoleon and Waterloo, representing Napoleon as a tyrant who had betrayed the glorious principles of the Revolution, and Waterloo as a victory for the people against their rulers. Paradoxically, it is in the chapter she omitted from her popular edition, the chapter on the great Welsh reformer, Robert Owen, that we find the clue to the direction her thoughts were taking from 1840 onwards.

Throughout her life, Flora was profoundly influenced by signs and portents, and of all her experiences in England, the one which had the most enduring effect upon her was the encounter with the madman Chabrier in Bethlem Hospital. She interpreted it as a heaven-sent confirmation that she was the prophet destined 'to free woman from enslavement to man, the poor from the rich and the soul from sin'. But she was also a practical woman, and her visit to England showed her how she could translate these ideals into action; she heard Daniel O'Connell address the House of Commons, and took note that it was the pennies of his impoverished compatriots in the Catholic Association that had enabled him to take his seat; she met the venerable Owen and knew, as all Europe knew, of his success in establishing a happy and well-ordered community centred on his factory at New Lanark; she attended a Chartist meeting, which impressed upon her the efficacy of association for political ends. Of all the social reformers whose theories she studied, it was unquestionably Owen who had the strongest and most lasting influence upon her, not least because he had achieved such spectacular results. Yet in the popular edition of her *London Journal*, Flora omitted any discussion of Owen's plans for a new moral order and retained only his ideas on education, which she incorporated into her chapter on infant schools. This was partly because she regarded education as the cornerstone of any programme for the emancipation of the oppressed classes and approved whole-heartedly of Owen's educational philosophy, but also because she detected flaws in his plans for the regeneration of mankind which she felt she was qualified to set right.

Flora criticised Owen for regarding man solely as the product of his environment and failing to take account of his spiritual aspirations, his 'presentiments of infinity'. She described Owen as 'the St John the Baptist who comes to prepare the way for Christ; he is the precursor of another, who will come to complete his creation, give this statue of Prometheus a soul, colour this material life with poetry, and raise a temple for the Arts to embellish with their prestige, a place where divine harmony will lift men's souls towards God and the Blessed Virgin Mary'. Who was to achieve this transformation if not Flora herself? She omitted her earlier appraisal of Owen's blueprint for a new society from the popular edition of the *London Journal* of 1842 because by now she was working on her own model, an improved version in which women were to play a central part as workers, wives and mothers. This was the substance of her new book *L'Union ouvrière* (1843).

Flora's rallying call of 1843 was echoed five years later by Marx. All that united the workers was their poverty, so their first task was to make themselves into a single class, putting behind them the bitter rivalries of the old trade guilds and striving to break down all the barriers between the sexes, trades and nations. Their besetting sin was an outmoded attachment to what they called their liberties, which made them reject any kind of organisation and prevented them from banding together even to fight for the right to work. If France's seven million men and women workers would each subscribe two francs a year to a central fund, they would soon learn that money meant power. Fourteen million francs would enable them to send their representatives to sit in the Chamber of Deputies, ensure that they were properly paid for their labours and enable them to give their children a good education. Only in this way could they eradicate their crippling poverty.

Flora prided herself on being practical and she elaborated a pyramidal structure for the Workers' Union, with ordinary members at its base electing local committees, which in their turn would elect a central committee of fifty (forty men and ten women). This body would be responsible for electing the people's leader, the Defender, who would take charge of the funds and be accountable to the people for his stewardship.

It distressed Flora that the workers had no opportunity to develop their aesthetic sense, so she planned that in every *département* there should be a 'palace', ideally a noble mansion or château with extensive grounds, to serve as a combination of school, leisure centre, hospital and rest-home. It was her cherished hope that celebrated artists and sculptors would contribute works of art to embellish the palaces, and she prepared a series of appeals to likely patrons, including the king, Louis-Philippe.

The new society would be based on belief in a beneficent God and the perfectibility of His creation; the progress of humanity would be fostered by a liberal education for boys and girls alike. Education was the keystone of the new order; children would be encouraged to ask questions and not burdened with useless or irrelevant facts. They would receive training in agriculture and industry as well as a formal education, and would be free to choose a profession or trade to suit their individual tastes and temperament; but whatever their first choice, they would be trained in two disciplines, to counter the risks of unemployment.

The unique and revolutionary aspect of Flora's system is her insistence on the importance of education for women of the working class. In her opinion, culture could not be constrained by divisive notions of class; anybody blessed with eyes and ears could be trained to appreciate art, music and literature. Now she developed the theme she had first expressed in *Méphis: all* women had a unique role to play in society as educators of the rising generation. For this reason their own education should be 'rational, solid, capable of developing all their good instincts', so that they would be 'efficient at their trade, good mothers capable of raising and training their children, natural willing teachers consolidating what their children learned in school, a moral influence on their menfolk from the cradle to the grave'. In other classes of society women were regarded as a refining influence; why should this not be true of working women as well? Begin by educating women, Flora declared, because they are responsible for bringing up male and female children. It was in men's interests to demand equal rights for women, because an educated woman was a companion, whereas an ignorant woman was a burden, resentful of her husband's concern with politics, and regarding all reading, writing and thinking as a waste of time. Flora was soon to discover the uncomfortable truth of this observation for herself, when she began to meet politically committed workers and was subjected to the abuse of their backward wives.

Meanwhile she had to find a publisher for her new book. The so-called progressive publishers refused to touch it, and even the editor of the workers' journal who had reviewed the *London Journal* so favourably declined to serialise it on the grounds that it was too Utopian. So Flora raised the money herself, tramping round Paris in all weathers to collect donations from rich and poor. After the book came out, in 1843, she set off to meet the workers of Bordeaux in person, as a trial run for an extensive tour of France she planned to make the following year, to explain her ideas and persuade workers to join the Union.

In her *Tour de France*, which remained unpublished until 1973, Flora has left us a day-by-day record of this extraordinary crusade which lasted from April to September 1844, and took her to a total of nineteen industrial centres. She found conditions in factories and workshops just as appalling as they were in England; the workers were so cowed that at first she had difficulty in making them understand anything she said, but she persevered. What appealed to them most was the idea of the workers' palaces which seemed like a vision of Paradise.

Flora had agreed in advance to notify the civil, military and ecclesiastical authorities of her presence in every place she visited, as she believed in open campaigning and had no intention of breaking the law. 'I'm here to prevent a revolution, not to start one!' she retorted to one officious police chief. But as her tour proceeded and interest in her ideas grew, she found herself increasingly harassed by the police, her hotel room searched, her papers confiscated, her meetings banned. As if this was not enough, the self-appointed spokesmen for the workers – local small-time politicians and newspaper editors – were jealous and suspicious, one even going as far as to accuse her of being a government agent sent to sow discord among the workers. Flora's comment is characteristic: 'If we're supposed to be making a revolution for people like this, I'd sooner stay with the Pope and Louis-Philippe until the end of time!'

In these trying months, Flora veered between moods of hope and despair. She suffered constantly from headaches, fever and colic – which one doctor treated with doses of arsenic and sulphur – and only her strength of will and faith in her mission kept her going. In her *Tour de France* she looks forward with longing to the vacation in Italy or Spain she plans to take – with her daughter and some congenial gentleman for company – when her tour of France is over.

It was in Lyons that Flora achieved her greatest success. The workers there raised enough money to pay for a third edition of the *Union ouvrière*. Here, too, Flora met Eléonore Blanc, the young laundress she came to look upon as a second daughter and beloved disciple. In Marseilles, Carcassonne, Avignon and Bordeaux, branches of the Union were formed, and in several towns the local press published articles supporting her efforts on behalf of the workers.

But by now Flora was exhausted after months of travel, public meetings, police harassment, and the constant battle against ill-health. She had in fact been fighting to stave off typhoid fever, and when she reached Bordeaux on 26 September, she collapsed; the following day, she had a stroke. A few days later, she rallied, but the disease had too strong a hold upon her weakened constitution for there to be any hope of her recovery. She died on 14 November 1844 at the age of forty-one, and was buried in the Carthusian Cemetery in Bordeaux. Her friends organised a campaign to raise money for a memorial which was unveiled in October 1848, the year of the revolution, at a ceremony attended by nearly eight thousand people. It was the fervent hope of all who had come under the spell of her remarkable personality that her tomb would become a place of pilgrimage for workers all over the world, but Flora's cult was short-lived; the piety of a handful of devoted disciples was not enough to keep her memory fresh. The failure of the revolution of 1848 and the accession to power of Louis Napoleon – the man Flora had derided as a buffoon – made a mockery of any hopes for a new moral order and the peaceful transformation of society.

A few months before her death Flora sent a mass of indecipherable notes to her friend Alphonse-Louis Constant for revision; he wrote them up, adding a good many touches of his own, and published the result as *L'Émancipation de la femme* in 1845. While the style may not be Flora's, the ideas are very much her own: abolition of capital punishment and all prisons, rehabilitation of criminals by humane methods in special centres, the evils of revolution by violence, and a reiteration of her appeal to women of all ages, ranks, opinions and nationalities to help the working classes in their struggle for emancipation.

It was Flora's firm belief that once men were freed from oppression they would work for the emancipation of women, but history had given her little reason for such optimism. In 1789 women threw themselves into the revolutionary struggle with all the fervour and resolution of the men – and what was their reward? Forbidden a voice in the various clubs and assemblies, they formed clubs of their own; one or two of these were too strident and dictatorial, which gave men the excuse they wanted to suppress them all; several of the outstanding women leaders were beaten and humiliated by female hooligans while the men stood by jeering. After the Revolution, women were in a worse position than before; even the limited franchise inherited from feudal society was swept away, together with all the gains of the Revolution, including the right of divorce. Only the law concerning inheritance remained, which decreed that property was to be shared equally between sons and daughters, and this material gain may even have been a drawback to further progress, because it tended to blind women to the fact that they still had no political rights.

Flora's hopes of inheriting great wealth were blighted at an early stage of her career, so she was able to concentrate her energies on reviving the demands made by the feminists of the French Revolution for political emancipation, equal education, entry to the professions, economic independence and the right to divorce. She had much in common with those flamboyant individualists: like Etta Palme von Aelders she exhorted women to educate themselves to be companions for men, not their playthings; like Théroigne de Méricourt she was an impressive orator; like Rose Lacombe she was fearless and excelled in action. Flora was particularly close to Olympe de Gouges, who by an odd coincidence had also been led to believe that she was illegitimate and thus deprived of her rightful inheritance. Olympe wrote plays, addressed a Declaration of the Rights of Women to Marie Antoinette in 1791, and stuck posters all over Paris demanding women's rights. She and Flora were alike in temperament as well; Olympe wrote, 'My first impulse is like a tempest, but as soon as the explosion is over, my mind is perfectly calm' – which is exactly how Flora saw herself.

But of all her feminist predecessors, Flora had most in common with Mary Wollstonecraft, whose *Vindication of the Rights of Woman* came out in 1792. In spite of the years that separate them they proclaim with one voice that men and women are potentially equal in intelligence and powers of judgement, which was just as blasphemous and revolutionary an idea in 1840 as it had been in 1792. They had both suffered at the hands of men, but refused to be trapped in conventional morality; their views on relations between men and women were sensible, compassionate and years in advance of their time – perhaps of ours as well. A woman should be allowed to love according to the dictates of her heart, and any relationship she formed should be condoned as long as it was based on love and not on money. In Flora's eyes an arranged marriage, with its settlement or dowry, was tantamount to prostitution. The impossibility of divorce made the position of an unhappily married woman more difficult, but Flora refused to condemn adulterous women, on the grounds that it was unnatural to insist on a permanent union between beings God had created incompatible. The only honourable course for a woman was to earn her own living, so that if necessary she could support not only herself but her children as well, as Flora had done.

This insistence that women should be self-supporting does not mean that Flora condemned the institutions of marriage and the family outright; but she regarded the self-absorption of the so-called 'happy family' as positively immoral. In her eyes it was a crime to live in oblivion of the poverty and suffering of mankind. When Flora stayed with her wealthy acquaintances Dr and Mme Goin, she was scandalised by the way their children were idolised and indulged: the food they wasted alone would have been sufficient to feed ten workers' families. Flora set a high value on the virtues of frugal living and self-denial she practised herself (though, as was normal in her day, she kept a personal maid, and it is clear from the *London Journal* how much she relied on the practical help of her numerous gentlemen friends). From various remarks scattered throughout her writings, particularly her correspondence, it seems that the paradoxical and elusive relationship she sought was one in which the two partners were united in tastes and temperament and a common desire to devote themselves to suffering humanity – yet free to cultivate intense, not to say passionate, friendships with members of their own and the other sex. This is very civilised but leaves undefined what part, if any, is played by sexual attraction, and there is more to the omission than considerations of decorum alone.

What complicated personal relationships at this time was genuine ignorance of the sexual nature of men and women. Neither sex expected marriage to bring sexual fulfilment. All-male medical opinion asserted that respectable women had no sexual desires anyway, and that men – once they had done their duty as regards the procreation of children – should repress, or sublimate, their own. If this proved impossible there was an expendable class of women available to satisfy their needs and preserve the sanctity of the family home (though one cannot help but speculate on the infections the returning husband brought *into* the sanctuary). Women went into marriage almost wilfully ignorant, and soon resigned themselves to having a houseful of children. There was little likelihood of a stern authoritarian husband unbending sufficiently to become a friend and companion, so they lavished their pent-up affection on women relations and friends. Men and women alike set great store by their intense attachments to members of their own sex, and within these limits they were permitted to demonstrate their affection and emotion to an extent that may seem excessive today. Thus they enjoyed a freedom that we, with our superior knowledge, have lost.

Flora went into marriage at eighteen just as ignorant as the young English girls she derides in her *London Journal*. She was tempted by the prospect of managing a comfortable bourgeois household, and vowed that she would prove a good wife and mother; but all marriage brought her was endless strife over money, impaired health, and three babies she was either unable or unwilling to nurse. Thereafter she went in constant search of a sublime relationship that transcended – or bypassed – sex, and, despairing of finding it in men, was prepared to turn to women, because here, at least, she felt there could be no tiresome sexual complications. Her striking beauty and magnetic personality attracted men and women alike. She found their attentions exasperating and often went to some pains to explain why. As late as 1843 (she was then forty) she received a proposition from a young student which offended her deeply. Her reply was characteristic; she explained that she was not *angry*; she wanted to discover his reason for writing in such a way. Had he read her novel *Méphis*, he would have understood that she held very strong views on love; now he must learn that – as a superior woman – she was not afraid to put them into practice. She claimed for women the right to take the initiative; she was strong enough to behave in the present as all women would behave in the future. If a man attracted her, she would tell him so, but she had never *belonged* to anybody. If her aspiring lover was man enough to accept his dismissal, he was welcome to visit her as a friend; if not, he must stay away for ever.

It was easy enough for Flora to treat male admirers in this way, because she knew perfectly well what they wanted of her. With women, she was not quite so sure: while she was in London in 1839, gathering material for her *London Journal*, she received an impassioned letter from her Polish friend Olympe Chodzko which, she said, sent a thrill of pleasure through her. It is worth quoting part of her long reply because it illustrates how completely Flora was possessed by the exalted spirit of Romanticism.

'. . . But perhaps you are playing with me – if so, beware! For a long time I have wanted to be loved passionately by a woman – oh, how I would have liked to be a man, so that I could have a woman's love. I have reached the point where no man's love is enough for me; perhaps a woman's love would give me what I seek, for a woman's heart and imagination are so much stronger than a man's, and her mind is much richer in resources. But perhaps you will tell me that as physical attraction cannot exist between two people of the same sex, this passionate exalted love you dream of can never be realised between one woman and another? Yes and no – there comes a time in life when the senses change places, or to put it another way, the brain takes them all in its embrace. . . . But you don't understand God, woman, man and Nature as I do – this winter I really *must* instruct you and a few kindred spirits in these things. Nowadays my life is so immense, so complete. Dear sister, I must make you understand: it is as if my soul had shaken off its outer covering; I live with other souls, I identify myself so completely with them that in a way I possess them. I've possessed you for a long time – yes, Olympe, I live in every breath you take and every beat of your heart. One day, even if it frightens you, I must tell you all your regrets, all your desires, and what it is that makes you suffer so. The power of second sight is the most natural thing, just the power of one soul to express what is going on in another. For me, love, *true* love, can exist only between souls. It is all so simple: two women can love in this way, so can two men. I am only trying to tell you that just now I feel an ardent desire to be loved, but I am so ambitious, so demanding, so fastidious and so greedy that nothing I am offered ever satisfies me. . . .'

Whether Olympe was satisfied with her letter, and whether she attended Flora's course of instruction, we do not know. At all events, Flora did not abandon hope of converting her friend to serve in her great crusade, but Olympe was not the stuff of which martyrs are made; her patriotism was shallow and she had no moral courage. She did not even dare to sign her name to the list of subscribers to the *Union ouvrière*, appearing as 'a Polish lady'. Flora treated promising male recruits to her cause just as she treated Olympe: she wrote to the young worker-poet Charles Poncy: 'I'm very interested . . . in taking possession of your soul, your heart and your mind, because I want to use everything that is fine and good in you to help achieve my great and beautiful work.' And during her tour of France in 1844 she was so elated at having made two converts to her Workers' Union that she wrote of them as 'another two beings I have created'.

On a less exalted plane Flora had many good friends among the socialists and feminists of her day, including Pauline Roland, who greatly admired the *London Journal*, wrote her own history of England, supported the revolution of 1848, and after Flora's death, took responsibility for Aline. Other friends were Eugénie Niboyet, who set up an institution for the higher education of women, and the Romantic poet Marcelline Desbordes-Valmore, 'the Christian Sappho' as Proust's friend Montesquiou called her. But Flora's biting tongue and imperious manner sometimes made her enemies. Her relations with George Sand were uneasy: she regarded the famous novelist as an 'armchair reformer' who accepted uncritically everything her worker-informants told her and used it in novels of working-class life which irritated Flora with their implausibility. In her *Tour de France* she ridiculed the notion that a highly-educated woman could ever fall in love with an uncultivated worker. A true reformer should go and live among the workers as she had done; it was a crime for intellectuals like George Sand and Victor Hugo to flatter the workers, because this made them conceited and incapable of contributing to the emancipation of their class. Whatever the cost, the workers must always be told the truth.

George Sand was just as uncompromising in her attitude to Flora, seeing her as a vain exhibitionist whom it was impossible to take seriously; she declined to contribute to Flora's memorial, saying the money would be better spent on Aline, the daughter she had neglected.

This lack of solidarity is inevitable when strong-minded individualists clash, and unfortunately it never fails to make the headlines. But there was an unchronicled surge of femi-nist activity at less prominent levels of society. In France the women's clubs had revived and there were at least two feminist publications in Paris. In England Robert Owen's ideal of a new society had captured the imagination of incalculable numbers of working men and women, and in the early 1830s women were forming their own trade unions. But Owen's Grand National Consolidated Trades Union lasted barely a year, thanks to persistent repression by both government and employers. Of course this does not mean that feminist aspirations were extinguished, but when the women's movement began to gather momentum in the 1850s, it was predominantly middle-class, made up of women such as Barbara Bodichon who concentrated primarily on property rights and the vote. Only later did they turn to the plight of women workers. And despite – or perhaps because of – the courageous fight of women like Josephine Butler against the Contagious Diseases Acts of the 1860s, and her defence of the civil rights of prostitutes, Victorian convention forced the movement to protect its respectable image. It could not risk involvement with women who were suspected of revolutionary sentiments or irregular morals.

This admittedly superficial outline of feminist activity is intended only to give Flora her place in that small band of reckless individualists who were not afraid to fight their private battles in the public arena. In England Caroline Norton, finding herself deprived of access to her children, mounted a brilliant campaign and enlisted the help of a sympathetic MP to get the Infants Custody Act through Parliament in 1839. Another gifted woman who escaped from an unhappy early marriage was Anna Wheeler. It was she who probably introduced Flora to Robert Owen in 1837, and who certainly accompanied her on her visit to Bethlem in 1839. She boldly declared that the equality of the sexes could be achieved only in a socialist society, a conviction shared by the women workers in England who answered Owen's call and formed their own unions in 1833–4. Flora has something in common with Caroline and Anna, but she is unquestionably unique for the way in which she was able to transmute her private griefs and misfortunes into a great campaign on behalf of an entire class of submerged men and women. Her reckless actions, unashamed fervour and extravagant language made her misunderstood and ridiculed even in her own times, so it is easy to understand the temptation to play down these aspects of her character today.

Flora's frequent mention of God perhaps demands some explanation. She was certainly a believer, brought up in the Catholic faith, but like several other reformers, she gradually evolved a doctrine to suit the needs of her personality and her life. She always wrote the name of God in the plural, as *Dieux*, to represent her personal trinity of Père, Mère, and Embryon, the active and passive instruments of generation and their seed. Flora endeavoured to render homage to her Creator by loving and serving her brothers and sisters on earth. Her love of God, humanity and individual men and women is all part of a consistent way of life which she strove to practise despite her many failings – pride, impatience, prejudice and chauvinism among them. She explained her creed in a letter to the mother of her friend Jules Laure: it was her destiny, she said, to reveal the gods to men in their true guise, as good, not evil; to teach men to love one another; to show them that self-seeking was pure childishness, that their future happiness lay in association, and that for this to endure every form of conflict must cease. 'As every act is ordained by Providence,' she wrote, 'we should consider suffering, not as an evil, but as a crisis of growth, a pain which is necessary to help us pass from our present state, which is good, to a future state, which will be better.' It was her destiny to love and to suffer, like poor Chabrier in Bedlam. Sometimes she found the burden almost intolerable, and then, with characteristic directness, she appealed to her comrade-in-arms. 'Oh, Jesus,' she wrote in *Le Tour de France* after a particularly frustrating day, 'how trivial your sufferings must seem to you, compared with mine!' On another occasion during this final tour, when she had stopped to rest in a quiet church and eat a crust of bread, two shocked ladies rebuked her for her irreverence, to which Flora retorted that God knew, and would forgive her. Flora's religion was the fabric of her daily life, an expression of revolution in action. She reached the point where her conscience refused to let her commit any mean or dishonest act. Once, while on her tour of France, she appropriated a little gold watch left in her hotel room, and spent a sleepless night agonising over her action before handing the watch to the proprietor in the morning. 'These tortures proved to me that it is impossible for me ever to betray justice,' she wrote. 'To respect the established order, while all the time working to demolish it – that is what I mean by justice.'

To represent her religious and political beliefs, Flora had two seals made for her personal use: both were triangular in shape, one with the word *Dieux* in the centre and *Père, Mère, Embryon*, on the three sides, and the other with *Unité* in the centre, and *Dieux, Franchise, Liberté* round the sides. She gave a drawing of these seals, as well as a copy of the *London Journal*, to the delegation of Owenists, led by John Barmby, who visited Paris in 1840. It would be interesting to know whether these tokens of her esteem have survived in any collection of Owenist mementoes.

It was not until the demand for women's suffrage was renewed in France after the First World War that interest in Flora Tristan began to revive, strengthened by the publication of J-L Puech's definitive biography in 1925. He is the ideal biographer, often sceptical but always affectionate, thorough but never dull. His book is an effective antidote to the touching and reverential account of Flora's life that her disciple Eléonore Blanc brought out in 1845. In England G D H Cole devoted a chapter to Flora in his *History of Socialist Thought* (1953) and C N Gattey published a full account of her life and work in *Gauguin's Astonishing Grandmother* (1970). Flora's daughter Aline had married the journalist Clovis Gauguin – although their son Paul was born too late to know the woman from whom he inherited his proud and wayward nature. In the last months of his life, when he could no longer paint, Gauguin strung together a collection of memories and jottings which was published in 1903 under the title *Avant et Après*. He devotes a page or two to recounting all he had ever heard about his unknown grandmother, which does not amount to very much and contains a good deal of nonsense, such as the story that Flora was the mother-goddess in a short-lived cult called Mapah.

In recent years a number of studies of Flora's life and works have appeared in France, including the first-ever edition of *Le Tour de France* with notes by J-L Puech and an introduction by M Collinet (1973); a new edition of the *Promenades dans Londres* by François Bédarida which came out in 1978; and a full critical edition of Flora's hitherto unpublished correspondence by Stéphane Michaud.

As if to emphasise the growing interest in Flora Tristan, an English translation of the 1840 edition of the *London Journal* was published in 1980, just as I was finishing my final draft, and it must challenge me to justify my preference for the popular edition of 1842. I have already outlined the differences in the two, without perhaps giving enough weight to the numerous lengthy quotations from scholarly works on social conditions Flora adds to her notes, which lend authority to the 1842 edition and make it so much more than just another entertaining but superficial travel book. (These notes appear at the end of each chapter in the text: Flora's are preceded by the letters FT, and my explanatory notes by the letters TN.)

But the principal difference in the two editions lies in a change of emphasis. By 1842 Flora was wholly committed to the submerged and oppressed classes: this is what makes her *Dedication to the Working Classes* a key to the workings of her mind. In it she anticipates the communitarian ideal summed up in Ivan Illich's term 'conviviality' – 'individual freedom realised in personal interdependence' – an ideal which is perhaps a little nearer attainment today, when a growing number of men and women are rejecting rival materialist dogmas and turning to ways of life which enable them to express their profound belief in spiritual and personal values.

It is perhaps inevitable that in the desire to restore Flora to the honourable place she unquestionably deserves in the history of socialism and feminism, there is a tendency to exaggerate her importance. Ellen Moers, in her splendid book *Literary Women*, gives the impression that Flora was profoundly versed in English literature, which was certainly not the case: that she received any education at all was largely due to her own efforts. Dominique Desanti takes Engels to task for borrowing extensively and without acknowledgement from Flora's *London Journal*, whereas the truth of the matter seems to lie rather in the fact that both used the same official documents for their material. And Hélène Brion has claimed that Flora was the true founder of the Workers' International, as she published her *Union ouvrière* five years before Marx and Engels published the *Communist Manifesto*. But there can hardly be a single writer or thinker who did not contribute in some measure to Marx's masterly analysis of human activity: it seems irrelevant to look to him for a long list of acknowledgements.

Flora Tristan, Robert Owen, Fourier and Saint-Simon based their different plans for a new world on profoundly moral principles, whereas Marx based his on economics alone and dismissed morality as a bourgeois concept. They saw the only hope for the future of man in voluntary association, and eschewed all forms of violence, whereas Marx called for an all-out confrontation between opposing classes. He admitted to Engels that while he knew it was politic to include in the Workers' International a commitment to all the principles so dear to the Utopian reformers, he had been careful 'to put them where they could do no harm'. Paradoxically enough, it is thanks to generous, impulsive, slightly absurd figures like Flora Tristan that these perennial principles survive.

xli

I leave the last word on Flora to Jules Puech: 'Nothing would have touched her more deeply than the discreet monument on her tomb and the few heartfelt words of the inscription; but she would have regarded all the learned studies on her unhappy career and the commentaries on her works as a waste of time and energy more usefully employed in action. . . . The best way of keeping her memory alive is to inspire readers with love and admiration for her.' This is what I have tried to do.

Jean Hawkes, 1981

Dedication To The Working Classes

Men and women of the working class, I dedicate my book *to all of you*; I wrote it so that you might understand your plight, therefore it belongs to you.

The horrifying oppression which the English aristocracy inflicts on the people of the British Isles – the labourers and workers who create all the wealth – offers a lesson of the greatest importance which the workers of the world should keep constantly in mind. Do you know how it is that a handful of lords, barons, bishops, landowners and sinecurists have the power to oppress, torture and starve a nation of twenty-six million people, beat them like animals, crowd them into workhouses, transport them to live among savages, and deny them clothes, even bread? Do you know the reason for these atrocities? It is because these twenty-six million human beings are brought up like slaves *in ignorance and fear*. It is because *the Church, the Schools and the Press* are in league with the oppressors. Do you think that if the English had been reared in accordance with the principles of freedom and equality, if they had learned that resistance to oppression is not only the *natural right* of Man but his *sacred duty*, they would have suffered the proprietors of feudal estates and the aristocracy – legislators *by right of birth* – to enact the *Corn Laws*[1], enabling them to exact a *higher price* for the workers' daily bread? No, of course not, for then the English people would have a sense of dignity and too proud a spirit to submit to a slow and painful death by starvation.

In 1831, when poverty and unemployment struck the workers of Lyons, those energetic and determined men chose to die fighting for their *rights* rather than see their numbers dwindle as they and their families died of hunger.

1

They took *a black flag* on which they wrote with a firm hand these memorable words: *Live working or die fighting*![2] Would to God that the workers in England would follow the splendid example of their brothers in Lyons! But, alas, for many years English workers have been on the brink of starvation; hunger, that implacable Fury, has so undermined their forces that today the unhappy people, spent and weary, hang down their heads and die in silence, for they no longer have the strength to protest. But their deaths will lie at the door of their cowardly assassins.

You would think that if a country were moderately well-governed, its citizens need only be diligent, thrifty and competent at their work to live in modest comfort. But in England you see a multitude of skilled men unable to find work and dying of hunger. This is because workers have to submit to exorbitant taxes which they cannot pay; because the fruits of their labours can no longer find markets abroad; because the aristocrats who govern England refuse to import grain, wine and livestock. This means that the worker has to pay more for the indispensable commodities of life – bread, meat and beer.

In England the people are free only in name; twenty-four million workers still labour under the yoke of the aristocracy. As yet they have not even begun the struggle for liberty and equality which you and your fathers won in glorious revolutions.[3]

Never forget that if the reign of justice – government *for the benefit of all men and women* – is won by the courage of the masses, it is preserved only by their most active vigilance. The privileged classes believe they are a law unto themselves, entitled to live a life of luxury at the expense of the rest of society. This means that in England the great landlords who dominate the elections have the power to starve the workers. When the members of legislative assemblies are elected by only a small number, it is for the benefit of this minority that the whole nation is governed.

So do not lose sight of your *political rights*, for if the law refuses to grant them to men of all abilities as they acquire that true, professional knowledge which enriches life and guarantees independence for everybody, if the law does not call upon an increasing number of citizens – increasing, that is, in proportion to their intellectual development – to exercise their political rights, you will fall beneath the yoke of a new aristocracy, the aristocracy of money – parsimonious, grasping, and a thousand times more tyrannical than the aristocracy from which your fathers were delivered.

However, take care that you look upon political rights as only the *means* which will enable you to strike, through the law, at the evil roots of society and at the abuses which dominate the social order today: abuses in the organisation of government and politics, commerce and agriculture, the family and religion. It is the social system, the base of the structure, which must concern you, not political power, which is but an illusion, supreme one day and overthrown the next, restored in a new form only to be overturned once more. For politics, properly speaking,[4] affects only special interests which differ from state to state, and concerns none but the privileged classes. Up to now the exercise of political power has been an egotistical science which governments have used with varying skill to exploit their peoples, whereas social science embraces the whole human race. The truly benevolent ruler acts for the common good and keeps the welfare of both the *individual* and the *community* constantly in mind.

But as in society today political power is still the keystone of the state, so you must continue to fight to extend your political rights. The able farmer and craftsman, the inventor of new products or methods, the skilled worker, artist, scholar, teacher, doctor, engineer, military or naval officer – all have a better claim to be electors or deputies than freeholders and petty landlords, who, in a word, *produce nothing*, and live *at the expense of the real producers of wealth*.

Fellow-workers, my book describes the great social drama

3

which England unfolds before the eyes of the world. It will acquaint you with the callous egotism, revolting hypocrisy and monstrous excesses of the powerful English oligarchy and its unpardonable crimes against the people. It will prepare you for the inevitable and terrible struggle between the proletariat and the aristocracy, and help you to judge whether the English people are destined to throw off the yoke and rise again, or whether this great nation must remain forever divided between a cruel and corrupt aristocracy on the one hand and a wretched and degraded people on the other.

Through the English example you will see how precarious is the existence of a people whose civil liberties are not guaranteed by political rights and social institutions, established *in the equal interests of all*. You will see how important it is for you to obtain these two guarantees and fit yourselves through education to make proper use of them.

Be sure of this, that your freedom and progress depend entirely on spreading throughout your ranks a thorough knowledge of every law and institution which either harms or benefits the workers' interests.

History shows us that urban and rural workers have been slaves for thousands of years. Their servitude might have endured for ever had not the advent of printing brought books within their reach. Reading has spread slowly among the working classes, but greater freedom has always followed in its wake. When people could read the Bible and the Gospels, they rejected the domination of Rome and the priests; when they had newspapers to instruct them in the *rights of man*, they demanded that their rulers should be accountable for their actions, that public office should be open to all, and that all (or at least all males) should have equal civil and political rights.

My brothers, we do not live in ordinary times: the people are no longer satisfied with partial emancipation; they understand at last that every man is a *citizen of the world*, all are part of the great human family, naturally dependent

4

one upon the other. It follows that they wish all who dwell upon this earth to be emancipated, free and happy.

Today the privileged classes are in the grip of a terrible fear; they threaten, the earth trembles. We must leave the songs of the bard to happier days, for now is not the time to amuse ourselves reading romances, poetry or drama. Usefulness first, *usefulness*. It is imperative for workers to learn *the causes of their sufferings and the means to remedy them*; they must understand the march of history and what lies behind the actions of the privileged classes. That is why they must make it a *duty*, an *act of conscience* even, to read and reflect on the works of their devoted champions. Let them study the books of Eugène Buret, Gustave de Beaumont, the Abbé Constant, Cormenin, Fourier – in short, the works of every human being to whom God has revealed the source of the evils which plague society and violate the laws of harmony.[5]

Workers, if you would persevere in the study and investigation of these evils and reflect on them calmly, you will need to steel your hearts and summon up all your courage, for you will uncover wounds too deep to heal.

I clasp your hands in mine, all you men and women who up to this day have *counted for nothing* in the world. I join with you in the common task, I live in you through love,

I am your sister *in humanity*,

Flora Tristan, 1842

NOTES

1(TN).   The Corn Laws were enacted at the end of the Napoleonic Wars, in 1815, at the instigation of the predominantly agricultural interest in Parliament. They were intended to keep the price of corn (as well as agricultural profits and rents) high by prohibiting foreign imports. Naturally the price of corn fluctuated from year to year, but the Corn Laws ensured that only when scarcity or other factors drove it above 80 shillings per quarter (28 lb.) could foreign grain enter the country.

2(TN).   This was the strike of the silk weavers. Flora's biographer J-L Puech has found no historical foundation for the incident of the black flag.

3(FT).   Although in France in some respects liberty and equality as yet exist only in name, a comparison of conditions in France and England shows the enormous and striking difference in the degree of liberty and equality the two peoples enjoy in laws and customs alike.

4(FT).   The origin of this word tells us its sense. It comes from the Greek for *city* and denotes the spirit of egotism, shrewdness and guile employed to defend the interests of cities or states. *Politics* is thus the very opposite of *society*; the workers must be quite clear about the difference between these two words – this is very important.

5(TN).   Eugène BURET (1810–1842) was a journalist. Flora quotes several extracts from his book, *De la misère des classes laborieuses en Angleterre et en France* (Paris, 1840); Gustave de BEAUMONT (1802–1866) went to America with de Toqueville to study the penitentiary system, and on his return wrote *Marie, ou l'esclavage aux Etats-Unis* (1835). Then he studied conditions in Ireland, and wrote the book that Flora stayed up the whole of one night to read: *L'Irlande sociale, politique et religieuse*, (1839). In the same year he was elected to the Chamber of Deputies. He subscribed to the publication of Flora's book *L'Union ouvrière*; Alphonse-Louis CONSTANT (1810–1875), the self-styled 'Abbé', was ordained a deacon but was never admitted to the priesthood, and later left the Church. He met Flora in 1837 and is said to have been her lover. He painted an idealised portrait of her in 1839. After her death he edited and published her posthumous work *L'Émancipation de la femme* (1845). A supporter of the feminist cause and a communist, he published several books, one of which, *La Bible de la liberté*

(1841), earned him a prison sentence. In later life he turned to magic and occultism, but was reconciled with the Church before he died; Louis-Marie de LAHAYE, vicomte de CORMENIN (1788–1868) was a member of the Chamber of Deputies, 1830–1836. A man of strong liberal views, he attacked Louis-Philippe and his rule, sometimes under the pseudonym of Timon. Later he became Vice-President of the Assembly (1848) and helped to draw up the new French Constitution; Charles FOURIER (1772–1837) was a social reformer for whom the happiness of mankind was bound up with the harmony of the universe. He believed that social arrangements based on competition and individualism were imperfect and immoral, and should be replaced by a communitarian society in which everybody worked. He elaborated his system in the minutest detail in his *Théorie des quatre mouvements* (1808) but it was not until the 1830s that his ideas began to gain support, and the only attempt made during his lifetime to set up a community based on his principles was a failure. But Fourierism led to some interesting experiments in communal living in the United States, notably at Brook Farm, Massachusetts, and the North American Phalanx near Red Bank, New Jersey, which lasted from 1843 to 1855. The community building used by the Phalanx was demolished sometime in the late 1930s, according to Edmund Wilson.

Foreword

England's important position in the world makes one wish to know the country better, but as it is not at all an agreeable place to live in, most travellers are satisfied with a superficial glimpse and, dazzled by the luxury of the wealthy and by the might of England's industrial power, they never suspect the wretchedness of the poor and the hypocrisy and selfishness of the upper classes, or the price paid for the immense riches they have acquired.

Fashionable visitors from the continent stay in the finest parts of London and show no interest in the considerable proportion of the population – very nearly half – employed in the workshops. Nor do they visit the Irish rural areas or the English industrial regions. They are unaware that in the metropolis itself there are many neighbourhoods which harbour all the misery, vice and evil known to mankind. They go to Richmond, Windsor and Hampton Court, they see the sumptuous palaces and magnificent parks of the aristocracy, and when they return home they dismiss as exaggeration or lies the reports of any observer who, penetrating *beneath the surface*, has seen the boundless immorality brought on by this greed for riches, and the horrifying sufferings of a people reduced to starvation and subjected to cruel oppression.

When General Pillet[1] published his book on England in 1814, the English aristocracy had the ear of Europe. Without anybody troubling to verify the picture painted by M Pillet, who had spent several years in England as a prisoner of war and was therefore in an excellent position to see for himself, he was accused of calumny. It is even said that the English Ambassador, at that time the Duke of Wellington, intervened. The fact is that the book was *suppressed*;

General Pillet was bribed to stop him from bringing out a second edition. Afterwards the English spread the rumour that the book was an *infamous libel* dictated by hatred.

At any other time such a violent reaction would have ensured that the book was widely read, on the reasonable assumption that if it angered the English so much, it must be *true*; but at that time political passions were running too high for matters to take their normal course. Since then, England's power has grown so great that all who have attempted to reveal the truth about her have received similar treatment. English malevolence has not spared even Baron d'Haussez,[2] though his book is a model of circumspection, and only recently the *Revue de Genève*, which for reasons best known to itself is devoted to the interests of the English government, attacked the eminent scholar Professor List[3], in language so intemperate that I forbear to repeat it, merely because he too committed the heinous crime of saying that 'English commerce *oppresses every nation*', and called upon Europe to *revive Napoleon's continental system* and close its ports to English merchandise.

My *London Journals* appeared in May 1840. M de Beaumont's book on Ireland had been published a few months earlier and was already beginning to attract attention, but M Eugène Buret's book on the poverty of the working classes in England and France did not come out until the end of the year. As my readers were accustomed to hearing England's prosperity extolled, and judged the country by the Englishmen they saw on the continent – very few of whom belong to the poorer classes – they believed I had *exaggerated*. In several quarters I was even accused of *slander*; people said that, envious and chauvinistic, I wanted to blacken England's reputation in the eyes of all Frenchmen. In reply to these accusations I can only say that the facts set down here are taken from *authentic documents*, that they are generally acknowledged as a *public scandal*, and that my account is a truthful one.

In any case, after what has happened in England in the

past six months,[4] I do not see how I can be accused of exaggeration. But in 1840 the French public still believed in England's *power*, her *philanthropy*, and her *strict moral code*. Today the mask has dropped.

As for the spirit in which my book is written, I beg that it be read with scrupulous attention. On every page the sincere reader will find that desire for *unity* which guides me in all things. I consider every question in the light of *European unity* and *universal unity*. Thank God I long ago renounced any notion of *nationality*, a mean and narrow concept which does nothing but harm. Nationalism is the source of so many evils and crimes that it cannot be too often attacked. So if I have spoken out strongly against the system of privilege and tyranny which oppresses the English people, against the monopolies England *imposes on her subject races* and *her lack of consideration in commercial dealings with other nations*, it is because this system forms an insurmountable obstacle to that European unity which I pray may come one day, as it is the sole guarantee of international prosperity and the only means of achieving world peace.

And before my readers reproach me for exaggerating my picture of England, may I beg them to read the books on Ireland and England by MM Gustave de Beaumont and Eugène Buret. There they will find *official documents, reports of government commissions, enquiries, memoirs, petitions*, etc. These materials will convince even the most sceptical that the misery of the poor in England has passed the *bounds of human endurance*. In this new edition I have quoted M Buret several times in support of my argument, which I was unable to do in my first edition, as his book did not appear until six months after mine.

To sum up, if I have attacked the English government, it is not from any spirit of denigration. It is because I see it as the greatest obstacle to the advancement of Europe and the rest of the world; because its power and prosperity are based on *the plunder of other countries*; because it destroys every sentiment of morality and love in man by using *all the means within its power* to attain its end – the acquisition of wealth for its own sake – at the cost of the blood and tears of all those it has been able to oppress and leave destitute.

November 1842

NOTES

1(TN).   General PILLET (1762–1816) spent a total of ten years in England: four as an émigré, six as a prisoner of war. He was freed in 1814, but his health was ruined. He published his book *L'Angleterre vue à Londres et dans ses provinces* in 1815 (not, as Flora said, in 1814). It was immediately banned because of its violent anti-British sentiments. He was made a Marshal by Louis XVIII.

2(TN).   Baron d'HAUSSEZ (1778–1854) was a Prefect under the Restoration and later served as Minister for the Navy. His involvement in drawing up the repressive July Ordinances of 1830, which cost Charles X his throne, forced him to go into exile in England, where he spent four years, out of which came his book *La Grande-Bretagne en mil huit cent trente-trois* (1833).

3(TN).   Friedrich LIST (1789–1846) was the German economist who championed the idea of the European Customs Union, the *Zollverein*. He maintained that protection was essential for Europe's growing industries if they were ever to prosper and hold their own against England.

4(TN).   A reference to 1842, when England was in the grip of the most serious economic depression so far that century, and one in every fifteen of the population was dependent on public assistance.

Preface

I have made four visits to England in recent years to study the manners and morals of its people. In 1826 I found the country very rich. In 1831 it was considerably less so, and I saw marked signs of unrest. In 1835 the middle classes were feeling the strain as well as the workers. In 1839 I returned to find the people of London sunk in deepest poverty; disaffection and discontent were rife at every level of society.[1]

In offering this work to the public, I do not pretend to describe the full misery of the English people. To do so would take several volumes and need the collaboration of several individuals, or the entire lifetime of one. I wish only to sketch the few things I saw in England and describe how they struck me. By speaking frankly, without fear or favour, I hope to clear a path for others to follow if they truly wish to serve the cause of the English people. To attack evil at its source, to discredit prejudice, to stamp out abuses, we must patiently trace them back to their cause; we must not shrink from sacrifice and toil, we must be as fearless as the Apostles and proclaim our findings to the world. I have resisted the dazzling temptations offered by the brilliance and richness of the English scene; I have penetrated backstage, I have seen the actors' paint and powder and the tinsel of their costumes; I have heard them speak in their natural voices. In the face of reality, I have judged everything at its true value. Mine is a factual book, and I have done my utmost to make it accurate. I have taken care not to let myself be carried away by enthusiasm or indignation. I have pointed out the evils in the English system so that we on the continent may make a deliberate effort to avoid them, and I should consider myself amply repaid if I were to succeed in disabusing my readers of any erroneous opinions and ideas they might thoughtlessly have acquired about a country one can know only after years of arduous study.

A friend of mine who has had relations with the English government over a period of thirty years, once gave me the benefit of his views on English politics at home and abroad, its commercial relations with foreign nations and with its subject peoples. I agreed so wholeheartedly with him that I published his article, entitled *A Glance at England*, at the beginning of my first edition.

In the past three years the newspapers have reproduced in some detail nearly all the ideas contained in his article, so I have not considered it necessary to reprint it. However, the same friend was good enough to let me have some further observations which I publish as a supplement, so to speak, to the first.[2]

I think it may be useful for anybody who wishes to learn about the morals, customs and politics of England to give them the titles of several impartial works.

FRENCH WORKS

Field-Marshal Pillet, *L'Angleterre vue à Londres et dans ses provinces* (1815).

Gustave de Beaumont, *L'Irlande religieuse, morale et politique* (1839).[3]

Eugène Buret, *De la misère des classes laborieuses en Angleterre et en France* (1840).

Baron d'Haussez, *La Grande-Bretagne en mil huit cent trente-trois* (1833).

Auguste Barbier, *Lazare* (a poem on London).

ENGLISH WORKS

M. Ryan, *Prostitution in London* (1839).

Mary Wollstonecraft, *A Vindication of the Rights of Woman* (1792).

NOTES

1(TN).   Flora's first visit to England in 1826 was forced upon her by sheer economic necessity, and in later years she would never speak of it. She was just as reticent about her second visit, in 1831, but circumstantial evidence makes it likely that this was when she went to the Houses of Parliament. 1833 was the year she went to Peru. She returned to Europe in 1834 or 1835 on a British vessel, the *William Rushton*. Landing at Falmouth sometime in 1835, she travelled across country by stage-coach as far as London, where she spent an unspecified time seeing the usual tourist attractions. An account of her impressions was published under the title of *Lettres à un architecte anglais* in the *Revue de Paris* in 1837. Her fourth and final visit to England, in 1839, lasted from mid-May to the end of August, a total of three and a half months. In a letter written from 10 Alfred Place, Bedford Square, on 24 May, she complained bitterly about the cold rainy weather which was causing her wound to pain her, and she consoled herself with the thought that in three more days she would be back in Paris. But she decided to stay longer; on 15 July, still complaining, this time about the formality and coldness of English manners and the unwelcome attentions of innumerable stuffy blond Englishmen, she announced that she was staying until the end of the month. Early in August she wrote that on the following day she was to visit Birmingham (see Chapter VII, note 5). Towards the end of the month she made her trip to Brighton by stage-coach. At the end of August or the beginning of September she was back in Paris, and soon after her return, she stayed up all night reading Gustave de Beaumont's book on conditions in Ireland.

As for conditions in England, summarised by Flora at the beginning of this preface, they were not steadily worsening between the years 1826-1839. Trade slumped in 1825-6 and again in 1831, but in the years 1833-1837 it revived – though this was not necessarily good news for the working classes, especially the unemployed, who under the provisions of the new Poor Law of 1834, were now supposed to enter the workhouse if they could no longer support themselves outside. From 1837 onwards, depression again set in and conditions grew progressively worse, culminating in the 'Hungry Forties'.

2(TN).   This expert has never been satisfactorily identified. The two articles referred to deal primarily with the imbalance in international trade caused by the supremacy of England. The author is suspicious of England's motives in seeking to lower import duties, and suggests that the best policy for Europe would be to unite in economic alliance against her.

3(TN).   The correct title of this book by de Beaumont is *L'Irlande sociale, politique et religieuse*.

I

The Monster City

London, four times the size of Paris; London, which
contains one eighth of the population of England,
two million people, whereas only one in thirty-two of
the French live in Paris; London, whose extravagant
immensity the traveller on foot could never hope to
cover in a day; London, the centre of such distressing
and magnificent power. . . .
Auguste Luchet, *Brother and Sister* (1833)[1]

. . . It is a multitude without disorder, a bustle without noise, an immensity without grandeur.
Baron d'Haussez, *Great Britain in 1833*

What an enormous city London is! Its huge size, out of all
proportion to the area and population of the British Isles,
simultaneously calls to mind the commercial supremacy of
England and her oppression of India![2] But riches gained by
dishonesty and force are by nature ephemeral; their very
existence violates the universal laws which decree that when
the time is ripe, the slave will break his bonds, the subject
peoples will throw off the yoke, and the light of useful
knowledge will spread across the earth and deliver mankind
from ignorance.

What then will be the fate of the sombre stretches of this
proud city? Will it survive on such a scale when mighty
England is no longer in the ascendant? Will the railways
which radiate in every direction from the monster city guarantee her unlimited growth? These thoughts are inescap-
able as one observes wave upon wave of people surging
silently through the long dark streets, the concentration of
buildings and vessels, the sheer mass of *things*; then one

must study very carefully the men of every class and the work they do to find answers to these disturbing questions.

At first sight, the foreigner is struck dumb with admiration for the creative powers of Man; then he is humbled and almost overwhelmed by so much grandeur. The ships of every size and denomination, far too numerous to count, which fill every inch of the river, making it seem no bigger than a canal; the heroic proportions of the arches and bridges which seem to have been erected by giants to span the two shores of the world; the docks, the huge wharves and warehouses which cover twenty-eight acres of land; the domes, towers and buildings looming out of the fog in fantastic shapes; the monumental chimneys belching their black smoke to the heavens to proclaim the existence of a host of mighty industries; these confused images and vague sensations press almost unendurably upon the troubled soul.

But it is especially at night that London should be seen; then, in the magic light of millions of gas-lamps, London is superb! Its broad streets stretch to infinity; its shops are resplendent with every masterpiece that human ingenuity can devise; its multitudes of men and women pass ceaselessly to and fro. To see all this for the first time is an intoxicating experience. Then again, in the daytime, the beautiful streets, the elegant squares, the austere iron gates which separate the family mansion from the common run of humanity, the vast expanse of gracious rolling parkland, the beauty of the trees, the number of superb carriages and magnificent horses which parade the streets – all this seems magical and blurs the judgment, so that no foreigner can fail to be entranced when he first enters the British capital. But I must warn you that the spell fades like a fantastic vision, a dream in the night; the foreigner soon recovers his senses and opens his eyes to the arid egotism and gross materialism which lurk behind that ideal world.

London is the commercial and financial centre of the British Empire and attracts a constant flow of new inhabitants, but the advantages it offers to industry are offset by the inconvenience of the enormous distances one has to travel; the city is several cities in one and has become too large for people to meet or get to know one another. How is it possible to maintain close relations with father, daughter, sister or friends, when for a visit lasting an hour, one has to spend three hours on the journey and eight to ten francs on a cab? The extreme fatigue of life in London can be understood only by those who have lived there for some time, whether in pursuit of business or diversion.

Any journey is likely to be of five or six miles, so however trifling one's business, one is obliged to travel over fifteen miles a day. It is not hard to imagine how much time is lost in this way; on average, half the day is spent going through the streets of London. If exercise is salutary when taken in moderation, nothing kills the imagination or paralyses the heart and mind like extreme and permanent fatigue. When the Londoner returns home in the evening, weary and exhausted by the day's travel, he is incapable of wit or gaiety and disinclined for the pleasures of conversation, music or dancing. Our intellectual faculties are destroyed by excessive physical fatigue, just as our physical strength is impaired by excessive mental stimulation; that is why, when the agricultural labourer returns home after twelve hours of painful toil, he feels only the need to eat and sleep to restore his strength, while his intelligence, whatever its potential, lies dormant; such is the fate of all who dwell in the monster city. They are always weighed down by fatigue which leaves its mark upon their faces and in their hearts.

London is divided into three distinct parts: the City, the West End and the suburbs. The City is the original town, and in spite of the Great Fire which took place during the reign of Charles II, it still has a number of narrow little streets, tortuous and poorly built, while the waters of the Thames lap the foundations of the houses which line its banks. So, apart from its more recent splendours, the City retains many traces of those times prior to the Restoration, as well as a number of churches and chapels of every religion and sect which commemorate the reign of William III.

People who live in the West End look down on the residents of the City as thorough *John Bulls*[3]; they are for the most part honest merchants who are shrewd enough where their own affairs are concerned, but care for nothing apart from business. The shops where many of them have made a fortune are so gloomy, cold and damp that the aristocrats of the West End would disdain to stable their horses in them. The dress, manners and speech of the City are marked by styles, customs and expressions which the fashionable West End condemns as unutterably vulgar.

The West End is inhabited by the Court, the high aristocracy, the genteel professions and trades, the provincial nobility, artists and foreigners from every country. This part of London is superb: the houses are well built and the streets, though extremely monotonous, are nicely laid out. Here one sees dazzling carriages, magnificently attired ladies, dandies parading on the most beautiful horses, and throngs of servants in rich liveries, armed with long gold- or silver-topped canes.

Lodgings are cheaper in certain parts of the south and north-east of the city, so this is where workers, prostitutes and a swarm of rootless individuals live – people reduced to vagrancy through unemployment or vice, or forced by poverty and starvation to beg, thieve or murder.

The contrast between these three districts is no more than civilisation has to offer in all great capital cities, but it is more striking in London than anywhere else in the world. One goes from the bustling population of the City, where the sole motive is the desire for gain, to the haughty aristocrats who come to London for only two months each year, to alleviate their boredom by a display of unbridled luxury or to revel in their wealth by contemplating the poverty of others. In the poor quarters one sees hordes of pale, thin workers and the pitiful faces of their dirty, ragged children; swarms of prostitutes with brazen looks and shameless manners; bands of professional thieves; and flocks of children who emerge every evening from their roost to descend upon the town like birds of prey and abandon themselves to plunder, safe in the knowledge that they can easily escape the clutches of the law, because the police force is insufficient to apprehend them in the vastness of the city.[4]

NOTES

1(TN).   Auguste LUCHET (1809 – 1872) was a popular novelist and playwright of strong democratic and republican convictions. His highly successful novel *Frère et Sœur* was published in 1838.

2(TN).   The census of 1841 gives the population of London as 1,950,000.

3(FT).   John BULL was the nickname given to the English in general twenty years ago; nowadays it is applied only to those who still cling to the old English habits, customs and prejudices.

4(FT).   . . . From six to eight years of age, poor children are sent forth by their parents across the city, with strict injunctions not to return home without having obtained a certain amount of money or quantity of provisions. They beg, and sell matches, tape, sand, and many of them are early instructed to add theft to their vagrancy.

From twelve to fourteen years of age, those with a strong tendency towards vice enter upon a permanent career of theft and prostitution.

Report on Young Delinquents, by Mr Beaver

(The full name of the author and his tract are: William Beaver Neale, *Juvenile Delinquency in Manchester: its causes and history, its consequences and some suggestions concerning its cure* (Manchester, 1840): TN.)

II

On The Climate Of London

In London there are eight months of winter and four months of bad weather.

> A tourist

Never has a ripe fruit, plucked in an English garden, appeared on the table of its owner. . . . Grass is cut when still green, grain is harvested green; there are no golden harvests, everything is dried after cutting. No plant or grain ever reaches maturity, despite the luxuriance of the vegetation. It is necessary each year to renew strains and import seed from the continent in order to avoid degeneration. Even the standard of the wheat could not be maintained unless farmers obtained their seed from the Baltic. Turnip seed comes from Sweden, hemp from Russia, sainfoin, lucerne, clover, peas, beans of various sorts, etc. from France, and all other vegetables from Holland and the Low Countries.

> Field-Marshal Pillet,
> *England observed in London and the Provinces*
> (1815)

Moral differences in people may well be due to differences in climate. In the south, where perception is keen and imagination intuitive, the pace of life is rapid but interspersed with long interludes of reverie and vague yearning. In the north, the mind is slower to respond to the promptings of the senses; investigation is calm and careful, action slow and steady. But it is a gradual progression from the Negro to the Laplander; as one goes north, the pressure of human needs increases, physical pleasure and pain become almost the sole preoccupation of Man, whereas in the South, prodigal

21

Nature allows the soul to bask in self-contemplation; awareness of life's blessings and misfortunes is less acute, and people are more open to the influence of mysticism than in the North.

Over every English town there hangs a pall compounded of the Ocean vapours that perpetually shroud the British Isles, and the heavy noxious fumes of the Cyclops' cave. No longer does timber from the forests provide fuel for the family hearth; the fuel of Hell, snatched from the very bowels of the earth, has usurped its place. It burns everywhere, feeding countless furnaces, replacing horse-power on the roads and wind-power on the rivers and the seas which surround the empire.

Above the monster city a dense fog combines with the volume of smoke and soot issuing from thousands of chimneys to wrap London in a black cloud which allows only the dimmest light to penetrate and shrouds everything in a funeral veil.

In London melancholy is in the very air you breathe and enters in at every pore. There is nothing more gloomy or disquieting than the aspect of the city on a day of fog or rain or black frost. Only succumb to its influence and your head becomes painfully heavy, your digestion sluggish, your respiration laboured for lack of fresh air, and your whole body is overcome by lassitude. Then you are in the grip of what the English call 'spleen': a profound despair, unaccountable anguish, cantankerous hatred for those one loves the best, disgust with everything, and an irresistible desire to end one's life by suicide. On days like this, London has a terrifying face: you seem to be lost in the necropolis of the world, breathing its sepulchral air. The light is wan, the cold humid; the long rows of identical sombre houses, each with its black iron grilles and narrow windows, resemble nothing so much as tombs stretching to infinity, whilst between them wander corpses awaiting the hour of burial.

On such black days the Englishman is under the spell of his climate and behaves like a brute beast to anybody who crosses his path, giving and receiving knocks without a word of apology on either side. A poor old man may collapse from starvation in the street, but the Englishman will not stop to help him. He goes about his business and spares no thought for anything else; he hurries to finish his daily task, not to return home, for he has nothing to say to his wife or children, but to go to his club, where he will eat a good dinner in solitude, as conversation fatigues him. Then he will drink too much, and in his drunken slumber forget the troubles which beset him during the day. Many women resort to the same remedy; all that matters is to forget that one exists. The Englishman is no more of a drunkard by nature than the Spaniard, who drinks nothing but water, but the climate of London is enough to drive the most sober Spaniard to drink.

Summer in London is scarcely more agreeable than winter; the frequent chilling rainstorms, the heavy atmosphere charged with electricity, the constant change of temperature, cause so many colds, headaches and bouts of colic that there are at least as many sick people in summer as in winter.

The climate of London is so trying that many Englishmen never become reconciled to its vagaries. Hence it is the subject of eternal complaints and maledictions.

ᥤᥱ III ᥲᥱ

On The Character Of Londoners

> There must be some kind of defect in the character,
> domestic arrangements and habits of the English, for
> they are not happy anywhere; they appear tormented
> by a need for movement that drives them from the
> town to the country, from their own land to others,
> from inland regions to coastal resorts. They care little
> for their comfort as long as tomorrow they are some-
> where else. That variety and diversion which other
> nations seek in the territory of their imagination the
> English seek simply in going about from one place to
> another. When they no longer know where to turn on
> land, they shut themselves up within the narrow con-
> fines of a yacht and brave the discomforts and dangers
> of the sea, sailing with no thought of time or place, no
> prospect of pleasure now or happy memories later,
> nothing to look forward to but the end of whatever
> they claim to be enjoying. This sort of folly is not con-
> fined to individuals, but is found in a large number of
> families, irrespective of class, rank or wealth.
>
> Baron d'Haussez, *Great Britain in 1833*

There is so great a difference between the climate of
England, of London particularly, and that of countries on
the continent in the same latitudes, that before I could talk
about Londoners and their characteristics, I had to work out
which aspects they owed to their climate.

Now it is not my intention to analyse the many and
diverse factors which modify human individuality, or to
examine the part played by climate, education, diet, customs, religion, government, profession, wealth, poverty,
history, in making one nation serious, arrogant and heroic,
and another convivial, cultured and fond of pleasure; in

making Parisians lively, gregarious, frank and brave, and Londoners grave, unsociable, suspicious and timid, fleeing like rabbits before policemen armed with truncheons. Nor do I seek to know why some affluent Member of Parliament is corrupt and some ineligible poet or artist incorruptible; why the rich man is so insolent and the poor so humble, the one so hard-hearted and the other so servile. For such a study the life of not just one but several German philosophers would be too short. I shall therefore confine myself to a rough sketch of the general character of the Londoner, and I make no claim that it holds good for everybody. Naturally there will be many exceptions. The man of genius is always a soul apart, owing more to his innermost nature than to outside influences. So I shall make ample allowance for exceptions, and trace only the common features which the monster city sets, like its seal, on all who dwell within its bosom.

The Londoner is not at all hospitable. The high cost of living, and the formality that governs all his relationships, prevent him from being so. Besides, his preoccupation with his own affairs leaves him no time to entertain his friends; he never sends out invitations, and is only as polite as self-interest demands. He is always punctual in his business dealings; the long distances he has to travel make this an absolute necessity. The Londoner would expect to forfeit public esteem for ever if he were to arrive *two minutes* late for an appointment. He is slow to come to a decision because he calculates to a nicety the various options open to him, but this is a sign of prudence rather than hesitation, for unlike his compatriots in other seaports the Londoner has a positive relish for great ventures; business is akin to gambling for him. Once he has made up his mind, he is straightforward and open-handed; he almost invariably provides more help and more of a service than he originally promised. In all his undertakings he carries determination to the point of stubbornness; he sets his heart on accomplishing whatever he has started, and nothing whether it is loss of time or loss of

25

money, or any other obstacle, can discourage him.[1]

In his family relationships the Londoner is cold and ceremonious. He insists on certain attentions, formalities and courtesies which he is scrupulous to repay. Towards his friends he is circumspect, suspicious, even; nevertheless, he goes to some pains to make himself agreeable, but he rarely carries friendship so far as to put his purse at their disposal. Towards foreigners he affects a modesty he does not possess or assumes an arrogance which is more than a little ridiculous. Towards his superiors he is obsequious to the point of servility when self-interest requires it. Towards his inferiors he is brutal, insolent, callous, inhuman.

The Londoner has no opinions or tastes of his own; his opinions are those of the fashionable majority, his tastes whatever fashion decrees. This subservience to fashion is general throughout the land; there is no other country in Europe where fashion, etiquette and prejudice exert such monstrous tyranny. Life in England is encumbered with a thousand absurd, puerile, excessively tiresome rules, like a monastic order. Should anyone chance to break them, the whole of society is up in arms; the rash offender is banished, excommunicated in perpetuity. This violent animosity against anyone who wishes to preserve his individuality cannot help but foster the suspicion that envy – the most ignoble passion of the human heart – is stronger in England than anywhere else in the world. Most of the English are nonentities, so it irks them to be outshone or reminded of their mediocrity; they take offence the moment one strays from the prescribed path. If a daguerreotype were made of the public in Regent Street or Hyde Park it would be remarkable for the same artificial expressions and submissive demeanour that characterise the crude figures in Chinese paintings.

The Londoner professes the greatest respect for tradition, faithfully observes the rules consecrated by custom, and defers to the prejudices of society and religion. Although his reason is often in revolt, he submits in silence and allows himself to be fettered by chains which he lacks the moral strength to break.

The aristocracy has been at great pains to foment hatred of foreigners – particularly of the French – among the workers, but this hatred is growing weaker every day, despite the efforts of the Tories to keep it alive. Londoners consider it good form to profess tolerance for fear of being taken for a regular John Bull from the City; nevertheless, they are all jealous of the French, whether it is from commercial rivalry or simple envy; the intensity of their hatred is betrayed in every word they utter and only increased by the pains they take to conceal it.

Luxury is the Londoner's dominating passion: to have fine clothes, a fine house, and a style of living which sets him on a pedestal of respectability; this is the dream of his existence and the goal of his ambition. His other consuming passion is pride – for which he is prepared to sacrifice everything, his love, his wealth, even his future. There is no room in his heart for any finer feelings, it is too full of pride, vanity and pretention. He is habitually gloomy and taciturn, and suffers greatly from ennui; his business absorbs his attention only so far as it involves great risks and profits; he goes in constant search of distraction, and although he spares no expense, he rarely finds it. Whenever his profession and finances permit he travels widely, dragging always in his wake a profound anguish that rarely lets a ray of light penetrate his soul. Sometimes, however, this being that one supposes to be uniquely destined 'to be the recorder of human distresses'[2] emerges from his silence. Then he goes to the other extreme: wild shouts, loud bursts of laughter, raucous songs – a contrast which makes a very painful impression on the observer.

To see the elegant comfort which the wealthy Londoner enjoys, you might think him happy; but look closely, and you will see from the expression of his features, which bear the imprint of boredom and lassitude, and from his eyes, in which the light of the spirit is extinguished and the agony of the soul laid bare, that not only is he unhappy, he is living in conditions which forbid him even to aspire to happiness.

NOTES

1(FT).   When Waterloo Bridge was under construction, the shareholders responded to three appeals for funds, even though they were to receive no more than two per cent in dividends. Nor were they deterred by the accidents which befell the tunnel.

2(TN).   This quotation derives from an English source which I have been unable to discover.

IV

Foreigners in London

BARON WORMSPIRE: You hesitate? Then let me
introduce myself . . . I am Baron —

ROBERT MACAIRE: Descended from the famous —

BARON WORMSPIRE: Precisely.

ROBERT MACAIRE: His name's in all the history
books.

BARON WORMSPIRE: I am, what is more, a Brigadier-
General . . . appointed in the old days . . . by the
Great Man himself! . . . There's a title for you, sir!

ROBERT MACAIRE: That settles it as far as I'm concerned.

BARON WORMSPIRE: Come now, my dear son-in-
law, a truce to these compliments. We veterans of
the Grande Armée don't need to stand on ceremony, we're a straightforward lot.

ROBERT MACAIRE: What a capital fellow: open, sincere, a man after my own heart![1]

London's great wealth and commerce attract large numbers
of foreigners, most of whom have business interests, some in
honest trade, others in speculation.

I am told that more than fifteen thousand Frenchmen live
in London, to say nothing of all the Germans and Italians.[2]
Recent events have brought an influx of Spaniards and Poles
as well, though I cannot be sure how many there are, nor can
I say how many other nationalities are represented in the
monster city; nevertheless it is worthy of remark that the
English call all foreigners Frenchmen no matter what their
country of origin. It is the same in the Orient where all
Europeans are called Franks – perhaps this is a sign that
one day the whole of Europe is destined to bear the name
Français or *Freeman*.

With the exception of refugees, all these foreigners are here on business; among them are numerous craftsmen in various trades, honest folk working hard to maintain their families; then there are wholesale and retail merchants, teachers dedicated to their profession, theatrical performers, doctors, members of the diplomatic corps, and lastly a floating population of travellers who stay in the country no more than a month or two. As for those who settle down and become what the English call 'householders', even the most touchy Englishman could never question their respectability, so they enjoy the esteem which is their due; the same is true of tourists, whose reason for being in England is plain for all to see.

Foreigners who possess no capital or credit, no profession or trade, still have to live, just like everyone else, and these are unquestionably the people who employ the greatest ingenuity to attain their ends. There is nothing more comical or ridiculous than the strategies they adopt to enter English society; once they have discovered the importance which not only nobles and financiers but even the middle class down to the smallest shopkeeper attach to *titles*, they do not hesitate to flaunt the rank of baron, marquis, count, duke, colonel, general, etc. They adorn their button-holes with the *croix d'Honneur* or the *croix de Saint-Louis*, and although in England decorations are worn only at Court, the English are delighted to welcome into their homes a *Chevalier de la Légion d'Honneur*. The *croix d'Honneur* is still a symbol of respectability in their eyes. Little do they suspect, alas, that it has now reached its nadir on the breasts of spies and informers.

It is droll to see a commercial traveller, a hairdresser, or some other totally uneducated person sign one of the noblest names of France with such ease and aplomb that one would think he had been *born* the Chevalier de Choiseul or the vicomte de Montmorency. All the older men have at the very least been marshals in the Grande Armée, decorated by Napoleon himself! The younger ones are invariably Carlists;

never less than colonels under Charles X, they declare they will not live in France now that their king has been driven out.

The mania for titles has now reached such a pitch in London that kept women and even prostitutes use them as a ladder to fortune; these ladies insist on being addressed as Madame la marquise de —, Madame la baronne de —, Madame la comtesse de —, and so on; they do not scruple to use the coat-of-arms of their adopted family, seal their *billets-doux* with one of those magnificent antique crests, have their linen and silver marked with the monogram of their house; even their footmen, when they have any (which is seldom), wear feudal livery. Naturally in a country where appearance is everything, a prostitute got up in all the trappings of the nobility is bound to make her mark – and sometimes makes her fortune into the bargain. French-women are no fools, and living in a country which is the traditional home of advertisement and exaggeration, they are quick to pick up the forms. You will hear Englishmen say of some lady of the streets, 'Oh, she comes from a very good family; she is a niece of the comte de La Roche-foucauld', or 'she is related to M de Broglie', and so on. Nobody but the English could be taken in by such humbug!

In England I have seen the oddest collection of barons, counts and marquises imaginable. Many are suspected of being in the pay of the French government, and the police are said to keep an eye on the movements of republican refugees in London. The rest of them are fashionable society gentlemen trying quite simply to make a living. . . .

These 'noblemen' boast of their military exploits, pay court to the daughter of the house, sing the latest drawing-room ballads – and at the same time endeavour to engage her father in some business venture. Nearly all of them claim to possess secrets of vital importance to industry. One can transform any kind of leaf into tobacco; another can make excellent paper out of some unidentified pulp costing next to nothing; yet another even bolder than the rest will have the effrontery to declare: 'Gentlemen, up to now you have used the most costly means to produce gas; but I have been fortunate enough to discover a new process which will yield shareholders a profit of 500 per cent! I make gas out of *nothing*! Just a little soil and a little air, that's all!'[3] Then there is the *giant filter* which will provide the whole of London with pure water. And what about the excellent beer made without benefit of hops or barley! Other gentlemen proclaim their desire to free the English from the crippling duty that their government, in its love of free trade, has imposed on wine, by making claret and champagne at prices so moderate that even ordinary people can afford them. They also make vinegar without wine, as good as vinegar from Bordeaux, and brandy that can hold its own with Cognac. If I were to list all the marvellous secrets of these gentlemen I should never finish.

The English are forced to acknowledge that far more inventions originate in France than in their own country. French imagination has often provided England with the means of making a fortune: without delving deep into the past, I could mention the mechanical dredger invented in the year VII (1799) by a French engineer from Saint-Germain, the process for making a continuous roll of paper by Didot, and the machine for spinning flax by Girard.[4] All these inventions were perfected and put into operation in England, then we had to buy them back again. The English are so persistent that by dint of successive modifications they succeed in exploiting inventions whose potential would never have been developed had they stayed in France. Girard's machines had been lying idle for some years when the English took them over, and now, after certain improvements, they have enabled English flax-spinning to make such rapid advances that our linen industry is on the brink of ruin, thanks to our government's absurd deference to a government which concedes nothing and is always on the look-out for dupes.

As a result, the English tend to take French inventions

seriously, because every day new chemical and mechanical processes reach them from France, as well as experts who help them to withstand the formidable competition from the continent. Unfortunately this tendency, which is wholly honourable and favours our best interests, is exploited by charlatans whose activities cause the French to be accused of bad faith and fraudulent practices, harm genuine inventors, deter investors from financing new ventures, and generally slow down the rate of progress.

Ingenious discoveries often raise hopes which are not fulfilled by first experiments, but this should not impugn the good faith of the genuine inventor, for this emissary of Providence and the charlatan have about as much in common as the music of Rossini and the banging of a drum, or the style of Walter Scott and the puff of a bookseller's advertisement. So if John Bull is made to look a fool, it is because he consistently overrates his own powers of judgment; if he had a thorough knowledge of his business he could never fall victim to the spurious claims of the charlatan – who has only to play skilfully upon his vanity to persuade him that he is perfectly capable of making up his mind unaided. John Bull's three guiding motives are so conspicuous that they are impossible to ignore: gluttony, cupidity and pride. The artful rogues I have already mentioned, having no culinary artists at their disposal, cannot take advantage of the first, but they exploit the other two with consummate skill, and when John Bull is properly duped, he breathes fire and flame against 'those villainous French'! He includes the whole nation in his stupid rage, calling it a rabble; for John Bull's money is always so honestly gained that it is a crime which calls to high heaven for vengeance if he is forced to forego even a penny of it. His cries of woe remind one of the crow in La Fontaine's fable who is tricked into letting go his piece of cheese.

If John Bull attached less value to titles and decorations, he would never give his daughter, with a rich dowry, to an adventurer with an implausible title and multi-coloured ribbons in his button-hole. Gentlemen who have lived in France are not deceived; they know very well that the French nobility has absolutely nothing in common with the self-styled noblemen who idle away their time on the streets of London.

That is why I decided to write this chapter on foreigners in London. I wanted the English to know us better, not to be taken in by appearances, but to learn how to distinguish the well-informed man from the charlatan, the nobleman from the impostor, the duke from his valet and the duchess from her maid. I would like John Bull to give up his absurd recriminations and stop venting his wrath on an entire nation when he has nobody to blame but himself![5]

NOTES

1(TN).   These are extracts from two separate and unrelated scenes from the 1834 version of *Robert Macaire*, by B Antier, A Lacoste, and the famous actor Frédéric Lemaître. The original play was a conventional melodrama with a different title, and gave the actor insufficient scope for his talents, so he gradually succeeded in transforming the character of the stock villain so that it dominated the play and turned its moral upside down. Macaire became a popular anti-hero, instantly recognisable with his battered hat, eye-patch, and the snuff-box with the creaking lid. (He makes a brief appearance in the film *Les Enfants du paradis*.) Charles Selby transferred him to the English stage (without acknowledgement) in his two melodramas *Robert Macaire* (1834) and *Jacques Strop* (1838).

2(TN).   Flora's informant exaggerated the number of French in London. The 1841 census did not separate foreign residents into their separate nationalities, but the 1851 census gives a grand total of 26,000 foreigners, of whom 5,900 were French.

3(FT).   This is absolutely true: for two years a Frenchman got shareholders to pay him a guinea a day, promising them all the time that he would make gas out of nothing at all. This is the most original trick I ever saw played in England, but it loses a great deal in the writing; to appreciate it to the full one needs to see and hear the story performed by the author himself.

4(TN). Didot SAINT-LÉGER (1767 – 1829) was a member of a celebrated family of printers and publishers; he invented the paper-making machine known in England as the Didot machine. Philippe de GIRARD invented a machine for spinning flax and patented it in 1810, in hopes of gaining the reward of one million francs offered by Napoleon for the inventor of the best· new machine, but he never received the money. As Flora says, his machines were not developed in France; in 1815 he accepted an invitation from the Austrian government to establish a spinning-mill near Vienna, which was run with his machinery for a number of years, but failed to prove a commercial success.

5(FT). In the first edition of my book this chapter was much longer; in it I mentioned Prince Louis-Napoleon Bonaparte and his retinue. My readers will recall that in 1840, M Louis Bonaparte was in London posing as the Pretender; he had himself addressed as 'Your Highness' and had a court; in a word, he set up as a celebrity and made himself ridiculous. It is well known that he founded the journal *Le Capitole* in Paris to serve as his mouth-piece and win support for his cause. The farcical episode which took place at Boulogne three weeks after the publication of my book, proved that I was right in my judgment of this aspirant to royalty and the crowd of sycophants who encouraged his folly because they were making a living from it.

The Bonapartists, who in their love for the late Emperor were determined to see him reborn in his nephew, have accused me of maliciously caricaturing their hero, but it seems to me that his descent on the French coast, his attack on Boulogne at the head of his valiant band, his trial, and the letters written in his own hand and dating from the time of his imprisonment at Ham, fully attest that all I have done is to copy Nature, which had cast the hero of Boulogne in the same mould as the hero of Cervantes.

V

The Chartists

Put your trust in God and keep your powder dry.

O'Connell

Chartist mottoes inscribed on the banners at their meetings:
Better to die by the Sword than perish with Hunger.
Patience and Perseverance, we shall win our rights.
He who would be free, himself must strike the blow!
Universal Suffrage.
Justice for the downtrodden producer!
One day of Freedom is worth an eternity of Servitude.
We live to die of hunger.
Freedom – whatever the cost!
Be free, or cease to be!
A man's a man for a' that!
Beat your ploughs into swords and your billhooks into pikes!
Let the weak say: I am strong!
Can the true soldier ever be made an instrument of oppression?[1]

In the British Isles, fanaticism and the hypocrisy it imposes on the people may still be strong. Nevertheless, the influence of religious beliefs on the formation of political parties is only secondary. Every man clings to his sect just as he does to his freedom of opinion, and resents having to pay money to priests whose doctrines he does not accept; but religious hatred is on the wane, in spite of all that is done to keep it alive, and it is principally in material interests that we must seek the motives of the different parties.[2]

My readers will all have heard of Whigs and Tories, Reformers and Conservatives, Radicals and Chartists. All these parties are at war among themselves, but the great struggle, the struggle which is destined to transform the social order, is between landowners and capitalists on the one hand, and urban and rural workers on the other: that is, between men who possess both wealth and power, and for whose profit the land is governed; and men who possess nothing – no land, capital or political power – yet pay two-thirds of the taxes, provide recruits for the army and navy, and are starved by the rich whenever it suits their interests to make them work for less pay.

In the three kingdoms, a very small number of families owns all the land; this is the result of feudal laws which control inheritance. Large farms predominate, arable land has reverted to pasture and common land has been distributed exclusively among the landed proprietors. The inevitable consequence of these measures has been the complete impoverishment of the rural working class, and as the administration, the police, and civil and criminal justice are all in the hands of the landlord class, it follows that the worker has sunk to being the landlord's slave, even worse off than the negro or the serf, because *their* masters would never leave them to die of hunger or rot in prison for having killed a partridge or a hare.

There have been three great revolutions in the manufacturing process. The division of labour has been carried to its utmost limit; machines have taken over every stage of production; the capitalist has the unlimited resources of the steam engine at his command. These three will bring about equally important revolutions in the political organisation of society. Isolated industries are gradually disappearing; there is hardly anything Man uses that cannot be made by machines in large factories; the work left for the worker to do demands so little skill that virtually anyone can do it.

At first the workers benefited from these advances in industry: the high quality and low price of goods increased the number of consumers and wages rose; but when peace came, competition from the continent began to develop.

The English manufacturer fought it with the help of the vast capital he had amassed, he built up enormous stocks in his warehouses at home and in the trading-posts the English had set up all over the world, and he successively reduced the worker's wages.

In this situation the English worker is entirely at the mercy of the capitalist manufacturer, who can continue to meet demand for a long time without needing to spare a thought for his workers. He takes every penny of the profits and the worker has nothing to show for his fourteen hours of toil except his daily bread.

The Radicals demand the abolition of the Corn Laws, but what the workers want is universal suffrage, because they know full well that if they had any hand in law-making they would very soon obtain the abolition of all duties affecting grain and every other kind of food, as well as the right to form unions to fight against the capitalists.

So far the Chartists[3] constitute the most formidable association that has arisen in the three kingdoms, and it grieves me to see that – whether from religious fanaticism or from the desire to preserve his dictatorship intact – O'Connell has forbidden the Irish to make common cause with their brothers in England. After all, their suffering comes from the same source: oppression weighs equally on them all, whether they live under the yoke of the English aristocracy or the Irish, whether they pay tithes to English or Irish agents, whether they weave cloth of cotton or linen; in a word, any man excluded from the present electoral system *ought* to join the Chartists, for now he is judged without a hearing and has no advocate to plead his cause. In time to come the Chartist league should number twenty million inhabitants united against the privileged classes in all three kingdoms. Already its branches spread far and wide; its members are to be found in every industry, factory and workshop; in rural districts poor cottagers join its ranks, and this holy alliance of the people, confident in its future, grows in strength and numbers with every day that passes.

Expenses are covered through monthly subscriptions, all activities are controlled from the centre, and never has there been an organisation so strong.

Although Chartism derives considerable power from its efficient organisation, its greatest strength lies in its unity of purpose. Every member without exception wants to see an end to aristocratic, religious and commercial privileges; all want equal taxation, equal civil and political rights; all know that to achieve their goal they must drive out the tyrannical aristocracy which uses the power it has usurped solely to further its own interests. They must seize power in order to restore it to the victims of oppression; what is more, they have the strength and intelligence to do so.

The Chartists are not to be fobbed off with half-measures; they will never trust a party whose object is to transfer the privileges of the aristocracy to the middle class, for this would only lead to more oppression. The workers, who have raised the fortunes of England to such heights, and to whom shopkeepers, bankers, businessmen and landowners all owe their wealth, are the pariahs of society; their name is never mentioned in Parliament, unless it be to propose laws to restrict their freedom; it is therefore their unshakeable conviction that any measure which is not based on the equality of political rights can be only an illusory gain.

If there were universal suffrage, would a government propose to raise the price of bread so high that the workers starve? Would there be a ban on importing almost every kind of foodstuff? Would the basic necessities of the poor be taxed three times more heavily than the luxuries of the rich? If all men could elect their representatives, would the administration of justice be so odious? Would the nobleman's son be fined a derisory sum for violating a woman or beating a subordinate almost to death, while the poor worker is mercilessly punished for some petty offence and sent to languish in prison and leave his family to die of hunger because he is unable to provide bail? Would fines be fixed in such a way that the *minimum* was equal to several weeks' wages for a worker, and the *maximum* half the daily expenditure of a rich man? Would there be more people in prison for infringing the game-laws than for all the felonies and misdemeanours put together? Would the military be sent out to do battle with poachers to avenge the death of a few pheasants? Would the Court of King's Bench decree that when common land was enclosed or expropriated, only the landowner was entitled to compensation, while the poor folk who had built dwellings on the land could be evicted together with the cow or pig they had raised? If the people who form the bulk of the army and navy were represented in Parliament, would soldiers and sailors still be beaten and flogged, would army commissions be sold, would a sailor be pressed into the service of the state, only to be paid less than he could earn ashore, and in all the long years that stretch before him between the press-gang and his last days in Greenwich Hospital, would he never dare aspire even to the rank of midshipman?[4]

At the first sign of organised activity in the working classes, the aristocracy sounded the alarm and declared that the workers were bent on destruction. Now the Chartists look forward to the reign of justice, so they must appear Vandals in the eyes of those who owe their wealth to privilege; and it is the virulence of this class which accounts for the repugnance and terror – whether real or feigned – that the Chartists inspire. But the workers who take an active part in the movement are the élite of their class: the leaders are educated men full of zeal and love of their fellow men. The workers do not indulge in dreams of agrarian laws, taxes on machines or a minimum wage. They feel they are oppressed by the capitalists and by the duties levied on the necessities of life; they are no longer prepared to submit to exploitation, they want to work for their own benefit and see an end to the laws that prohibit association. As manufacturers they would like to follow the example of the Greek and Italian sailors who own shares in the ships they sail on, and in this way supplant the merchantmen of other nations in the Mediterranean. Their claims, which baser men have sought to impugn, are founded on the idea of justice which God imprints in our hearts. A well-organised union of workers in any industry ought to obtain more credit than a comparable private company, because the risks of production are shared by all its members, whereas in a private business they are borne by only one or two.

The lords of industry understand the implications of these new ideas only too well, which is why they have misrepresented the intentions of any workers who plan to set up in competition with them; there are, however, a few honourable exceptions. Some manufacturers are sufficiently enlightened to make common cause with the workers and realise that both sides stand to gain from the formation of joint associations.

In the national petition presented to Parliament on 14 June 1839[5], the workers and the more enlightened among the manufacturers exposed their grievances. They attributed the cause to the massive taxation which weighed so heavily upon the people, and to the squandering of public resources. They declared that electoral reform was a derisory measure which no longer deceived anybody and had done nothing but transfer power from one faction to another, leaving the people as wretched as before; that the capital of the master could no longer be deprived of its rightful interest or the worker's labour of its due reward; that the laws which made food dear, money scarce and labour cheap must be abolished; that as the good of the greatest number was the only legitimate goal, it should also be the chief study of government; that the present state of affairs could not continue much longer without serious danger to the stability of the throne and the peace of the kingdom; and that if legal means proved of no avail, they were resolved to take action themselves. As an indispensable preliminary to the changes which the welfare of the people required, they demanded universal suffrage, the secret ballot, annual Parliaments, the abolition of all voting qualifications and the payment of members of Parliament.

The mammoth petition of 1842, based on the above, is very much more explicit, but as all its parts would not be of equal interest to our readers, we present them with a summary:[6]

1. The petitioners submit that the government can demand obedience and enact laws only by virtue of delegation from the people; that it is responsible to the people; that the government which is not elected by universal suffrage is unconstitutional and tyrannical, and that it is the duty of all to resist it.

2. They inform the House that, as at present constituted, it has not been elected by, and acts irresponsibly towards, the people, and hitherto has represented only certain interests and benefited the few, regardless of the wretchedness, suffering and grievances of the many.

3. They accuse the government of having enacted laws contrary to the expressed wishes of the people and of enforcing obedience to those laws by unconstitutional means, thereby creating despotism and the most degrading servitude.

4. They emphasise the disproportion between the number of inhabitants and the number of electors, stating that the population of the three kingdoms is twenty-six million and that only 900,000 are entitled to vote. They point out that the electoral law not only destroys the rights of the people but gives a preponderant influence to the landed and monied interests to the utter ruin of the small-trading and labouring classes, by the unequal distribution of members, according to which the large industrial centres elect, in proportion to their size, a far lower number of representatives than the boroughs and towns of the agricultural counties; and that it is a public scandal that every election of this so-called national assembly is dominated by intimidation and corruption.

5. They complain that they are enormously taxed by men not authorised by the people in order to pay interest on a debt currently standing at £800 million − a debt which these men term *national* although it was they alone who incurred it by waging wars for the suppression of all liberty.

6. They describe the appalling poverty of the people and the miseries which the new Poor Law has inflicted on them; they call attention to the immense disparity between the wages of the producing millions and the salaries of those persons whose comparative usefulness ought to be questioned.

7. Thus, they say, Her Majesty receives £164.17s.10d. daily for her private use, while thousands of workers' families receive only 3¾d. per head per day; H.R.H. Prince Albert receives £104.2s. daily, while thousands have to exist on 3d. per head per day; the King of Hanover (the Queen's uncle) receives £57.10s. while thousands of taxpayers have only about 2¾d; the Archbishop of Canterbury receives £52.10s. while thousands of poor families have only 2d. per head per day.

8. They say that in spite of the undoubted constitutional right of the people to meet freely in order to air their grievances, discuss political subjects or frame petitions, this right has been unconstitutionally infringed; that five hundred citizens have been unlawfully arrested, and subjected to excessive demands for bail; that they have been tried by packed juries, convicted, and treated as felons of the worst description.

9. They denounce the organisation of a new tyranny: a vast unconstitutional multitude of armed men in the pay of the police, recruited into their ranks at enormous cost and dispersed all over the country to prevent the due exercise of the people's rights. They are of the opinion that police stations and Poor Law Bastilles (workhouses) originate from the same cause: the increased desire of the irresponsible few to oppress and starve the many.

10. They add that a huge unconstitutional army is maintained for the purpose of repressing public opinion and to intimidate the millions in the exercise of their legal rights.

11. They depict the sufferings of the people; they complain that the hours of labour, particularly of the factory workers, are protracted beyond the limits of human endurance, that the wages earned are inadequate to procure them the means of subsistence, and that agricultural workers are dying of hunger.

12. They deplore the existence of any kind of monopoly,

and condemn without distinction any tax upon the necessities of life. They demand the suppression of all monopolies: the existing monopolies of the suffrage, of paper money, of the press, of religious privileges, of the means of travelling and transit, and of a host of other evils too numerous to mention, all arising from class legislation, and which Parliament has consistently favoured.

13. They say that, from the numerous petitions presented to the House, it is fully acquainted with the grievances of the working men; so they pray the House to take counsel and redress these wrongs, for it is the worst species of legislation which leaves the grievances of society to be removed only by violence and revolution, both of which are to be feared if just complaints continue to be rejected.

14. They say that £9 million per annum are exacted from them to maintain a church establishment from which they dissent; that it is unjust, and not in accordance with the Christian religion, to enforce compulsory support of religious creeds and expensive church establishments with which the people do not agree.

15. They say that the people are subject to the rule of irresponsible law-makers, to whom they have given no authority or mandate, and are saddled with enormous taxes to uphold a corrupt system to which they have never given their consent.

16. They affirm that according to tradition and ancient practice, every male inhabitant of the United Kingdom, he being of age and of sound mind, and not convicted of any crime, has the right to choose Members to represent him in Parliament; and that it is equally easy to prove, by the customs and statutes of the realm, that there should be annual Parliaments.

17. They strongly object to any form of property qualification, because it is contrary to the ancient usages of the country. They add that influence, patronage and intimidation prevent free elections; enormous sums are paid for a seat in Parliament, which proves the existence of fraud and corruption in the highest degree.

18. They acknowledge that the Irish people have many grounds for complaint, and contend that they are fully

entitled to demand the repeal of the Union.

19. They have viewed with profound indignation the partiality shown to the aristocracy in the courts of justice, and the cruelty of that system of law which deprived Frost, Williams and Jones of the benefit of the objection offered on their behalf by Sir Frederick Pollock during the trial at Monmouth, and which a majority of the judges approved.

20. They say that within the limits of their petition they cannot set forth even a tenth of the many grievances of which they justly complain; but should the House be pleased to grant their representatives a hearing at the Bar, they would unfold a tale of wrong and suffering – of intolerable injustice – which would create utter astonishment in the minds of all benevolent and good men, that the people of Great Britain and Ireland have so long quietly endured their wretched condition, brought upon them by unjust exclusion from political authority and by the manifold corruptions of class legislation.

21. Therefore, exercising their just constitutional right, they demand that the House should remedy the many gross and manifest evils of which they justly complain, by adopting as law the document entitled 'The People's Charter', which embraces the representation of male adults, vote by ballot, annual Parliaments, no property qualification, payment of Members, and equal electoral districts.

It is with the desire to promote the peace of the United Kingdom, security of property and prosperity of commerce that they earnestly press their petition on the attention of the House.

As may be seen, the conclusions of the two petitions are the same, but what a world of difference lies between them! In 1839, men who were still prepared to *reason* with their rulers soberly pointed out the inevitable consequences of the existing state of affairs; they demanded that all should share the same political rights, because the corruption, greed, plundering and oppression of the aristocracy reduced them to the most appalling poverty, destroyed public prosperity and threatened the peace of the realm by driving people to despair.

Today it is 3,317,702 individuals, nearly one half of the male population of the three kingdoms over the age of twenty-one, who inform the House that it has no authority to enact laws and demand obedience to them; that the people will *resist* Parliament because they have not appointed it. They are no longer begging for concessions, they *demand their rights*, and will seize them *by force* if they continue to be withheld. They protest against Parliament for using the powers it has *usurped* to rob and plunder the people; against the scandalous rapacity of the clergy imposed on them against their will; against organised tyranny with its police, its soldiers, its arbitrary imprisonment and the iniquitous partiality of its law courts; they contrast the income of eminent sinecurists from the Queen downwards with the wages of productive workers, and consider the comparative usefulness to society of each.

This petition is nothing less than the English people's declaration of war against the aristocracy, and now we wait to see if words will be followed by deeds; if our brothers in Great Britain will imitate the example we have set them since 1789; if they will engage in battle, burn down castles and resolve never to lay down their arms until they have won back their rights!

These two petitions are based on principles which conform so closely to the concept of universal justice that only bad faith, tyranny or stupidity could oppose them. The men for whose profit the land is governed, who owe their income to monopolies, draw large salaries or enjoy sinecures, all proclaim that the workers seek to destroy property, as if property could ever be justified by usurpation or recognise any legitimate claim but labour. However, these impassioned accusations are no more effective than the cries of papism with which a few fanatical Tories seek to arouse the masses. Just now England presents a bizarre anomaly: among the workers, prejudice is gradually dying out, religious and national hatreds are on the wane; whereas in the upper ranks of society the aristocracy, terrified by the spread of enlightenment, withdraws into impenetrable darkness, buries itself in the obscurity of the Middle Ages, evokes the memory of Crécy and Agincourt and the shades of Henry VIII and Mary Tudor. At a time when the people are dying of hunger, the aristocracy seeks to embroil them in religious controversy and longs to return to the benighted days when men would cut one another's throats over a theological quibble. And these are the men who claim the right to lead the nation!

As for the Whigs, they still live in the century of Louis XIV; look how important they think it is that one royal family should govern a country rather than another![7] They imagine that in Europe it is kings who decide what people think and that rulers may act as they please without the assent of their subjects. Poor creatures! they do not see that national prejudice is declining, that every day the people are becoming more closely united, that the interests of the masses dominate every issue on the continent as well as in England, and that an unpopular war could no longer succeed in any country in Europe, but would spell eternal ruin for the aristocracy which provoked it!

The Chartists were so often mentioned in the newspapers, and I had heard so many different reports of them, that I wanted to get to know them better. The Tories told me they were abominable scoundrels, the Whigs – with their customary fatuity – said they were impudent upstarts, while the Radicals, who have great hopes of them, spoke of them as the saviours of the country. To hear such conflicting opinions filled me with the strongest desire to meet the leaders of this great popular movement and to attend a meeting of its central committee. I had no confidence in the biased testimony of party politicians; I wanted to judge for myself whether the Chartists really *were* bloodthirsty monsters, madmen betraying the people's cause, or angels sent from God to deliver England from slavery. A friend who is closely connected with two of the Chartist leaders took me to the place in Fleet Street where the National Convention was holding its meetings. No doubt this spot has often been the object of Tory ridicule in the House – these Tories are *so* witty! Indeed it is not very impressive: a shabby tavern in one of the dirty narrow little alleys just off Fleet Street.[8] When you go inside, a pot-boy comes and asks if you want beer; from your reply he guesses your business and takes you through the back-shop to the assembly room – but what does the place matter? Was it not in crypts, cellars and caves that the first apostles gathered the Christians together, yet their words were mightier than the power of the Caesars, for they were inspired by faith, and on the wooden cross each clasped in his hands was inscribed the word *Redemption*!

My friend asked for Messrs O'Brien and O'Connor;[9] they came, I was introduced, and they showed me into the room. Nobody is admitted unless he is sponsored by two members, yet even these wise precautions do not prevent spies from penetrating to the very heart of the assembly.

I was immediately struck by the lively expression on every countenance; at other English meetings I had seen only faces of the dreariest uniformity, devoid of any memorable feature, as if they had all been cast in the same mould. Here, on the contrary, each face had a marked individuality; there were thirty or forty members of the National Convention present and probably as many supporters, the latter from the working class and nearly all young; among them I noticed four or five French workers and two women. There was not a single interruption, no whispering, no private conversations – quite unlike the House of Lords! Everybody gave his undivided attention and followed the debate with interest. Occasionally, in accordance with English custom, the speaker would venture a humorous remark which made everybody laugh.

O'Connor is a vigorous, fiery orator whose brilliance is inspiring. O'Brien is remarkable for his sound reasoning, his lucidity, his calm manner and his profound knowledge of history. Dr Taylor[10] is ardent and impassioned – the

Mirabeau of Chartism. These three, together with Lovett,[11] are the people's leaders at the present time; but there are also men of outstanding merit in the ranks immediately below them.

At the meeting I singled out three young men, the eldest of whom could hardly have reached the age of twenty-six: the first, Dr Stephens,[12] has a charming head; everything about him denotes the man with a genuine vocation for study, who wears himself out through sheer hard work. A man of strong views, he defends them with the energy of the advocate determined that they shall prevail. He expresses himself with ease and fluency, is quick to score a point, and seizes upon the most subtle shades of meaning with rare intelligence. This young man has a brilliant future before him, for God has endowed him with every talent necessary for the apostle of the people's cause. The next to claim my attention was Palmer, a man from the ranks of the people whose towering height proclaims his strength. He has a remarkably fine head, a well-proportioned body, and a proud, even menacing, appearance. He is the typical handsome Irishman – regular features, a mass of black hair, dark skin, flashing deep blue eyes, a mouth and chin expressing the depth of his passions, and an air so resolute and martial, not to say terrifying, that just to look upon him evokes the sight and sound of battle. You can see that this child of unhappy Ireland is aware of his manly dignity and that his soul is in revolt against the yoke. Oh! I will vouch for it that this young man will play a great part in the revolution should Providence permit it to come within the next ten years, for his arm is mighty and his implacable hatred will pursue the aristocracy even as Marius pursued the Roman senators. His speech betrays his lack of education, nevertheless I could not help noticing how impressed the assembly was by the words that burst unbidden from his heart, and how much his opinion was respected. A somewhat trifling difference had arisen between Mr O'Connor and a contentious old lawyer; several members had tried to appeal to the old windbag's commonsense, but in vain, for he had spent a lifetime arguing the pros and cons, going to inordinate lengths to prove the incontrovertible, gliding lightly over uncertainties, and looking at every side of the question, so he kept up a rapid fire and showed no sign of running out of ammunition.

The young Irishman rose to his feet, and in a sonorous voice that drowned the words of the old lawyer, he said, 'Sir, we are not here to bandy words but to debate important matters; our time is precious, we must spend it in deeds not idle phrases.' Coming from this young man, these few words had an indescribable effect; the entire audience showed their approval. This time the old lawyer stopped short, no longer sure of his ground. The young Irishman had gone straight to the point, a practice the veteran of the law-courts had either forgotten or thought beneath him.

The third Chartist to catch my eye was another Irishman. Imagine a thin, pale young man with a delicate constitution, one of those frail beings for whom existence is perpetual suffering, who lives only through his imagination, abandons the real world for fantasy and allows himself to die of hunger while lost in dreams of enchanted palaces: one of those poetic souls who think only of human progress and are happy only in the happiness of others. You can see that the poor boy believes in God, in Woman, in self-sacrifice. He is twenty years old, his great love embraces all humanity, hope shines on his brow, his trust is boundless. As yet he has no inkling of the masks self-interest assumes; he dashes recklessly into the abyss we call Society, little suspecting the cruel rivalry, envious hatred and bitter disappointments that await him, or the agonies he is fated to endure. Every time my eyes lighted on this frail creature, I was reminded of Camille Desmoulins, Madame Roland, Saint-Just and all the others full of faith and devotion who perished, victims of our own civil strife.[13]

I left this assembly feeling edified and well content. I had seen order prevail in its deliberations and felt this augured

well for the talents, sincerity and dedication of the men God
has raised up to lead this people.[14]

NOTES

1(TN).   The first quotation is Cromwell's exhortation to his
troops, and has nothing to do with the great Irish patriot Daniel
O'Connell, who consistently opposed violence in any form (see
Chapter VI note 2 (TN)). He prevented Chartism from taking
root in Ireland and disassociated himself from the 'physical force'
faction inside the movement led by his compatriot Feargus
O'Connor. A possible explanation for Flora's unfortunate mis-
take is that she heard the words quoted at a Chartist rally, misunderstood the implication, and misheard the attribution.

As for the Chartist slogans, they come from a wide variety of
sources. The first is from the Old Testament (Lamentations,
ch. 4, v 9): 'They that be slain with the sword are better than they
that be slain with hunger.' The third is from Byron's *Childe
Harold*, Canto II, Ixxvi:

Hereditary bondsmen! know ye not
Who would be free, themselves must strike the blow?

Flora mistranslates 'strike the blow' as '*donner le signal*'. This
motto was very popular in both the Irish and Chartist movements
and survives on some of the magnificent silk banners of individual
trade union branches. Further down the list is the famous line
from Robert Burns, followed by another quotation from the Old
Testament (Joel, ch. 3, v. 10): 'Beat your ploughshares into
swords and your pruning hooks into spears: let the weak say, "I
am strong".' I am most grateful to Dorothy Thompson for identifying the Bible quotations.

2(TN).   Flora, even if not a conventional practising Catholic,
was nevertheless raised in the traditions of that faith and was by
temperament antipathetic to Protestantism. She seriously under-
estimates the conflict between the Established Church and the

Dissenters, and the political and social divisions to which it gave rise. But she does not exaggerate the survival of hostility towards Roman Catholics – exemplified in the speeches she heard at the meeting of the Home and Colonial Infant School Society (see Chapter XVI).

3(TN). Chartism represents an extraordinary and unprecedented nation-wide upsurge of working-class consciousness, combining the demands of the educated worker for a share in government with the general protest against low wages, long hours, widespread unemployment and appalling living conditions. Discontent was aggravated by the new Poor Law of 1834 (which abolished outdoor relief for the able-bodied and made entry into the workhouse a condition of relief) and by the government's policy of suppressing any attempt to form trade unions. In 1836 a group of radical artisans formed the London Working-men's Association, and in 1837 they drew up a petition containing the famous Six Points: universal male suffrage, vote by ballot, equal electoral districts, the abolition of property qualifications for MPs, payment of members, and annual Parliaments. This was the basis of the Charter, which became a rallying-point for popular discontent. The Chartist movement was formally inaugurated at a huge public meeting in Birmingham; as the next step, groups were formed all over the kingdom to elect delegates to the first People's Convention, which met in London in February 1839 and made preparations to submit the Charter to Parliament.

4(FT). I am not one of those who see in universal suffrage a remedy for all our ills. Political measures are only a means to an end, but there is room to believe that giving all men the vote would send to the House members who were truly devoted to the public welfare, and that in number they would far outweigh the representatives of private interests. It is in this hope that I desire universal suffrage, so that a better social order may be brought about.

5(FT). See the first edition in which this petition is translated in full.

6(TN). This is a direct translation of the principal clauses of the

Charter rather than a summary of the whole, so I give the original text with only slight modifications. See G M Young and W D Handcock, *English Historical Documents Vol XII (1) 1833–1874* (Eyre and Spottiswoode, 1956). Apart from substituting 'iniquitous' for 'unequal' in Cl. 4, and missing the significance of 'packed juries' (Cl. 8) and the functions of the Court of Exchequer as a court of appeal (Cl. 19 – she refers to the judges as jurymen), Flora's translation is admirable.

7(TN). This refers to the dynastic quarrels of 1833–1834 in Spain and Portugal, both of which were settled by English intervention. The Whigs were in power and Lord Palmerston was Foreign Secretary. His high-handed behaviour made him intensely unpopular abroad.

8(TN). The National Convention opened on 4 February 1839 at the British Coffee House in Cockspur Street; it later moved to the tavern in Bolt Court off Fleet Street which Flora describes. Between 13 May and 5 July the Convention transferred to Birmingham, a far more politically active place than London at the time. The final meeting there on 5 July was broken up by the police, the Chartist leader William Lovett (a moderate opposed to O'Connor's 'physical force' faction) was arrested, and the Convention returned to London. The first Charter was rejected by Parliament on 12 July, and on 16 July the Convention debated the proposal to declare a 'sacred month' of strikes to begin on 12 August. The debate continued over the three days of 22–24 July, but the proposal was finally dropped for want of support. It is impossible to be sure which of these July meetings Flora attended, because the names she mentions do not correspond with those listed in the reports of Convention meetings published in the two Chartist newspapers *The Charter* and the *Northern Star*. One of the women Flora noticed might have been Lovett's wife who was elected secretary after his arrest.

9(TN). James Bronterre O'BRIEN (1804–1864) was, like Lovett, a moderate, an advocate of 'moral force'. He qualified for the Bar in Dublin and went to London for further study, but devoted his time to radical politics instead, editing various newspapers and spreading radical ideas to such effect that he became known as 'the schoolmaster' of Chartism. His aim was the expropriation of the propertied classes and the establishment of communities run on co-operative, Owenist principles. Feargus O'CONNOR (1794 – 1855) was a tremendously powerful orator and an advocate of physical force within the Chartist movement. He was an Irish squire elected to Parliament in 1832, but O'Connell found him such a liability as a colleague that he had him prevented from taking his seat. O'Connor founded the *Northern Star*. His vacillating policies contributed to the collapse of Chartism. He started a company for settling townsfolk on the land, but it went bankrupt. In 1847 he was elected MP for Nottingham, but he was by then showing signs of mental instability, and in 1852 he was pronounced insane.

10(TN). John TAYLOR (1805 – 1842) was a Scottish naval doctor who came into contact with republican ideas in France. Thereafter he devoted his life to the Chartist movement; he was arrested with Lovett in Birmingham on 5 July 1839, but cannot have been detained for long, if he was present at a meeting of the Convention later the same month; however, he was re-arrested in November. As Flora prophesied, he wore himself out and died before his time.

11(TN). William LOVETT (1800 – 1877) was born in Cornwall and came to London in 1821. He was a founder-member of the London Workingmen's Association and its first secretary. He drew up the petition which formed the basis of the Charter. After his arrest in Birmingham, already mentioned, he was tried and imprisoned in Warwick Gaol. He remained consistently opposed to violence, putting his faith in the extension of the franchise, which he thought would lead to the social and economic regeneration of society. His autobiography was *Life and Struggles in Pursuit of Bread, Knowledge and Freedom* (1876).

12(TN). Joseph Rayner STEPHENS (1805 – 1879) was a Wesleyan minister, a Tory radical and a bitter opponent of the Poor Law. His vigorous defence of workers' rights made him a popular speaker at the huge Chartist rallies, and it is possible that Flora attended one of the mass meetings he addressed in London in 1839.

As for the giant Palmer and the delicate young Irishman who made such a deep impression on Flora, they have not been identified.

13(TN).   Jeanne ROLAND (1754 – 1793) belonged to the relatively moderate party of the Gironde. After the execution of Louis XVI her political enemies had her arrested and she went to the guillotine in 1793. Camille DESMOULINS (1760 – 1794) was a member of the extremist group known as the Mountain which voted for the king's death. He and Danton were outmanoeuvred in the struggle for leadership. Robespierre had them arrested and they were guillotined in April 1794. After Robespierre seized power, he and his principal supporter Antoine SAINT-JUST (1767 – 1794) wanted to establish a dictatorship, but this roused the enmity of their colleagues on the Committee of Public Safety, who sent them to the guillotine in July 1794.

14(FT).   This was already written when the Chartist rising led by Frost took place at Newport with such deplorable results.

We French are so accustomed to seeing citizens pitted against regiments that we find it hard to understand why the English offer no resistance to a handful of soldiers and let themselves be defeated. Perhaps we should remember that whereas in France conscription is responsible for teaching most of the population how to handle weapons, in England the army is recruited from soldiers who sign on for life and thenceforth not only cease to belong to the people but are also totally isolated from them through constant surveillance. Then again, in France the officers and other ranks of the insurrectionary forces are admitted to membership of the inner councils which plan the various risings only after undergoing tests of character which gauge how far they are to be trusted. In a word, numbers alone are insufficient to stand up to well-trained, well-armed soldiers and good artillery; it is not exuberant enthusiasm that is needed, but the irresistible courage that springs from the soul. Men must be prepared to sacrifice their lives by throwing themselves in a body upon the cannons as they fire, for those who are not hit are certain to reach the gunners before they have time to reload. To be sure, some men will fall; the cannon-balls and grapeshot of despotism will send some martyrs in the holy cause to Heaven, but ultimately, by

55

reason of their courage and their numbers, the people are bound to be victorious. If the English workers wish their revolution to succeed, they must unite with their French brothers and take inspiration from their example.

(This rising took place on the night of 3 November 1839, and was the only occasion when the advocates of 'physical force' inside the Chartist movement had their way. A force of about three thousand men, mainly Welsh miners, converged on Newport, led by John Frost, William Jones and Zephaniah Williams, three men well known in the district. Frost was a former mayor of the town. A detachment of infantry was sent out against them and opened fire: fourteen men were killed and a further ten died of their wounds later. The three leaders were charged with treason and tried at Monmouth in December. For the defence, Sir Frederick Pollock, twice Attorney-General and a Tory MP, raised a point of procedure which could have invalidated the trial; this resulted in an appeal being made to the Court of the Exchequer. The appeal judges overruled Sir Frederick's objection and all three defendants were sentenced to death. The sentences were later commuted to transportation and by the end of January 1840 the three men were on their way to Australia. TN)

A Visit to the Houses of Parliament

Members are extremely careless of their appearance: they present themselves in frock-coat, riding-boots, hat on head, umbrella under their arm. They pay little attention to most of the speeches.

Baron d'Haussez, *Great Britain in 1833*

In France our liberties are established by custom long before they are confirmed by law. In vain did Napoleon and the Restoration repeal the laws which marked the beginning of woman's emancipation; this tyranny merely served to awaken universal resistance. Women are proving daily that they are men's equal in intelligence, and public opinion is growing correspondingly more enlightened. But in England intellectual ideas have no power to extend the bounds of freedom; there, freedom has never advanced a step without the aid of insurrection. While women authors illuminate the entire British horizon with their brilliance, not only do laws and prejudices combine to keep women in the most atrocious bondage, but even the House of Commons, that body which claims to represent the *whole* nation, if not in reality, at least on paper, and which goes down upon its knees to receive the orders of a queen, carries inconsistency to such lengths that it *refuses women* the right of admission to its sittings![1]

In this country, which claims to be free – if we are to attach any value to the rhetoric of journalists and politicians – one half of the nation is not only deprived of its civil and political rights, it is also in many ways virtually enslaved; women can be *sold* in the market-place, and the legislative assembly *denies them a place* in its bosom. Oh shame! Shame on a society that persists in such barbarous customs! What ridiculous arrogance that England should insist on the right to impose her principles of liberty throughout the world! Yet where is there a country more oppressed than England? Even the Russian serf is happier than the English factory-worker or the Irish peasant. Is there any place on earth where women do not enjoy more freedom than in the British Isles?

Being forbidden to attend a sitting of the honourable gentlemen made me want to gain admittance all the more. I was quite well acquainted with a member of the House, a Tory, not an unreasonable sort of man; he had travelled a good deal and prided himself on being free from prejudice. I was innocent enough to believe that his deeds would match his words; I asked him – thinking it the most natural thing in the world – to lend me some men's clothes and take me with him to the sitting. My proposal had the same effect on him as had, in days gone by, sprinkling holy water on the devil! What! Lend men's clothes to a woman and insinuate her into the sanctuary of male power? What an abominable scandal, what depravity, what fearful blasphemy! My friend the Tory turned white with fear, red with indignation, snatched up his hat and stick, rose without a glance in my direction, and declared that he could have nothing more to do with me. His parting words were from the Gospel: 'Woe to that man by whom the offence cometh!' to which I added the verse: 'And woe to that man by whom offence is taken!'

This incident showed me the omnipotence of prejudice in England, but I could also see that the ruling classes are not taken in by it; they accept its demands out of hypocrisy, because this enables them to exploit the dogmas of religion to keep the masses in their place.

The will of woman is the will of God; this proverb is so often borne out that I feel it augurs well for woman's future emancipation. My resolution was not shaken in the least. To me all obstacles are a challenge which only make me persevere the more. I saw very well that I could have no further recourse to any member of Parliament, whatever his political colour, nor to any other Englishman. I therefore approached in succession several gentlemen attached to the French, Spanish and German embassies, but met with refusals everywhere, not for the reason that the Tory had given, but because they feared to compromise themselves by offending against accepted custom. At last, strangely enough, I found an eminent Turkish gentleman, sent to London by his government, who not only approved my plan, but helped me carry it out by offering me a complete set of clothes, his admission card, his carriage, and his own amiable company as escort. How gratefully I accepted his offer!

We settled on a day. I repaired to his lodging with a French gentleman we had taken into our confidence. Here I changed into an elaborate Turkish costume; it was much too big and I felt very uncomfortable in it – but he who desires the end must accept the means!

London and its buildings are so well lit that one sees better by night than by day. We get out of our carriage at the door of the House of Commons. Our costume attracts attention; everybody stares at us, follows us, and I hear murmurs all around me: 'The young Turk appears to be a woman.' Since in England all is scrupulous formality, the usher asks the real Turk for his admission card, takes it to show I don't know who, then makes us wait for more than ten minutes. There we stayed, surrounded by row upon row of inquisitive onlookers, both men and women, assembled in this lobby to enjoy the interesting sight of watching their representatives pass by. Two or three ladies fixed their gaze upon me and repeated out loud, 'There's a woman in Turkish clothes!'

My heart was beating violently and I blushed despite myself; I was in agonies during that long wait for fear that people would complain and prevent me from being admitted. However, my appearance inspired respect. I overcame my agitation and preserved a calm demeanour, for such is the influence of costume that, in donning the Turkish turban, I had acquired the serious gravity habitual to the Moslem.

At last the usher returned and told us we could go in. Quickly we made for the little staircase on the left and took our places in the back row so that we would have nobody behind us; but here too our costumes excited attention, and soon the rumour spread throughout the gallery that I was a woman in disguise. In that one evening, I learned more about Englishmen in high society than ten years of ordinary residence in London would have taught me; no words could express their extreme discourtesy, coarseness – brutality, even – towards me.

Although the Turk and I outwardly maintained the calm bearing of the true Ottoman, they must have guessed how distressed and embarrassed we were feeling. Yet without the slightest respect for my status as a woman and a foreigner, or for the fact that I was there in disguise, all these so-called gentlemen passed in front of me, staring at me boldly through their lorgnettes and exchanging remarks about me in loud voices; then they stopped behind us in the stairway, and – speaking loud enough for us to hear – exclaimed in French:

'What is that woman doing in the House?'

'What reason can she have for attending the session?'

'She must be French; they have no respect for anything.'

'Such conduct is most improper.'

'The usher should make her leave.'

Then off they went to speak to the ushers, and *they* came to stare at me as well; others hastened to inform members of the House, who left their seats to come and stare in their turn. I was on thorns; what a gross breach of good manners and hospitality! But I shall pass over these painful memories and speak about the House itself.

In appearance nothing could be meaner or more commonplace; it puts one in mind of a shop. It is rectangular in shape, small and very cramped; the ceiling is low, the galleries above overhang and partly hide the aisles beneath; the wooden benches are stained a walnut-brown colour. The chamber has no outstanding feature, nothing to show it has a lofty function to fulfil. It could just as well serve as a village chapel or house an assembly of grocers, what you will; its architecture and furnishings have no dignity whatsoever. The gas-lighting, however, is absolutely magnificent, and this is the only thing that I can find to praise.

The honourable members recline on the benches in bored and weary poses – several even stretch right out and *go to sleep*! The English, who make martyrs of themselves in strict observance of the rules of etiquette; who attach so much importance to dress that even in the country they must change three times a day; the starchy English, who take offence at the least lapse or the slightest negligence, display an utter contempt for every convention of polite society when they are in the House. It is good parliamentary form to appear at a session in everyday clothes, covered in mud, an umbrella under one's arm; or to arrive at the House on horseback and enter in full hunting array, complete with spurs and riding-crop. The insignificant creatures who are so numerous in the British Parliament hope in this way to show how urgent are their pursuits and how fashionable their diversions; and although I presume that not one of them would take the liberty of visiting any of his colleagues without removing his hat, they all make a point of keeping their hats on in the House; well, at least they demand no more courtesy from others than they have for themselves! Nobody in the galleries removes his hat either. In France this mark of courtesy is required in every public meeting; but in England, one assumes, the House of Commons does not claim any such right.

Only when a member addresses the House does he take off his hat; he leans upon his stick or umbrella, sticks his thumbs in his waistcoat or his trouser pockets. They all tend to speak at great length and do not expect anybody to pay any attention to what they say – indeed, they do not seem to be very interested in it themselves! Certainly a far deeper silence reigns there than in our Chamber of Deputies, as most of the members are either asleep or reading their newspapers.

We had spent more than an hour in the chamber; a second speaker had succeeded the first without attracting the slightest attention, and I was beginning to feel extremely fatigued; my understanding of English was insufficient for me to follow the debate, but I am sure I would have understood it better had not the monotonous voices of these *waxworks* grated so intolerably on my nerves. We were preparing to leave for the House of Lords when O'Connell[2] rose to his feet. Immediately everyone awoke from his parliamentary torpor; the recumbent members sat up, rubbing their eyes; newspapers were set aside, whispering ceased, and on every pale impassive face there appeared an expression of the keenest attention.

O'Connell is a bull-necked, commonplace sort of man; his face is ugly, red, blotchy and wrinkled; his gestures brusque and unrefined. His dress matches his person – he wears a wig and a wide-brimmed hat. To see him in the street, you would take him for a cabman in Sunday best – but I would swiftly add that beneath this gross exterior God has concealed a being full of fire and poetry, and there is a world of difference between the two!

The spokesman for the people looks no different from any ordinary citizen, and this may be one reason for the power he exerts, for in this corrupt society, elegant manners make one suspect the truth of a man's words and the purity of his heart. When O'Connell speaks in defence of his people or in the name of his religion, he is inspiring, sublime – how he makes the oppressor tremble! His ugliness vanishes, his face becomes as impressive as his words. His little eyes flash fire, his voice rings out, resonant and clear; he speaks with such emphasis that his words go straight to his listeners' hearts, where they kindle every emotion from pity to rage. At meetings he provokes his audience to tears, anger, enthusiasm – and revolt! I truly believe that this man could work miracles. If Queen Victoria were to rely on so powerful an adviser, if she could set aside religious differences and unite in fraternal embrace the people of her three kingdoms, she could achieve in a few years what Louis XI failed to accomplish in his entire reign, and her liberated people would bless her name. But to succeed in this great task, it would need a follower of Machiavelli to sit upon the throne.

We proceeded to the House of Lords. There, too, they guessed my sex, but the manners of these gentlemen were very different from those I had been exposed to by the representatives of shopkeepers and financiers. They kept their distance; there were some smiles and whispers, but I heard no unseemly or discourteous remarks. I saw that I was in the presence of true gentlemen, tolerant of a lady's whims and even making it a point of honour to respect them. The English nobility, despite its aloofness, possesses an urbanity of manner, a politeness one seeks in vain amongst the overlords of finance – or in any other class.

As we entered, the Duke of Wellington was addressing the House; he spoke in a cold expressionless drawl, and what he said, though received with deference, made little impression. Then Lord Brougham delivered two or three facetious pleasantries which provoked uproarious laughter from their lordships.[3]

Their chamber is hardly any better than the Commons; it is built on the same plan, with the same rough unfinished masonry devoid of any decoration.

The noble lords conduct themselves no differently from their fellows in the lower chamber; they too keep their hats upon their heads, but this is from pride in their rank rather than lack of manners, and they require spectators in the public galleries and witnesses summoned to appear at their Bar to bare their heads, even if they are members of the Commons.

When Lord Wellington had finished speaking, he

sprawled across his bench with his legs on the back of the bench above and his head lower than his feet – a most grotesque posture, just like a horse with its legs in the air, as we French would say.

I left these two chambers hardly edified by what I had seen, and certainly more scandalised by the behaviour of the gentlemen of the House of Commons than they had been by my clothes!

NOTES

1(TN). The Houses of Parliament, as described by Flora, were almost completely destroyed by fire in October 1834, and from that date until the opening of Barry's new buildings in the 1850s, both Houses were in temporary accommodation.

Parliament voted to admit ladies to its sittings in 1835, four years before Flora published her *Promenades dans Londres*.

It therefore seems reasonable to infer that the events described in this chapter took place during Flora's second visit to London, in 1831. All three speakers she mentions by name could have spoken on the same evening; Daniel O'Connell took his seat in the Commons in 1829, Lord Brougham moved from the Commons to the Lords in 1830, and the Duke of Wellington had been entitled to a seat in the Lords since 1808.

2(TN). Daniel O'CONNELL (1775–1847) was known as 'the Liberator' for his lifelong efforts on behalf of the Irish people. A lawyer by training, he exploited every legal loophole to outwit repressive landlords and administrators as he laboured to build up the Catholic Association in his native land. In 1828 he was elected an MP but was unable to take his seat until 1829 when the Catholic Emancipation Act was passed. O'Connell used his remarkable powers of oratory to advance the Irish cause by constitutional means; throughout his life he remained opposed to subversion and violence. He worked to free the predominant Catholic majority in Ireland from the burden of the tithes they were compelled to pay towards the upkeep of the Church of Ireland, and to improve the lot of the impoverished tenants of Anglo-Irish land-lords. In these two causes he had some support from his colleagues in the House, but in his agitation for the repeal of the Union with England, he was alone.

3(TN). The Duke of WELLINGTON was leader of the Tory Opposition in the House of Lords in 1831, and again in 1835–1841. Henry BROUGHAM (1778–1868) became a Baron in 1830. He was renowned in both Houses for his wit and eccentricity. Flora took a dislike to him because he adopted some of the ideas of Malthus and the utilitarianism of Jeremy Bentham; she distrusted the liberal doctrines of free trade, as propounded by the Whigs. She probably did not know that he also voted against the admission of ladies to parliamentary debates.

Factory Workers

Children of our glorious land,
Up! To arms! and watchful stand!
Militants of industry,
Constant must your vigil be.

Vainly the parasite
Mocks at your labours;
You are the masters now,
Rouse yourselves, neighbours!

Producers all, impose your will,
Show the hacks who scribble still
What the peaceful future plans
For deserving artisans!

Up! To arms! etc.

> *A Call to Arms* (song by Vincard,
> a worker and a disciple of Saint-Simon)[1]

The workers are now the pariahs of society; not a voice
is ever raised in the legislature for their good, except it
be for some restraint upon their liberty, or curtail-
ment of their pleasures.

> *London & Westminster Review*
> April 1839, vol. XXXII, 2, p.494

In the beginning all societies go through a period of slavery,
but the evils it produces make it essentially transitory, and
its duration is in inverse ratio to its harshness. If our fathers
had not treated their serfs with more humanity than English
industrialists treat their workers, servitude would never have
lasted all through the Middle Ages. The existence of the

English worker, whatever his occupation, is so appalling that the negroes who left the sugar plantations of Guadeloupe and Martinique to enjoy English 'freedom' in Dominica and St Lucia are glad to return, when they can, to their former masters. But do not think for a moment that I should want to commit the sacrilege of condoning any form of slavery! I only want to show that English law treats the workers more harshly than the autocratic French master treats his negroes, and that the slave of English capitalism has a far heavier task to earn his daily bread and pay his taxes.

The negro is exposed only to the caprice of his master, whereas the English worker and his family are at the mercy of the manufacturer for their very existence. If calico, or any other product, suddenly falls in price, all employers affected by it, whatever their business – spinning, cutlery, pottery, etc. – immediately agree among themselves to reduce wages, without troubling to consider whether the new rates are sufficient to feed their workers or not; at the same time they increase working hours. When the worker is on piecework they demand better quality work, yet pay less for it, and if they are not satisfied with the standard of work, they refuse to pay for it. Cruelly exploited by his employer, the worker is also squeezed dry by taxation and starved by the landlords, so he invariably dies young, his life shortened through overwork or through the nature of the work itself. His wife and children do not long survive him: harnessed to the same machines, they succumb to the same causes; or if winter comes and they have no work, they die of hunger by the wayside.

When the division of labour is carried to extremes, industry makes enormous progress, but it dispenses with Man's intelligence and reduces him to the function of a mere cog in the machine. If the worker were still capable of performing more than one stage in the manufacturing process, he would enjoy more independence and his greedy employer would have fewer opportunities to torment him; if he spent no more than a few hours at the same task, his constitution would be able to withstand the harmful effects of his work. In no English factory will you ever see a grinder over the age of thirty-five; yet the use of the grinding-machine has no ill-effects on our workers at Châtellerault,[2] because grinding is only one part of their work and takes up only a little of their time, whereas in the English factories grinders do nothing else. If the worker were engaged in various stages of production, he would not feel crushed by a sense of his utter insignificance, nor would his intelligence become dulled through constant repetition of the same actions; he would·not feel the need for strong liquor to rouse him from the torpor induced by the monotony of his work, nor would drunkenness add the final touch to his misery.

Unless you have visited the manufacturing towns and seen the workers of Birmingham, Manchester, Glasgow, Sheffield, Staffordshire etc., you cannot appreciate the physical suffering and moral degradation of this class of the population. It is impossible to judge the plight of the English worker by French standards. In England the cost of living is half as much again as it is in France, and since 1825 wages have fallen so low that the worker is nearly always forced to claim parish relief to keep his family alive. As the parish authorities are overwhelmed by the increased demands on their resources, they regulate the amount of relief according to the worker's wage and the number of children he has, in relation to the price of potatoes, not bread, for to the English worker bread is a luxury! Skilled workers fare little better, as their higher wages make them ineligible for relief. The average wage they earn, I am told, does not exceed three or four shillings a day, and they have, on average, four children, so if you relate these figures to the price of necessities in England, you can easily imagine their distress.

Most workers lack clothing, bed, furniture, fuel, wholesome food – even potatoes![3] They spend from twelve to fourteen hours each day shut up in low-ceilinged rooms where with every breath of foul air they absorb fibres of cotton, wool or flax, or particles of copper, lead or iron. They live suspended between an insufficiency of food and an excess of strong drink; they are all wizened, sickly and emaciated; their bodies are thin and frail, their limbs feeble, their complexions pale, their eyes dead. They look as if they all suffer from consumption. It is painful to see the expression on their faces, which is common to all workers, and I do not know whether it comes from the stress of permanent fatigue or the black despair that corrodes their hearts. It is difficult to get them to look at you for they all keep their eyes lowered and only occasionally steal a sly, sidelong glance at you; then their normally impassive faces, wrapped in profound gloom, assume a stupid, brutish, thoroughly evil expression.[4]

In English factories, unlike ours, you never hear snatches of song, conversation and laughter. The master does not like his workers to be distracted from their toil for one moment by any reminder that they are living human beings; he insists on silence, and a deathly silence reigns, so much does the worker's hunger reinforce the employer's command! Between master and man there exists none of those bonds of familiarity, courtesy and concern one finds in France: bonds which soften the feelings of hatred and envy that the rich, with their disdain and harshness, their excessive demands and their love of luxury, always arouse in the hearts of the poor.

In an English factory you would never hear the master say to a worker, 'Good day, Baptiste, how is your wife and the little one? Good, that's splendid! Let's hope she'll soon be quite well again; tell her to come and see me as soon as she's up and about.' An English employer would think it demeaning to speak to his workers in this way. In every factory owner the worker sees the man with the power to dismiss him from his job; that is why he touches his cap so humbly every time they meet, but the employer would think it beneath his dignity to return the greeting.

In my eyes slavery is no longer the greatest human misfortune since I have become acquainted with the English proletariat, for the slave knows he will get his daily bread all his life and be cared for when he falls ill; but there is no bond between the English worker and his master. If the employer has no work to offer, the worker dies of hunger; if he falls ill, he dies on his wretched straw pallet, unless when he is on the point of death, he has the good fortune to be taken into hospital – for it is a special favour even to be admitted. If he is old, or crippled in an accident, he is dismissed and has to resort to begging, but then he has to be careful not to be arrested for vagrancy. All in all, his position is so appalling that you feel he must be possessed of either superhuman courage or total apathy to be able to endure it.

Cramped conditions are a commonplace in English factories; the space allowed each worker is calculated with a careful eye. The yards are small, the staircases narrow; the worker is obliged to move around his machine or loom *sideways*. If you visit a factory it is easy to see that the comfort and welfare, even the health, of the men destined to spend their lives within its walls, have never entered the builder's head. Cleanliness, one of the surest roads to health, is sadly neglected; the more meticulously the machines are painted, varnished, cleaned and polished, the dirtier are the floors, the dustier the windows, the more squalid the yards with their pools of stagnant water. It is a sad truth that if the buildings and workshops were clean, trim and well maintained, like our factories in Alsace, the rags of the English worker would appear even more hideous in contrast. But no matter what the reason for the lack of cleanliness, whether it is due to accident or design, it is none the less an extra burden for the worker to bear.

England has no greatness left save in her industry, but this is truly colossal, in terms of the mechanical inventions she owes to the mathematical genius of modern times. These magical machines seem to turn everything around them to stone! The docks, the railways, the immense size of the factories, all testify to the importance of British commerce and industry.

The sheer power of the machines and their universal application amaze the mind and stupefy the imagination. Human science in a million different guises has usurped the functions of the intellect; with machines and the division of labour, motors are all we need; reasoning and reflection are no longer necessary.

I have seen a steam-engine with the power of 500 horses![5] Nothing could be more impressive and awe-inspiring than the sight of these iron masses in motion; their gigantic dimensions strike terror into the imagination and dwarf the capacities of Man. This mighty engine is housed in an enormous shed where it controls a considerable number of machines working on iron and wood. The huge bars of gleaming iron, raised and lowered forty or fifty times a minute to set the monster's tongue darting in and out as if to devour everything in sight; the dreadful groans it emits; the rapid revolutions of the immense wheel that issues from its entrails only to return before it has revealed more than half its vast circumference; all this fills the soul with terror. In the presence of the monster, you have eyes and ears for nothing else.

Recovering from your fear and stupor, you look about you for Man, but you hardly see him, reduced to the size of an ant by the giant proportions of everything around him. He is busy feeding enormous iron bars between two great blades curved like the jaws of a shark, which cut through them as cleanly as a Damascus steel slicing through a turnip.

If at first I felt humiliated to see Man brought so low, his functions reduced to those of a machine, I was quick to realise the immense advances which all these scientific discoveries would bring: brute force banished, less time expended on physical labour, more leisure for Man to cultivate his intelligence. But if these great benefits are to be realised, there must be a social revolution; and that revolution will come, for God has not revealed such admirable

71

inventions to men only to have them remain the slaves of a handful of manufacturers and landed proprietors.

Beer and gas are the two main products consumed in London. I went to see the superb brewery of Barclay-Perkins[6] which is certainly well worth a visit. This establishment is very spacious; no expense has been spared in its equipment. Nobody would tell me how many litres of beer it produces each year, but to judge from the size of the vats, it must amount to an extraordinary quantity. It was in one of these vats – the largest, it is true – that Messrs Barclay and Perkins once invited a member of the English royal family to a dinner at which more than fifty guests were present. This particular vat is 30 metres high! Everywhere that steam can be used, manpower is excluded, and what strikes one most about this brewery, is how few workers are employed in such a vast enterprise.

One of the largest gas-works is in Horseferry Road, Westminster; I have forgotten the name of the company. You cannot visit it without a ticket of admission.[7]

In this palace of industry the abundance of machinery and iron is quite overwhelming; everything is made of iron – platforms, railings, staircases, floors, roofing etc.; plainly no expense has been spared to ensure that buildings and equipment alike are made of the most durable materials. I saw cast-iron vats with the dimensions of a four-storey house. I wanted to know how many thousand tons they hold, but the foreman with me was just as uncommunicative as the foreman at the brewery, and preserved an absolute silence.

We went into the big boiler-house; the row of furnaces on either side were burning brightly; the scene was not unlike the descriptions the poets of Antiquity have left us of Vulcan's forges, save that the Cyclops were animated with divine activity and intelligence, whereas the black slaves of the English furnaces are sullen, silent and impassive. There were about twenty men present, going about their work in a slow, deliberate fashion. Those with nothing to do stood motionless, lacking the energy even to wipe away the sweat streaming down their bodies. Two or three turned their blank gaze towards me; the rest did not even raise their heads. The foreman told me that only the strongest men were selected as stokers; even so, they all developed chest diseases after seven or eight years of the work, and invariably died of consumption. That accounted for the misery and apathy depicted on every countenance and apparent in every movement the poor wretches made.

The work demanded of them is more than human strength can endure. They wear nothing but cotton drawers; when they leave the boiler-house they merely throw a coat over their shoulders.

Although the space between the two rows of furnaces must have been fifty or sixty feet, the floor was so hot that the heat penetrated my shoes immediately and made me lift up my feet as if I had stepped on live coals. I stood upon a large stone slab, but even this was *hot*, although it was well off the ground. I could not stay in this veritable hell; the heat was suffocating, the smell of gas was making me dizzy, and my chest felt as if it would burst. The foreman took me to a gallery at the end of the boiler-house where I could see everything in relative comfort.

We made a complete tour of the establishment; I was lost in admiration for all the machines, for the meticulous care that marks every stage of the work; but in spite of all precautions there are frequent disasters in which men are injured and even killed. O God! Can progress be bought only at the cost of men's lives?

The gas produced at this factory is taken by pipes to light the Oxford Street area as far as Regent Street.

The air is horribly tainted; at every instant you are assailed by poisonous fumes. I emerged from one building, hoping to find the air purer in the yard outside, but everywhere I went, the foul exhalations of gas and the stench of coal and tar pursued me.

What is more, the entire premises are very dirty. The yard

– with its pools of stagnant water and piles of rubbish – testifies to a total neglect of hygiene. It is true that the materials used to produce gas are of such a nature that it would require vigorous measures to keep the place clean, but two men would be sufficient for the task, and for a trifling increase in outlay, the entire establishment would be healthier.

I was on the point of suffocating and could not wait to escape from such an evil-smelling place when the foreman said, 'Stay a moment longer, there's something very interesting for you to see; the stokers are just about to remove the coke from the ovens.'

I returned to my perch in the gallery; the sight that met my eyes was one of the most appalling that I have ever seen.

The furnaces are above ground level, with a space below to catch the coke. The stokers, armed with long iron rakes, opened the ovens and raked out the coke, which fell in blazing torrents into the chamber below. Nothing could be more terrible or majestic than the sight of so many mouths all pouring forth flames: nothing more magical than the cavern suddenly illumined with living fire, descending like a waterfall from a rocky height, only to be swallowed in the abyss: nothing more terrifying than the stokers, their bodies streaming as if they had just emerged from the water, lit on both sides by the dreadful braziers that thrust out their fiery tongues as if to devour them. Oh, no! a more frightful spectacle it would be impossible to imagine!

When the furnaces were half-empty, men perched on vats in the four corners of the lower chamber threw water on the coke to extinguish it. The scene changed; there arose a dense hot whirlwind of black smoke which ascended majestically through the open skylight. Now the furnaces were visible only through this haze, which made the flames seem even redder and the fire more menacing; the stokers' bodies turned from white to black, and the unfortunate wretches were swallowed up like demons in some infernal chaos. I was caught unawares by the smoke, and barely had time to make a hasty descent.

I awaited the end of the business, anxious to see what would become of the poor stokers. I was astounded that not one woman appeared. Dear God! I thought, have these men no mother, sister, wife or daughter waiting at the door as they emerge from that hell, to wash them in warm water, to wrap them in shirts of flannel; to give them something nourishing to drink; to greet them with friendly words that would give them heart and help them to endure their cruel lot? I was in a fever of anxiety; not one woman appeared. I demanded of the foreman where these men, soaked in sweat, would go to take their rest. 'They'll lie down in this shed,' he replied, quite unconcerned, 'and in a couple of hours they'll go back to their stoking.'

This shed, open on all sides to the wind, was really no more than a shelter from the rain, and inside it was as cold as ice. A sort of mattress lay in one corner, almost indistinguishable from the coal around it. I saw the stokers stretch out on their stony bed, with no covering but a greatcoat so stained with sweat and coal-dust that it was impossible to tell its original colour. 'There,' said the foreman, 'that's how these men get consumption; they don't look after themselves, going straight from the heat into the cold like that.'

This last observation by the foreman was all it needed to send me out of the factory in a state of exasperation.

So this is how men's lives are bought and sold; and when the work required of them kills them, at least the capitalist is spared the expense of increasing their wages! But this is even worse than the *slave trade*; I can think of no crime more monstrous, except cannibalism! There is no law to prevent factory-owners from disposing of the youth and strength of their workers exactly as they please, purchasing their existence, sacrificing their very lives, just for the sake of making money – and all the workers get is seven or eight shillings a day!

I do not know whether any owners of similar factories have had the humanity to provide a warm room equipped with tubs of warm water, mattresses and woollen blankets, where stokers could go after their work to wash, wrap themselves up and rest in a temperature more in keeping with the one they had just left. It is a shame and a scandal for a country that the things I have described should ever happen.

In England, when the coach arrives at a post, ostlers come running to throw cloths over the horses' backs, rub them down, wash their feet and lead them to a warm stable strewn with dry straw.

Several years ago a number of extra staging-posts were introduced, because people realised that excessively long relays shortened the lives of the horses. Yes, but a horse costs the capitalist £40 or £50 sterling, whereas the state provides him with men for *nothing*!. . . .

NOTES

1(TN). Jules VINÇARD (1796 – 1879) was a skilled worker who became a follower of the social reformer Saint-Simon and founded the journal *La ruche populaire* (The People's Beehive) which reviewed Flora's *Promenades dans Londres* favourably, but declined to serialise her *Union ouvrière* on the grounds that it was too Utopian. In his day, Vinçard was probably best known for his popular songs.

2(TN). Châtellerault is a town in the west of France, not far from Poitiers and situated on the river Vienne; it is famous as the home of the national small arms factory, established in 1819.

3(FT). 'It is on record that many workers in the manufacturing towns of England do not attend church because they have no clothes.

On 31 May 1840 I visited the district of Bethnal Green in the company of the parish officers responsible for distributing relief in this part of the city of London. . . .

Among the wooden hovels scattered all over the "gardens" we

noticed one which stood out from the rest by reason of its even more wretched appearance. It might have been taken for a pile of rotting timber thrown upon a dunghill; the fence separating it from the other hovels consisted of broken planks interspersed with scraps of iron and metal all in an indescribable state of filth and dilapidation. In one room on the ground floor – the only room in the house – with its floor a few inches lower than the pile of rubbish in the yard outside, lived a family of ten. This hovel which measures less than ten feet square by seven feet high has a rent of 1s. 6d. a week. It is even more difficult to convey an idea of the state of the family than to describe their dwelling. The man, the head of the family, was shaking with fever; illness and hunger had reduced him to extreme emaciation, and nothing about him seemed alive except his gaze, transparent and animated by the heat of his fever; it was impossible to endure his anguished expression. This man, thirty-seven years of age, English by birth and a silk-dyer by trade, told us that he could earn up to 15s. a week when employed, but that he had been unable to find work for five months. The relief officer confirmed that he had always been of good character, and that neither laziness or vice had brought him to this state. His wife, crouching by the broken hearth, held an infant to her breast, and three more barefoot young children were outside. Their father confessed to us that the other children had gone out ''in the hope of finding something, either by begging or otherwise''. For five months he had had no other means of existence than what the parish allowed him and what the children brought home. Despite the extreme destitution of this family, they refused to take refuge in the workhouse.

In another yard of this abominable quarter we found a family which seemed to us even more wretched than the first, if that is possible. They were living in one upstairs room, quite spacious and light, but approached by a dark and dirty staircase where every stair shook beneath our feet. This family consisted of eight people, all present at the time of our visit. The head of the family was a weaver of velvet, still young, and English by birth. He earned 7s. 6d. per week, but he was not continuously employed. His lodging cost him 2s. 6d. per week, and for nearly two months he had been unable to pay his rent. The only article of furniture in the room was his loom; there were no chairs, no table, no bed. In one corner was a big heap of straw, half hidden by a scrap of cloth, and in it were buried three children, stark naked like animals, with not a single rag between them. The woman had her back turned to us and was vainly trying to fasten about her what remained of her clothing so that she would be fit to be seen. The man was wearing a blue coat with two or three shining engraved buttons still on it; he had no shirt. He received us with courtesy, and sadly yet calmly told us the full horror of his plight. When we entered he was holding a Bible, and when the parish officer asked him why he did not go to church, he pointed to his bare chest, to his wife standing motionless with shame in the corner, and his children hiding one behind the other to avoid our gaze, and replied that soon he would not even be able to go out looking for work. This family was accounted honest, and the officer had already distributed clothes to them several times, but lack of work had forced the father to trade these gifts of charity for bread. . . . And this is not the only part of London privileged to suffer such wretchedness. Shoreditch, Whitechapel, Shadwell, St Giles and St Olave would provide us at every step with scenes similar to those we have just described.'

Eugène Buret, *De la misère des classes laborieuses en Angleterre et en France* (Paris, 1840).

4(FT). This expression, which I have also noticed in slaves in America, is not confined in the British Isles to factory workers alone. It is found wherever people are dependent or subordinate; it is one of the most characteristic features of a working class twenty million strong. There are some exceptions, nevertheless, and it is nearly always among women that they are to be found.

5(FT). I saw it in Birmingham. The proprietor of the factory assured me that the power of the machine equals that of 500 horses; it turns more than 200 driving-wheels and sets in motion wood-saws, shears for cutting iron, rollers of every size and an assortment of machines for various purposes such as making zinc spoons etc. While I was there, a sixpenny piece was placed under a press to give me some idea of the power exerted – and out came a ribbon of silver paper forty-two yards long and as thin as an onion-skin.

6(TN). Barclay Perkins' brewery in Southwark was one of the great tourist attractions: the largest brewery in the world with the biggest output of beer – 400,000 litres a day.

7(TN).   This was the Gas, Light and Coke Company, founded in 1812 and first in the field for the commercial exploitation of gas. It established its works in Horseferry Road in 1813 and one of its first achievements was to light the approaches to the Houses of Parliament. By the time of Flora's visits to London in the 1830s there were nearly a dozen other companies, all in fierce competition.

Prostitutes

Prostitution is not a crime: it is a punishment. Just as man has an instinctive horror of death, woman has an instinctive abhorrence of prostitution. We should weep over the fallen woman, not laugh in her face.

Alphonse-Louis Constant,
The Assumption of Woman (1841)

There is no country, or city, or town, where this evil is so systematically, so openly, or so extensively carried on, as in England and her chief city.

Report of Mr Talbot, secretary of the London Society
for the Prevention of Juvenile Prostitution[1]

Now I ask anybody with a modicum of intelligence whether, in the interest of present and future generations, it is useful to observe and study prostitutes or not, and whether the man who devotes himself to this task, who confronts its horrors, who sacrifices to it his time, his trouble and his fortune, truly deserves the contempt that prejudice, begotten by ignorance, has kept alive to this day. As for myself, I believe I see the matter in its true light; I know that research is not always respected in proportion to the difficulties it involves or the services it renders, so I put my faith in the judgment of sensible men who understand and appreciate my intentions; as for the rest, while I respect their opinions, I deplore their blindness.

Parent-Duchâtelet,
Prostitution in the City of Paris (1836)[2]

I have never been able to look upon a prostitute without being moved by compassion for our society, contempt for the way it is organised, and hatred for those who dominate it: strangers to any sentiment of shame, any respect for humanity or love for their fellows, who reduce the work of God's hand to the depths of humiliation and debase her below the level of the brute.

I can understand the brigand who robs travellers on the highway and forfeits his life on the guillotine, the soldier who gambles with death every day in return for a few pence, the sailor who exposes his life to the fury of the sea, for all three find a sombre and terrible poetry in their calling. But I cannot understand the prostitute. To surrender all rights over herself, annihilate her will and feelings, deliver her body to brutality and suffering, her soul to contempt! The prostitute is an impenetrable mystery to me. . . . I see prostitution as either an appalling madness or an act so sublime that my mortal understanding cannot comprehend it. To brave death is nothing – but what sort of death faces the prostitute? She is wedded to sorrow and doomed to degradation: physical torture endlessly repeated, moral death every moment, and – worst of all – *boundless self-disgust*![3]

I repeat, this is either sublime, or it is madness![4]

Prostitution is a blight on the human race, the most hideous of all the evils caused by the unequal distribution of wealth, an even more damning indictment of society than crime. Prejudice, poverty and servitude combine to produce this revolting degradation. Yes, for if you men did not impose chastity on women as a necessary virtue while refusing to practise it yourselves, they would not be rejected by society for yielding to the sentiments of their hearts, nor would seduced, deceived and abandoned girls be forced into prostitution. If you allowed women to receive the same education and follow the same professions as men, they would not be crushed by poverty while men prospered. If you did not expose them to the violence and abuses that parental despotism and the indissolubility of the marriage bond entail, they would never be forced to choose between oppression and dishonour.

The concepts of vice and virtue imply the freedom to do

good or evil, but what moral sense can a woman have if she cannot call her soul her own, possesses nothing in her own name, and has been accustomed all her life to use her guile and seductive charms as a means to escape from tyranny and constraint? When she is tormented by poverty and sees the wealth of this world reserved for men's sole enjoyment, does not the art of attraction in which she has been schooled since childhood lead her inevitably into prostitution?

Then let the society man has made be blamed for this aberration of nature, and let woman be exonerated. As long as she remains the slave of man and the victim of prejudice, as long as she is refused training in a profession, as long as she is deprived of her civil rights, there can be no moral law for her. As long as she can enjoy wealth only through the power she exerts over men's passions, as long as she has no independent legal status and her husband can rob her of any property she has earned or inherited, as long as she can ensure her right to her property and her freedom only by renouncing marriage, there can be no moral law for her. And it is my firm belief that until women are emancipated, prostitution will continue to grow.

Nowhere but in England is wealth so unequally divided; this is why there is so much prostitution. English law places no restrictions on a man's right to make a will, but the precedents set by the aristocracy and followed by everybody from the lord of the manor to the humble cottager accept that in every family there is one male heir; consequently a daughter's dowry is pitifully small, unless she has no brothers.

Yet there are very few occupations open to the woman of some education: furthermore, the fanatical prejudices of the various religious sects ensure that the girl who has been seduced and betrayed is banished from every house, even from her own home. Most wealthy landowners, industrialists and manufacturers regard it as a sport to take advantage of young girls. It is to the workers who labour fourteen hours a day for a crust of bread that such men owe their wealth, yet far from devoting any of it to redress the evils and disorders which are a direct consequence of the accumulation of so much wealth in so few hands, they nearly always use it to swell their pride and increase their intemperance and debauchery, while the people, already demoralised by their appalling poverty, are further corrupted by the vices of the rich.

Girls born into the lower classes are driven to prostitution by hunger; women are barred from working on the land, so when they can find no work in the factory, their only resources are servitude or prostitution.

'We must go walk the streets, my sisters, love is our
    shameful trade,
Never complain though the hours be long and our
    work so poorly paid,
Fate has decreed that we serve men's need and forfeit
    our worthless life,
All to defend the family home and protect the virtuous
    wife.'[5]

There are so many prostitutes in London that one sees them everywhere at any time of day; all the streets are full of them, but at certain times they flock in from the outlying districts where most of them live, and mingle with the crowds in theatres and public places. It is rare for them to take men home; their landlords would object, and besides, their lodgings are unfit. They take their 'captures' to the houses reserved for their trade; these are scattered throughout the city, and according to Dr Ryan they are as numerous as gin-shops.[6]

Between seven and eight o'clock one evening, accompanied by two friends armed with canes, I went to take a look at the new suburb which lies on either side of the long broad thoroughfare called Waterloo Road at the end of Waterloo Bridge. This neighbourhood is almost entirely inhabited by prostitutes and people who live off prostitution; it is courting danger to go there alone at night. It was a hot summer evening; in every window and doorway women were laughing and joking with their protectors. Half-dressed, some of them *naked to the waist*, they were a revolting sight, and the criminal, cynical expressions of their companions filled me with apprehension. These men are for the most part very good-looking – young, vigorous and well-made – but their coarse and common air marks them as animals whose sole instinct is to satisfy their appetites.

Several of them accosted us and asked if we wanted a room. When we answered in the negative, one bolder than the rest demanded in a threatening tone, 'What are you doing here then, if you don't want a room for you and your lady friend?' I must confess I would not have liked to find myself alone with that man.

We went on our way and explored all the streets in the vicinity of Waterloo Road, then we sat upon the bridge to watch the women of the neighbourhood flock past, as they do every evening between the hours of eight and nine, on their way to the West End, where they ply their trade all through the night and return home between eight and nine in the morning. They infest the promenades and any other place where people gather, such as the approaches to the Stock Exchange, the various public buildings and the theatres, which they invade as soon as entry is reduced to half-price, turning all the corridors and foyers into their receiving-rooms. After the play they move on to the 'finishes'; these are squalid taverns or vast resplendent gin-palaces where people go to spend what remains of the night.[7]

The 'finish' is as much a part of life in England as the beer-cellar in Germany or the elegant café in France. In the tavern the clerk and the shop assistant drink ale, smoke cheap tobacco and get drunk with tawdrily dressed women; in the gin-palace, fashionable gentlemen drink Cognac, punch, sherry, port, and French and Rhenish wines, smoke excellent Havana cigars, and flirt with beautiful young girls in splendid gowns. But in both places scenes of orgy are acted out in all their brutality and horror.

I had heard descriptions of the debauchery to be seen at finishes, but could never bring myself to believe them. Now I was in London for the fourth time with the firm resolve to discover everything for myself. I determined to overcome my repugnance and go in person to one of these finishes, so that I might judge for myself how far I could trust the various accounts I had been given. The same friends who had accompanied me to the Waterloo Road again offered to be my guides.

What goes on in these places ought to be seen, for it reveals the moral state of England better than any words could express. These splendid pleasure-houses have an appearance all their own. Those who frequent them seem to be dedicated to the night; they go to bed when the sun begins to light the horizon and awaken after it has set. From the outside, these 'gin-palaces' with their carefully fastened shutters seem to be quietly slumbering; but no sooner has the doorkeeper admitted you by the little door reserved for initiates than you are dazzled by the light of a thousand gas lamps. Upstairs there is a spacious salon divided down the middle; in one half there is a row of tables separated one from the other by wooden screens, as in all English restaurants, with upholstered seats like sofas on each side of the tables. In the other half there is a dais where the prostitutes parade in all their finery, seeking to arouse the men with their glances and remarks; when a gallant gentleman responds, they lead him off to one of the tables loaded with cold meats, hams, poultry, pastries and every manner of wines and spirits.

The finishes are the temples which English materialism raises to its gods; the servants who minister in them are dressed in rich liveries, and the capitalist owners reverently greet the male guests who come to exchange their gold for debauchery.

Towards midnight the regular clients begin to arrive; several finishes are frequented by men in high society, and this is where the cream of the aristocracy gather. At first the young noblemen recline on the sofas, smoking and exchanging pleasantries with the women; then, when they have drunk enough for the fumes of champagne and Madeira to go to their heads, the illustrious scions of the English nobility, the very honourable members of Parliament remove their coats, untie their cravats, take off their waistcoats and braces, and proceed to set up their private boudoir in a public place. Why not make themselves at home, since they are paying out so much money for the right to display their contempt? As for any contempt *they* might inspire, they do not care in the least. The orgy rises to a crescendo; between four and five o'clock in the morning it reaches its height.

At this point it takes a good deal of courage to remain in one's seat, a mute spectator of all that takes place. What a worthy use these English lords make of their immense fortunes! How fine and generous they are when they have lost the use of their reason and offer fifty, even a hundred, guineas to a prostitute if she will lend herself to all the obscenities that drunkenness engenders. . . .

For in a finish there is no lack of entertainment. One of the favourite sports is to *ply a woman with drink* until she falls dead drunk upon the floor, then to make her swallow a draught compounded of *vinegar*, *mustard*, and *pepper*; this invariably throws the poor creature into horrible convulsions, and her spasms and contortions provoke the *honourable company* to gales of laughter and infinite amusement. Another diversion much appreciated at these fashionable gatherings is to empty the contents of the nearest glass upon the women as they lie insensible on the ground. I have seen satin dresses of no recognisable colour, only a confused mass of stains: wine, brandy, beer, tea, coffee, cream etc., daubed all over them in a thousand fantastic shapes – the handiwork of debauchery! The human being can sink no lower than this.[8]

The sight of this satanic revelry fills the soul with terror and revulsion; the atmosphere turns the stomach. The air is heavy with the noxious odours of food, drink, tobacco, and others more fetid still which seize you by the throat, grip your temples in a vice and make your senses reel: it is indescribably horrible!. . . . However, this life, which continues relentlessly *night after night*, is the prostitute's sole hope of a fortune, for she has no hold on the Englishman when he is sober. *The sober Englishman is chaste to the point of prudery*.

It is usually between seven and eight o'clock in the morning when people leave the finish. The servants go out to look for cabs, and anyone still on his feet gathers up his clothes and returns home; as for the rest, the pot-boys dress them in the first garments that come to hand, bundle them into a cab and tell the cabman where to deliver them. Often nobody knows their address; then they are deposited in the cellar and left to sleep in the straw. This place is known as the drunkards' hole, and there they stay until they have recovered their wits sufficiently to say where they wish to be taken.

Needless to say, the prices charged in these establishments are exorbitant, so the noble lords depart with an empty purse, fortunate if their greedy temptress has had the grace to leave them their watch, their gold-mounted lorgnette, or any other article of value.

In this city of intemperance, the working life of a prostitute, whatever her class, is of short duration. She is forced to drink alcohol whether she wants to or not.[9] What constitution could stand up to such constant excess? This is why half of London's prostitutes die after three or four years; some may last for seven or even eight, but this is a limit that few reach and fewer still exceed. Many die in hospital of bad diseases or pneumonia; or if there is no room for them there, they die in their sordid lodgings, deprived of food, medicine, care, and everything else.

The dying dog is favoured with a kind look from his master, but the prostitute dies alone in the gutter with nobody to spare her a pitying glance.

In London between 80,000 and 100,000 women, the

flower of the population, live by prostitution.[10] Every year from 15,000 to 20,000 of these poor creatures sicken and die the death of a leper in total neglect, and every year a still greater number springs up to replace those whose dreadful life is over.[11]

In order to account for vice on such a colossal scale it is necessary to bear in mind the immense increase of wealth in England over the past fifty years and to remember that in every society at every age, debauchery has increased with wealth. The pursuit of trade has reached such a pitch in England that it outweighs every other consideration; there is not one man whose dominant passion is not to make money. Even the younger sons of the wealthiest families are under the same compulsion, and nobody is content with what he already possesses.

The love of money is instilled in the heart of young people from the most tender age; it destroys family affection together with any compassion for the misfortunes of others, and leaves no room for any sentiment of love to take root. Love counts for nothing in their lives: they seduce a young girl without love, they marry without love. The young man *marries for a dowry*, then forsakes his wife and dissipates her fortune in the gaming-houses, clubs and finishes of the West End. How repulsive it is, this materialistic existence devoted entirely to the gratification of selfish appetites! Did society ever before wear so hideous a face as now, when money is the only preoccupation, and wine and prostitutes the only pleasure?

In London every class of society is rotten to the core. In the child, vice precedes experience; in the old man, it outlives potency. Not one family has escaped the taint of the diseases associated with debauchery. My pen refuses to describe the depths of depravity and perversion to which men sink when they are surfeited with material pleasures, when they live only through their senses and their souls are dead, their hearts withered, their minds a desert. What would St Paul have done in the face of such lasciviousness? He would surely have called down curses upon all fornicators and shaken the dust of these islands from his feet!

In the monster city there is no compassion for the victims of vice: the fate of the prostitute inspires no more pity than that of the Irishman, the Jew, the worker or the beggar. The Romans were no more indifferent to the fate of the glad-iators who perished in the arena. Men – when they are not too drunk – will kick any prostitute they pass in the street; they would beat her if they were not afraid of attracting the attention of the police or provoking a fight with her protec-tors.[12] Respectable women look upon prostitutes with harsh contempt, and the Anglican priest, unlike his Catholic brother, is not the comforter of the distressed. He has no pity for the prostitute; from his pulpit he will deliver a moving sermon on the loving kindness Jesus showed towards Mary Magdalen, but for the thousands of Magdalens who die every day in all the horrors of poverty and desertion, he has no tears to shed. What do these creatures matter to him? His duty is to stand up in church and preach a well-phrased sermon at a fixed time on a fixed day, and that is all. In London a prostitute has no right to anything but the hos-pital, and then only if there is an empty bed for her.

National vanity makes us want the country where Provi-dence ordained our birth to reign supreme. This malevolent disposition towards other nations, the bitter fruit of past conflicts, constitutes the greatest obstacle to progress and often prevents us from acknowledging the causes of the evils which the foreign visitor calls to our attention. Then the old hatred revives, and we challenge him to furnish proof for phenomena as obvious as a Thames fog! All nations have a common interest, but as yet only a few enlightened individ-uals understand this, so the foreigner who dares to criticise is taken for an enemy who slanders us.

Prostitution is found everywhere, but in London it is so widespread that it seems like an omnivorous monster. I knew that the ordinary reader might find this hard to believe and accuse me of exaggeration, so I resolved to arm myself with *proof* and cite authorities to confirm the testimony of my own eyes.

I had read the book by M Parent-Duchâtelet, so I knew that even if it was impossible to give exact figures for a phenomenon which eludes official statistics, nevertheless by dint of prolonged investigation it was possible to get very near the truth. I inquired whether there was a philanthropist in England sufficiently devoted to humanity to dedicate his life to the study of prostitution in London with the same unconquerable tenacity that M Parent-Duchâtelet had shown in his study of prostitution in Paris. I learned that there *was* such a man, a Dr Ryan whose book *Prostitution in London* was already arousing a storm of recrimination and hatred.

Dr Michael Ryan is an established author whose large following bears witness to his talents, so he did not need to publish this book to acquire a reputation. This publication, which was to provoke an outcry from the upper classes whom it unmasked, and outrage the hypocritical conventions of English morality, is an act of supreme devotion on his part. Dr Ryan knew his country and was fully aware of what the consequences of publication would be, yet endowed with the courage and energy that soar above the clamours of a corrupt world, he boldly revealed the facts and exposed the depravity and vileness which the monster city strives to conceal.

Dr Ryan's book was published in London last year (1839) and contains the most accurate information on prostitution in London that it is possible to obtain, given the present state of the English police. In support of his facts, Dr Ryan quotes from the reports made to a parliamentary committee by the Society for the Suppression of Vice[13] in 1837 and 1838; the report of the Metropolitan Police for the same two years; reports of the Society for the Prevention of Juvenile Prostitution for 1836, 1837 and 1838; reports made by Mr Talbot, the Society's secretary, and the police commissioners before Parliament; and Home Office reports for 1837 and 1838.

From these documents it transpires that in 1793 Mr Patrick Colquhoun, a stipendiary magistrate and a person of some consequence, estimated after prolonged research that the number of prostitutes in London was 50,000. But this was only an approximate figure, for even now that the police force is better organised, they have no means of obtaining accurate statistics. The population of London has doubled since 1793, therefore it is not unreasonable to suppose that vice has more than doubled in proportion, seeing that the distribution of wealth is still as unequal as ever, that employment has not increased in step with the population, that wages have consequently decreased, and that so far the government has failed to effect any real improvement in the lot of the workers. However, on the basis of information supplied by the police, magistrates and by Messrs Prichard and Talbot, the secretaries of the two societies already mentioned, Dr Ryan estimates that there are between 80,000 and 100,000 prostitutes in London, of whom half – some claim two-thirds – are less than twenty years old.

One can only guess at their average lifespan as prostitutes, for up to 1838 there was no law in England requiring the registration of deaths. Mr Clarke, the last chamberlain of the City of London, puts it at four years, others say seven, while the Society for the Prevention of Juvenile Prostitution estimates the annual mortality of prostitutes at 8,000. From his researches, Mr Talbot concludes that there are 5,000 brothels in London – that is, as many as there are gin-shops. He also estimates that there are 5,000 men and women in London employed in procuring girls for these houses, and between four and five hundred persons he calls *trepanners*[14] employed to entrap girls aged from ten to twelve and take them – of their own free will or by force – to these frightful dens. He calculated that 400,000 people have a direct or indirect interest in prostitution, and that eight million pounds is spent on this vice annually in London alone.

The Society for the Prevention of Juvenile Prostitution

91

was founded in 1835. In its first public statement it exposed the depravity of the lower classes in London, claiming that schools existed where boys and girls were taught all kinds of fraud and immoral practices, that prostitution and theft were *openly encouraged* by those who stood to profit by them, and that crime was highly organised. It called the attention of the public to outrages of the most scandalous nature, committed with impunity in broad daylight to feed this most infamous traffic. It said there were large numbers of men and women whose business it was *to sell girls between ten and fifteen years of age whom they had caught in their traps*. These children, enticed on some plausible pretext into collecting-houses or brothels, were kept in close confinement for a fortnight or so and thus forever lost to their parents.

In its annual report in May 1836, the Society remarks:

> Although the metropolis too frequently presents scenes of open and undisguised vice, distressing to every moral and religious person, yet no picture is perhaps more revolting than the frightful increase of juvenile prostitution. Under the shadow of night, and even at mid-day, the streets are perambulated by unhappy children, decoyed from the paths of virtue and the protection of their parents by miscreants, for the mere purpose of gain, and who, though the authors of their destruction, yet remain unpunished.[15]

During the first year of its work the Society came to the help of a number of young girls who had been led astray, among them a child of thirteen or fourteen; the dealer responsible for her abduction and detention was brought to judgment and acquitted! The Society's reports for 1837 and 1838 mention several similar cases in which the traffickers in human flesh escaped with *a few months' imprisonment*.

After describing some of the methods used to trap children, the Committee adds:

> To detail the numerous artifices employed to draw unwary children of both sexes into this vortex of misery would be

impossible, they are so complicated and varied; the Committee will therefore only allude to the treatment experienced by these unfortunate children after being trepanned. As soon as the female is decoyed to a brothel, she is no longer allowed to wear her own clothes, which become the prize of the keeper; she is decked with second-hand trappings, once the property of some wealthy lady. The regular clients are notified, and when she no longer attracts customers to the house, her master sends her to walk the streets, where he has her closely watched so that it is impossible for her to escape, and if she attempts it, the spy, often a bully or a procuress, charges her with stealing from the master of the house the clothes she wears on her back. Then the policeman arrests her, and sometimes he takes her to the station-house, but more commonly he gives her up to the brothel-keeper, who rewards him. . . . When the forlorn unfortunate wretch returns to her infamous abode, she is maltreated and *kept nearly naked* during the day, so that she cannot attempt to run away; she is often *half-starved*, and at night her trappings are restored to her and she is sent into the streets again, always followed by a spy. Failing to bring home nightly a certain number of men, she is severely punished. She is not permitted to appropriate one penny to her own use.[16]

Brothels are forbidden in England by law, so it is difficult to furnish proof of their existence. Persons who frequent such places are unlikely to testify against them in court out of shame, and as the police have no power to enter a house unless there has been a disturbance, they cannot establish that an offence is being committed. The neighbours can have them suppressed by parish officers only on the charge that they disturb the peace of the neighbourhood.

In any case, to prohibit brothels by law is absurd, for as prostitution is an inevitable consequence of the way European society is organised, governments at the present time ought to be dealing with the factors which cause it, and thus bring it under control.

In its reports of 1837 and 1838 the Committee of the

Society gives an account of the actions it has brought against brothel-keepers and other individuals guilty of corrupting juveniles between the ages of ten and fifteen; but the penalties imposed for such offences never exceed *one year's imprisonment* and are generally from one to six months. Sometimes the accused is acquitted on the grounds *that the boys and girls in question freely consented either to go to the house, or to live there*. This is the kind of protection the law affords the family of the worker! As for the children of the wealthy, who are always under the eyes of the various servants employed to watch over them, they are far less exposed to the danger of abduction.

Moral depravity is so widespread and the price paid for children so high that these people will go to any lengths to procure them. In 1838 the Committee called the attention of all upholders of patriotism, virtue, religion and humanity to 'the shameless efforts constantly being made to offer up new victims to debauchery. Scarcely a street can be passed through without meeting some storehouse of obscenity. Agents are employed for the purpose of entrapping the unwary and innocent. The suburban villages, the bazaars, the parks, the theatres, continually furnish new victims. Your Committee has authority for stating that the keepers of brothels and procurers are frequently in the habit of obtaining females from the workhouses and penitentiaries.'[17]

The upper classes pose as the guardians of morality with the object of perpetuating intolerance among the people, but they have not shown the slightest disposition to support the work of the Society for the Prevention of Juvenile Prostitution; on the other hand, ever since the Society for the Suppression of Vice was formed thirty-seven years ago for the sole purpose of enforcing observance of the *Sabbath* and prohibiting *fortune-telling* and the sale of *obscene publications*, it has received their constant and unanimous support, because it is perfectly acceptable to sleep all through the Sunday sermon, renounce the paintings of Aretino and keep one's vices intact; moreover, by subscribing to a society which professes to work for the suppression of *vice*, one acquires a reputation for *virtue*, which is very precious in the eyes of these English Macaires.[18]

The Committee of the Society for the Prevention of Juvenile Prostitution said in May 1838:

> While carrying forward the operations of the Society, the members of the Committee have had to encounter obstacles of no ordinary character, arising from the almost universal apathy and indifference prevailing upon the subject. They have been met in their course by the sneers and contempt of the profane and immoral, the censures and condemnation of those who believe that licentiousness is *necessary* for the well-being of society, the supineness and negligence of the religious; nowhere have they encountered aid or encouragement; but amidst the buffetings of all, they have been able to persevere, supported by a consciousness of the importance of the objects they have in view, and by the sympathies and kindness of their subscribers.[19]

English depravity has produced nothing more odious than those monsters of both sexes who scour England and the continent ensnaring young children, snatching them from their fond parents, exciting insidious hopes in their breasts, telling them wicked lies, sometimes unwittingly caught in the very traps they use to entice the children; then they return to London to sell their spoils to the virtuous aristocracy and the new moneyed class. Some of these agents working for the slave markets of the West End move in the most respectable circles, yet these are the people who are often sent to various towns and villages in Holland, Belgium, France and Italy. They negotiate with the parents and engage the daughters as embroiderers, milliners, seamstresses, musicians, ladies' companions, maids etc., to allay their suspicions; sometimes they even go as far as to advance a quarter's wages to the parents, and when they have obtained a certain number of young girls they return to London.[20]

In 1838 the Committee of the Society for the Prevention of Juvenile Prostitution instituted proceedings against a Frenchwoman named Marie Aubrey who was forced to abandon her infamous trade and flee to France in order to escape several months' imprisonment.

The house in question was situated in Seymour Place, Bryanstone Square. It was an establishment of great notoriety, visited by some of the most distinguished foreigners and others and carried on in a style little short of that observed in the richest and noblest families. The house consisted of twelve or fourteen rooms, besides those appropriated to domestic uses, each of which was genteelly and fashionably furnished. The saloon, a very large room, was elegantly fitted up; a profusion of valuable and splendid paintings decorated its walls, and its furniture was of a costly description . . . a service of solid silver plate was ordinarily in use when the visitors required it, which was the property of Marie Aubrey. At the time the prosecution was instituted, there were about twelve or fourteen young females in the house, mostly from France and Italy. There was a medical practitioner in the neighbourhood who was employed as agent. It was his duty to attend the establishment. He was frequently sent either to France, Italy or the villages near London, to procure females. . . . Marie Aubrey had lived in the house a number of years, and had amassed a fortune. Shortly after she left, the inmates were sent away, and the house is now shut up and the furniture disposed of. Upon receiving a fresh importation of females, it was the practice of this woman to send a circular, stating the circumstance, to the parties who were in the habit of visiting the establishment.

At the present time there are in the metropolis a great number of young females from France and Italy, and other parts of the continent, a large proportion of whom have been decoyed from their homes, and introduced into the paths of iniquity by Marie Aubrey or her infamous agents. There are a number of houses of this description at the West End now under the cognizance of the Society, and whose circulars are in its possession, who adopt this plan, and, by means of the Court Guide and twopenny post, are forwarding notices of their establishments indiscriminately to all.

Your Committee desire to lay before this meeting the means adopted by the agents of these houses. As soon as they arrive on the continent they obtain information respecting those families who have daughters, and who are desirous of placing them in respectable situations; they then introduce themselves, and by fair promise induce the parents to allow their children to accompany the stranger to London, with the understanding that they are to be engaged as tambour workers, or in some other genteel occupation. A sum of money is left with the parents, as a guarantee for the due performance of the contract, with an agreement that a certain amount shall be forwarded quarterly. . . . While they remain in the house they were first taken to, the money is duly forwarded, and their parents are thus unconsciously receiving the means of support from the prostitution of their own children; if they remove, letters are sent to the parents to apprize them that their daughters have left the employ of their former mistress, and the money is accordingly stopped; they fail not to inform the parents that they have obtained other respectable situations, and are doing well.[21]

The profound corruption of the wealthy classes and the high prices they can afford to pay, protect and encourage this obscene trade. Mr Talbot states that in the seraglios of the West End, newly imported slaves sell for between twenty and two hundred pounds, and if one considers the luxury of these establishments and the cost of maintaining them, together with the agents' travelling expenses, prices of this order cannot be an exaggeration. When the young women become well known to all the regular clients and no longer excite their fancy, they are passed on to a second-rate house and after a year or eighteen months the wretched creatures die in hospital or are left to fend for themselves on the streets.

The demand for children is so enormous that traps are set for them in every imaginable place to catch them and give their guardians the slip. Mr Ryan describes how women lie in wait at coach stages for young girls who come to London in search of a place, and offer them lodgings; others present themselves at workhouses and orphanages on the pretext of hiring servants, and children are often entrusted to their care, for these women are well-dressed and their manner inspires confidence; in shops they enter into conversation with the assistants and they frequent the best fashion-houses and dressmakers' establishments, where they charm the apprentices with their winning ways. Their employers make them travel far, and they often go as much as eighty miles from London in search of their prey.

'The other modes by which infamous houses are supplied,' says Mr Talbot, 'as death, disease or demand require, is that the keepers employ agents, young women of about eighteen years, to perambulate the streets, and decoy any children they may meet with, under pretence of taking them to see a relative, or going for a pleasant walk, or inviting them to a theatre, or getting them a place of service. The most subtle artifices are employed on these occasions, both by day and night. The Sabbath is a favourite day with these wretches, and they watch young children go to Sunday schools, and entice them to their haunts; nay, I believe children have been actually *taken from the school* in the sight of teachers and companions, they having no idea of so shocking a system being in operation. As soon as the children are secured, they are *sold*, and their doom sealed, perhaps, by some hoary-headed debauché at an enormous price.'[22]

Mr Talbot recounts many facts which have come to his knowledge regarding children of ten and eleven years of age violated in brothels. These crimes are a commonplace, and he says that so little is done to curb them that keepers negotiate with carters to supply them with children *at so much per head*, whom they have enticed to come to London on various pretexts. These carters are often brought before the magistrates for crimes of this sort, but because of the shortcomings of the law, they suffer only the lightest penalties, if they are punished at all.

'Testimony in my possession,' says Mr Talbot, 'shows that a considerable number of keepers lure *young boys* to their houses. This happens all the time, and I think I am right in estimating that out of 5,000 etablishments, 2,000 encourage the corruption of young boys.'

'*Sunt lupinaria nunc inter nos, in quibus utuntur pueri vel puellae*![23] Mr Talbot mentioned localities,' says Dr Ryan, 'which of course cannot be printed. These most infamous and horrible dens are partly supplied by children and young persons who are observed gazing at the windows of the improper print-shops, and as much as ten pounds has been expended to secure one boy.'[24]

The police have no power to set foot inside a house of any description unless the noise and disorder within can be clearly heard outside; consequently most brothels – with the exception of houses concerned to establish a reputation in fashionable society – are in dangerous and remote places. They afford shelter to burglars, pickpockets and rogues of every description, and the keepers are frequently brought before the local magistrate because of disputes and disturbances, or on suspicion of theft. Thieves resort to the brothels to lie low and divide the spoils obtained from their depredations upon the public; the keepers traffic in stolen goods and, in the event of the thieves being apprehended, come to their aid and provide money to subvert the course of justice and ensure an acquittal. Nearly all prostitutes have as their protectors men engaged in some business or other, who spend the night at the brothel and are always ready at the slightest signal to pounce upon a victim and rob or even murder him.[25]

Dr Ryan mentions a part of London called Fleet Ditch where almost every house is the lowest and most infamous brothel. There is an aqueduct of large dimensions running through it which empties into the Thames some distance away. The murderers and criminals of every description who inhabit these houses precipitate the corpses of their victims into the aqueduct without the slightest risk of discovery.

He has also heard of two influential men in the City who let two houses in the vicinity, in reality not worth thirty pounds a year each, for two pounds a week each as common brothels! The rental of such houses varies from a hundred to five hundred pounds a year, and a premium of one to three hundred pounds is asked for the goodwill of a first-rate establishment. Dr Ryan tells another story of two gentlemen who were enticed to spend the night in a disreputable house situated in a notorious square, and the fierce struggle they had the following morning with the protectors of their charming young ladies.[26]

Apart from the brothels to be found in every part of London, where prostitutes take the men they accost in the streets, there are also lodging-houses kept by receivers of stolen property in some quarters, where thieves of every description congregate; several such houses contain as many as fifty beds and may be occupied by either sex, but there are some where only boys are admitted, because they wish to escape the control of persons stronger than themselves. As these boys are equal and often superior to grown men in skill, presence of mind and knowledge of their business, the lodging-house keeper, wanting to reap as much as possible of the boys' plunder, will not admit men because they might rob the boys. Women, however, are not excluded – or more correctly, girls between ten and fifteen years old, for it is seldom that the female companions of thieves live to be women. These girls are admitted as the *mistresses of the young boys* who introduce them. Dr Ryan says that 'the scenes of profligacy that occur in these dens are indescribable and would be *incredible* if described'![27]

Nearly all the boys between twelve and fifteen years of age committed to prison have had relations with prostitutes, and are visited every day by their mistresses posing as their sisters. Mr Talbot estimates that in London there are always between 13,000 and 14,000 young prostitutes *from ten to thirteen years old*. He says that over a period of eight years, the number of venereal cases treated at Guy's Hospital was 2,700; these were children *aged from ten to fifteen*, and a far greater number than those admitted were *refused for want of accommodation*. 'In one day,' he adds, 'I have seen *as many as thirty of them* turned away from one hospital, some of them in the most direful state, scarcely able to walk.' Dr Ryan also says that a great number of applications are made every day at the Metropolitan Free Hospital, most of them by girls of twelve to sixteen suffering from syphilis. 'As a physician to different public charities in the metropolis,' he continues, 'I have often been shocked by the number of young lads, or rather children, presenting themselves for advice on venereal diseases.'[28]

In London there are five institutions set up to help prostitutes who wish to abandon their dreadful career, but they are generally badly organised and lack sufficient resources to be able to do much good.[29] The total number of prostitutes offered refuge in these five shelters annually does not exceed five hundred. Five societies – and they can help and provide work for only five hundred of these unfortunate women! The only organisation to attack the evil at its source is the Society for the Prevention of Juvenile Prostitution, which actively exploits existing laws, but despite all its efforts, it can do little to curb abuses, because the assistance it receives and the law as it stands are both inadequate. So the brothel-keeper who is guilty of abducting young children and selling them into a life of depravity will escape with no more than *eight or ten days* in prison – if he is not acquitted – whereas some poor honest working woman arrested for selling fruit or some such thing in the street is sent to prison for thirty days. Of course, for the keeper of a brothel a few days in prison is hardly a punishment at all, for he is dead to any sense of shame; his cronies do not esteem him any the less – on the contrary, they show him every sympathy, do what they can to shorten his imprisonment, and keep him company to relieve his boredom. But for a virtuous young woman guilty of only the most trifling

101

infringement of the law, thirty days in prison almost inevitably spells her ruin. But what do the wife or child of a worker matter? It is in the shopkeeper's interest to see that goods are not peddled on the public highway; he and the brothel-keeper have *political rights*; they are electors and jurymen, whereas the worker and his family are nearly always dependent on the parish. Evidently the annual consumption of between eight and ten thousand children by the moneyed classes fits neatly into the Malthusian system for decreasing the surplus population; and from this point of view, the keeper of a brothel is a *pillar of respectability* and a useful citizen of his country!

NOTES

1(TN). James Beard TALBOT (1801–1881) founded the Society for the Prevention of Juvenile Prostitution in 1835. The estimate that there were eighty thousand prostitutes in London originated with him.

2(TN). Alexis Jean-Baptiste PARENT-DUCHÂTELET (1790–1836) was an internationally recognised authority on health and hygiene, whose great work *De la prostitution dans la ville de Paris, considérée sous le rapport de l'hygiène publique, de la morale et de l'administration* was published in two vols. in 1836.

3(FT). 'They know how vile they are and seem to have a profound awareness of their abject state; they are a subject of horror to themselves; the loathing they have for themselves is if anything even greater than the loathing they inspire in virtuous people. They bitterly regret their fall; they plan and even strive to escape from their predicament, but all their efforts are in vain, and what drives them to despair is the knowledge that in the eyes of the world they are the dregs of society.

'Anyone who has reflected on human nature will easily understand how painful such a state must be; nothing is more natural than the desire to be liked by one's fellow men. Who could endure the general neglect, and even worse, the hatred, contempt and universal disdain of society without feelings of terror, panic and despair? Only to think of it is enough to drive some prostitutes out of their minds. Not long ago, M Pariset called my attention to a prostitute confined in the hospice of La Salpêtrière. This woman spoke to nobody, but when she thought she was alone, she repeated over and over again, "How unhappy I am that I left the path of virtue! how can I bear to be despised by everybody; how can I live in such humiliation?" '

Parent-Duchâtelet,
De la prostitution dans la ville de Paris (1836)

4(FT).   'One of the facts which has struck me most in the course of my researches in the Department of Public Morals and in police records is the frequency with which mental weakness and a state bordering on insanity occur in prostitutes. In reports of legal proceedings this is constantly being advanced to justify either their release, or a lighter sentence than their various offences would normally incur.

'A valuable document on the mental derangement of prostitutes has come to us from a colleague, M Esquirol, who has for many years been entrusted with the care of the inmates of La Salpêtrière. From a careful analysis of the records kept by this doctor, it emerges that in the five years between 1811 and 1816, 105 prostitutes were admitted to the hospital, that is on average twenty-one every year, which is more than would have been expected. Less from police submissions than from his own research and investigations into the previous life of the patients admitted, M Esquirol was able to establish what all these women were, or what they had been; and he is certain that several escaped his investigation and must be somewhere among the embroiderers, linen-maids, milliners, clothes-dealers and so on who fill the pages of his voluminous registers. One woman became mad as a consequence of the distress she suffered at being recognised by someone from her old home as she went about her trade.

'It is interesting to note the particular nature of the derangement suffered by patients of this class:

Melancholia 36
Mania 43
Dementia 18
Undiagnosed 8

Total   105'
Parent-Duchâtelet, op. cit.

5(TN).   Auguste BARBIER (1805 – 1882) was a poet and dramatist who was inspired by the July Revolution of 1830 to write a series of vigorous poems on the social evils of the time. This extract from his long poem about London, *Lazare*, was written in 1837.

6(TN).   Michael RYAN (1800 – 1841) was a doctor at the Metropolitan Free Hospital and editor of the *London Medical and Surgical Journal* from 1832 to 1838. His *Philosophy of Marriage in its Social, Moral and Physical Aspects* (1837) was reprinted twelve times in the space of thirty years. The full title of the book so frequently quoted in this chapter is *Prostitution in London, with a comparative view of that of Paris and New York.* . . . *with an Account of the Nature and Treatment of the Various Diseases* (London, 1839). Mayhew's collaborator Bracebridge Hemyng discounts some of the allegations made by Ryan and quoted by Flora, and challenges Ryan's informants to identify themselves (see Mayhew, *London Labour and the London Poor*, vol.IV).

7(FT).   'There are also many splendid saloons in different parts of the town in which as many as two hundred dashing prostitutes assemble at the same time. Fashionable and wealthy young men visit these places and choose their mistresses from those assembled. These saloons are also attached to taverns, and are the source of great wealth. They are not exculsively confined to the west-end of the town, or London, beyond Temple Bar. They are known in other parts under the name of 'long rooms', particularly along the banks of the Thames, where sailors abound. Some of these long rooms can accommodate five hundred persons.

'Prostitutes are arranged in rows in these houses, like cattle in Smithfield market, until sailors and other visitors select their ''wives''. The suited then enter another capacious apartment in the establishment, and after every kind of revelry, drinking and dancing, proceed to brothels, where they are stupefied by

poisoned drink, fleeced, robbed and beaten by the bullies.'
Dr Ryan, Prostitution in London, p. 189

8(FT). In this finish I saw four or five superb women; the most remarkable was an Irish girl of extraordinary beauty, and although she was well known there, her entry caused a sensation and excited a murmur of admiration. As for me, my eyes filled with tears at the sight of such a beautiful creature; had she been queen of England, men would have come from all over the world to admire her.

It was almost two o'clock in the morning when she made her appearance, dressed with an elegant simplicity that enhanced her beauty. She was wearing a gown of white satin and half-length gloves which displayed her lovely arms; charming little pink slippers showed off her dainty feet and a diadem of pearls crowned her head. Three hours later this same woman was lying on the floor dead drunk! Her gown was a disgusting sight; everybody was throwing glasses of wine, etc. all over her beautiful shoulders and magnificent bosom. The pot-boys were trampling her underfoot as if she were a bundle of rubbish. If I had not witnessed such shameful desecration of a human being, it would have been impossible to believe it.

9(FT). 'All the information I have collected proves that they begin to drink only in an attempt to forget; then by imperceptible degrees they grow accustomed to alcohol, and in a short while the habit becomes so strong that it prevents them from returning to the path of virtue; this fact alone makes all the efforts of the charitable institutions fruitless.

'This is the main reason for their drinking and it influences all the rest, but there is another even more powerful reason which however applies only to the lowest and most numerous class of prostitutes; it is commonly held, particularly by soldiers and sailors who know from experience how the abuse of strong liquor aggravates syphilis and allied diseases, that the prostitute who does not drink to excess remains sober only because she is diseased; therefore they force her to drink in order to reassure themselves that she is not, and insist on her drinking all the time they are with her. Now imagine the state of the wretched woman who is forced to endure the attentions of two or three different individuals in the course of the same day.'

Parent-Duchâtelet, op. cit.

10(TN).   Visitors to London were appalled at the number of prostitutes thronging the streets, but it is impossible to accept that there were ever as many as 80,000 or 100,000; the total female population between the ages of fifteen and fifty was only 596,000 in 1841. As Flora points out, all these calculations can be traced back to an earlier estimate of 50,000 made in 1793 by Patrick Colquhoun, a police magistrate, in his *Treatise on the Police of the Metropolis*. As the population of London had doubled since then, so, it was assumed, had the number of prostitutes, hence the estimate of 100,000. Talbot's figure of 80,000 was arrived at by a more complicated process. He and a number of other investigators carried out a survey comparing the degree of licentiousness with the size of the population in four cities: Norwich, Belfast, Liverpool and London, from which he estimated the number of prostitutes in London as 52,000. But as over the past twenty years the increase in crime (300 – 400%) was out of all proportion to the increase in London's population (33%) he adjusted his figure to 80,000. Engels was content to leave it at 40,000. The police estimate, confined to the number of prostitutes who got into trouble with the law, was somewhere between 7,000 and 10,000. All these conflicting figures may be due in part to the fact that prostitution was, as William Acton put it, 'a transitory state through which an untold number of British women are ever on their passage.' There was so much casual prostitution that it was impossible to assess exactly how much. Women drifted in and out of it as their circumstances dictated; many regular prostitutes left the trade to open a shop or business, to get married and settle down, sometimes to emigrate. Mayhew records instances of decent unmarried couples with a perfectly satisfactory relationship who sometimes found themselves in such desperate financial straits that the only remedy was for the woman to go on the streets for a night to earn enough for a meal or to pay the rent. There was constant temptation for young girls to prostitute themselves, as even a chance encounter in a dark street could give them more money than they earned in a week of drudgery. (In Paris, statistics were more reliable, as prostitutes had to register. The figure for 1842 was 46,089.)

106

11(FT). The Bill requiring the registration of deaths is very recent and as yet there is no means of determining with strict accuracy the figure for the mortality of prostitutes.

12(FT). While I was in London, a city merchant who was suffering from a bad disease imagined that he had contracted it from a prostitute of his acquaintance; he arranged to meet her at a house of assignation, where he tied her skirts above her head so that from the waist upwards she was confined in a sort of sack; then he beat her with a birch-rod until he was worn out, and finally threw her out into the street just as she was. The wretched woman was suffocating for want of air; she struggled, shouted and rolled about in the mud, but nobody came to her aid. In London people never interfere in what happens in the street; 'that is not my business,' an Englishman will say, without even stopping, and he is already ten paces off by the time his words reach your ears. The poor woman lying on the pavement was no longer moving and would have died had not a policeman come and cut the string which tied her clothes. Her face was purple and she was hardly breathing, she was asphyxiated. She was taken to hospital where prompt treatment restored her to life.

The man responsible for this abominable assault was summoned before the magistrate and fined six shillings for offending against morality on the public highway.

In a nation so ridiculously prudish, the penalty for outraging public decency is clearly not very high . . . but what is surprising is that the magistrate saw nothing in this act but a misdemeanour and judged it accordingly.

13(TN). The Society for the Suppression of Vice was founded in 1802; its first secretary was William Wilberforce. Henry Prichard was secretary for more than thirty years (1836 – 1869).

14(FT). 'Trepanners' are setters of traps and snares.

15(FT). Ryan, *Prostitution in London*, p. 124.

16(FT). *Ibid.*, pp. 129 – 130; p. 179.

17(FT). *Ibid.*, p. 146.

18(TN). The name given to charlatans and frauds after Robert Macaire, a character in the play of the same name (see Chapter IV, Note 1).

19(FT). *Ibid.*, p. 144.

20(FT). *Ibid.*, p. 181.

21(FT). *Ibid.*, pp. 151–153.

22(FT). *Ibid.*, p. 182.

23(FT). *Ibid.*, p. 199. I copy the Latin given by Dr Ryan, which out of decency he has not translated ('There are now in our midst brothels where they sometimes use young boys, sometimes very young girls:' TN).

24(FT). *Ibid.*, p. 166. In support of the quotation from Dr Ryan I set before my readers an extract from the *Calcutta Courier* of February 1841. Here is proof that the English take their corruption with them wherever they go.

'According to information supplied by the *Calcutta Courier* and reprinted in the *Anti-Slavery Journal*, there exists in British India, and notably in Calcutta, an infamous trade hardly known in the most corrupt days of the Roman Empire. This trade, which the English tolerate just as they tolerate slavery, is in young children of both sexes. Far from decreasing, it is growing daily and takes place on a large scale. To keep up the supply, it is not only children from Indian families who are bought and sold, but even *Christian children* of both sexes. . . . What is one to think of these abominable practices and the state of society they expose?'

If the English, who in the name of humanity and morality are working for the abolition of slavery on this side of the globe, can permit such a state of affairs to exist in their dominions, how can they be sincere or consistent?

(Flora is quoting from an unnamed French source at second-hand, from which she infers that the English not only tolerated slavery and child prostitution, but actually introduced the latter practice into their Indian dominions.

The original extract, from the *Anti-Slavery Reporter* of Wednesday, 29 December 1841, reads as follows:

From the *Calcutta Courier*. 'We have more than once adverted to a custom indulged in to an extent but little imagined in this city, at which humanity shudders. The custom to which we refer is the sale of female children for the vilest purposes. The practice is, we learn, not a whit abated; nay, we fear, on the contrary, that it is rather on the increase. It is a well known fact, that female children are disposed of for pecuniary considerations to the procuress of the public stews of Calcutta; and that these poor wretches, after having served the purposes of their depraved purchasers, are cast helpless and discarded to seek either a mere existence or a premature grave in the lowest haunts of vice. Nor, from what has recently come to our notice, is this practice wholly confined to strictly native children; but even some who have a still stronger claim on our sympathy have been and are made the subjects of shameful barter in this city. Christian youth have been so disposed of.'

The British authorities in India uncovered similar practices, including cases where parents were murdered and their children abducted. They are cited in the *Anti-Slavery Reporter*, a fortnightly paper printed in London and financed by subscribers to the Anti-Slavery Society. In British India, slavery was declared illegal in 1843: TN.)

25(FT).   Ryan, op. cit. pp. 176, 192.

26(FT).   *Ibid.*, p. 177.

(What Dr Ryan said was, 'An enlightened medical gentleman assured me that near what is called Fleet Ditch, almost every house is the lowest and most infamous brothel. There is an aqueduct of large dimensions into which murdered bodies are precipitated by bullies and discharged at a considerable distance into the Thames without the slightest risk of discovery.' This is the story that Bracebridge Hemyng challenged: TN.)

27(FT).   *Ibid.*, p. 201.

28(FT). *Ibid.*, pp. 185, 186.

(Flora does not always make clear whether it is Dr Ryan speaking, Mr Talbot, or one of their anonymous informants. The information about the number of venereal cases treated came from a surgeon at Guy's Hospital and the figure of 2,700 applied to three hospitals, not just Guy's. As for Dr Ryan's own observation at the end of the paragraph – he refers to 'beardless boys': TN.)

29(FT). The Magdalen (1758); the London Female Penitentiary (1807); the Guardian Society (1812); the Maritime Penitent Refuge (1829); the London Society for the Prevention of Juvenile Prostitution (1835). As for the Society for the Suppression of Vice, founded in 1802, it professes five aims:
1. The prevention of the profanation of the Lord's day.
2. The suppression of blasphemous publications.
3. The suppression of obscene books, prints, etc.
4. The suppression of disorderly houses.
5. The suppression of fortune-tellers.

The Society is actively concerned with little more than promoting the observance of the Sabbath. It sees idleness on the seventh day of the week, and time spent in taverns, as the only manifestation of religion among the people. Its members sometimes take action against obscene books and pictures, and to tell the truth, this is the only useful thing they do. The abduction of eight or ten thousand children sacrificed every year to the vices of the wealthy does not seem to interest them in the least. The Society is looked upon favourably by the aristocracy and the Church of England, which is probably why it has stopped persecuting fortune-tellers, as these people are now in the good graces of the clergy.

Prisons

For the English the penalty of imprisonment is not intended to reform, but quite simply to repress; its aim is to punish the guilty man as he deserves, to teach him a severe lesson, and to deter those who might otherwise be tempted to follow his example.

Moreau-Christophe,
Report on the Prisons of England, (1839)[1]

The enormous growth of wealth and poverty throughout Europe is causing such an overwhelming increase in crime that its consequences are arousing serious public concern.[2] At last governments are realising that so far prisons have been schools where crime obtains its fatal energy. In recent years there have been numerous investigations, and in several countries experiments are being tried to remedy this growing evil. No doubt this is all to the good, but it is only part of the problem; eventually people will see that to curb the growth of crime it is not enough to establish penitentiaries in an attempt to reform the guilty through education and a strict régime, and that it is impossible to achieve any improvements in society by these means unless there are corresponding reforms in all other institutions.

If in fact, far from diminishing, the causes which *make men criminals* multiply every day, what guarantee is there that a man who has had some sort of training in prison will not relapse into crime? What good is served by solitary confinement and the rule of silence? The newly reformed criminal finds he is unable to earn a living from his trade; he sees all around him the evidence of crime, so he very soon lapses into his former ways. As things stand at present, what nation in Europe has the resources to set up enough penitentiaries

111

to contain the growing number of criminals? Can nobody see that if governments persist in a system which condones privilege, fetters trade, taxes workers and indulges in massive unproductive expenditure, they will have to carry out mass deportations, erect scaffolds at every crossroad, and arm one half of the population to mow down the other when it comes begging for bread?

Poverty on the scale that exists in England and Ireland can lead only to revolt and revolution; but hunger is not the only reason for attacks on property. Since in our society money can satisfy every passion and surmount every obstacle, since money is a substitute for talent, honour and probity, since money opens every door, then man will stop at nothing to acquire it. Nobody is content with his position in life, everybody seeks to rise in the world; and the crimes committed in the name of this universal ambition are incalculable.

As for the crimes of murder, poisoning and infanticide, it is well known that it is the indissolubility of the marriage bond that places the dagger or the poison cup into the hands of the unhappy spouse, and that the barbarous and fanatical prejudice against the unmarried mother may turn her into a criminal. Moreover, as women are excluded from every profession, when their children have no father to provide for them, their only resources are infanticide, theft or prostitution.

Legislators, statesmen, and all you to whom God has entrusted the destiny of men, before you think of reforming the criminal, concentrate on abolishing the causes of crime, and the criminal will cease to exist! The mother does not punish her child because he has fallen into the fire; she puts a guard around the hearth, and her maternal solicitude and foresight avert every possible danger.

I had heard conflicting accounts of English prisons, and my interest in social questions was increased by the wish to clarify my uncertainty about the true nature of conditions in England; but as any foreigner in London who does not have the advantage of being a duke, a marquis or a baron and staying in the best hotels meets with the greatest difficulty in accomplishing even the simplest things, it was only after repeated applications that I obtained permission to visit Newgate, Coldbath Fields and Millbank Penitentiary. Apart from these three, there are eight other prisons which national vanity forbids any foreign eye to see; I was told that this is because of their unprepossessing exteriors, badly-planned interiors and all the other abuses and irregularities which prevail in these veritable cesspools of English civilisation.[3]

Newgate has a singularly repulsive appearance:[4] it is how one would imagine a prison of the Dark Ages. It is a vast rectangular complex of buildings: the stone blocks are of massive dimensions, their face chiselled like the markings of a tiger's skin, their colour a sombre grey which gives the prison a more forbidding and terrifying aspect than any other London landmark. A few windows fitted with thick iron bars are hardly seen, lost in the thickness of the walls. The main door is nothing short of a masterpiece; I wish I could tell my readers how much iron had gone into its manufacture, so that they could share my stupefaction. If the mere sight of it is enough to strike fear into the heart of the visitor, what must the wretched criminal feel when its great iron mass clangs shut behind him, and he finds himself in the lodge of this dreadful jail?

The great defect of Newgate is its lack of daylight, but this was probably considered a virtue, a credit to the moral sense of its architect, in the days when man's idea of justice demanded vengeance on the lawbreaker. This antechamber is not quite as dark as the rest of the prison, but it still takes a little time for the eye to discern the nature of the objects around its walls. Why leave such horrifying objects there to torment the prisoner's imagination? Perhaps so that his fear and ignorance will make him confess; perhaps to make him believe that he is to be subjected to the tortures he remembers from stories told him long ago in his village; perhaps to warn him to beware of the justice of men who only yesterday were still using these very means to extort the truth. But surely it is more important for the lawbreaker to have his trust in the law, and in the impartiality of the officers who administer it, restored? Do you wish him to be in permanent revolt against society or do you wish to reform him? These objects would not look out of place in an historical collection to commemorate the reign of Henry VIII or Charles IX, but in the nineteenth century they have no place in a prison lodge; this is the arsenal of Newgate! The walls are covered with hooks on which hang every article of torture used since its foundation. They are the prison records: massive iron collars with fetters attached, saws for hacking off limbs, racks for breaking bones, clubs, axes, swords, and an assortment of instruments for extorting information from prisoners.

I confess I felt very ill at ease in this lodge. There is no fresh air or daylight; the prisoner can still hear the noise of the street outside, and beneath the door he can still see the sunlight shining in the square. What a dreadful contrast, and how he regrets the loss of his liberty! But once past the lodge he hears nothing more; the atmosphere is as cold, damp and heavy as in a cellar; most of the passages are narrow, and so are the stairs leading to the upper wards.

First I was taken to see the women's wing. Over the past few years several changes have been made at Newgate, and now it houses only prisoners awaiting trial, not convicted prisoners; in this respect it corresponds to the Conciergerie in Paris. It is here too that most executions take place.

The governor was kind enough to accompany me over the prison; he told me that thanks to the writings of philanthropists and the constant complaints of humanitarians, Newgate had undergone all the improvements of which it was capable. Mr Cox was particularly happy that prisoners were now divided into different classes, whereas formerly they had all been confined together.

The internal arrangement of the prison is not very satisfactory and there is not enough space for individual cells. In each ward the beds, wooden constructions six feet long and two feet wide, are arranged in two or three tiers like berths on board a ship. There is a large table in the middle with wooden benches all round it; this is where the prisoners eat, work, read and write. On close examination I found the wards very clean and well-kept, but as they are dark and poorly ventilated and the floors are very uneven, their general appearance is unpleasing.

Nearly all the women I saw there were of the lowest class: prostitutes, servants or country girls accused of theft. Four were on charges carrying the death penalty for crimes classified as felonies under English law. Most of them seemed to be of low intelligence, but I noticed several whose tight thin lips, pointed nose, sharp chin, deep-set eyes and sly look I took as signs of exceptional depravity. I saw only one woman there who aroused my interest. She was confined with six others in a dark, damp low-ceilinged cell; when we entered they all rose and made us the customary servile curtsey which had embarrassed and irritated me from the moment I set foot in the prison. One alone refrained and it was this sign of independence which attracted my attention. Picture a young woman of twenty-four, small, well-made and tastefully dressed, standing with head held high to reveal a perfect profile, graceful neck, delicate well-formed ear, and hair a model of neatness and cleanliness. My readers have already had occasion to remark the effect that beauty has upon me and will readily understand my feelings at the sight of this pretty creature; my eyes filled with tears and only the presence of the governor prevented me from going up to her and taking her hand so that she might understand my interest in her fate and so that my sympathy might calm for a few moments the sufferings of her heart.

Beauty can only be supreme when it reflects the noblest qualities of the soul. Without that inner radiance even the most beautiful woman in that sad place would have left me unmoved; but there was such dignity in this beauty which bore the depths of misfortune with pride and courage that I was overwhelmed with emotion and could not believe for one moment that she was wicked. Her soul was pure: I could tell it from her expression, the set of her head, her whole person. Violent passion could have driven her to commit a crime, but this creature made in God's image was still conscious of her dignity and had not been degraded.

I asked the governor and the wardress on what charge this young woman had been committed to Newgate; what was her social position, how had she behaved in prison, what standard of education had she, and so on. My eagerness betrayed the concern I felt for the unfortunate woman and aroused the interest and sympathy of my listeners.

'Oh! Madame!' replied the wardress, 'this poor young woman deserves your pity; she is six months gone with child and has three other children. Alas! it was to give them bread that she committed the theft which brought her here: she is married to a sailor, a drunkard who left her without a shilling, and as she had nowhere to turn, she sold one by one every article she possessed, but the day came when she had nothing left to sell, and her three children were begging for bread! So the poor mother, driven out of her mind by poverty and the cries of her starving children, sold some of the furniture of the room she rented, and the owner had her arrested. She has been here for two months awaiting trial.'

I had guessed right; such a woman could never be a prostitute or a professional thief! She was a *mother* who had felt the pangs of hunger devouring her unhappy children. . . . She had stolen, it is true; she had acted wrongly when she was desperate and overwrought. But which is the more guilty, this woman or the unjust inhuman society which abandons the poor to a frightful death and turns them into madmen and criminals?

The wardress told us all this in a low voice because she did not want the other prisoners to hear, and because she did not want her words to hurt the feelings of the young mother whose predicament she pitied and whose misfortunes she respected. But the cell was small and the young woman

knew very well that we were speaking about her. Nevertheless, during the quarter of an hour or more that she was the
object of our attention, she preserved her proud demeanour;
her expression did not falter; her face was calm and betrayed
no sign of agitation, because in her eyes her maternal devotion redeemed her crime and increased her self-respect. She
knew her duties as a mother and rejoiced in having fulfilled
them even at the price of her good name and the agonies of
imprisonment. In some women maternal love is so strong a
passion that no man-made law can touch it. I was lost in
admiration for the courage that God had implanted in this
mother's heart and I felt a poignant grief that her life was to
be ruined; that she would come before judges incapable of
feeling or *understanding* the sacred duties of motherhood
because they respected only the rights of property. Forget-
ting that they owed their very existence to a mother's tender
affection, they would sacrifice her on the altar of property
and condemn her to the same punishment as a professional
thief. I cursed the laws which made no distinction between
crime and virtue; I cursed the property which has to be
defended against the assault of hunger by imprisonment
and suffering. The luxuries of the landowners are paid for
with the blood of the poor.

While the wardress was speaking to the governor, I
observed the prisoner, hoping that she would eventually
look in my direction, but she remained calm and motionless. A sigh escaped me and she heard it; quickly she turned
her head and our eyes met. How could I ever describe the
tenderness and pride I read in the eyes of this poor victim of
our society? A halo seemed to encircle her head; her eyes
veiled with tears, her quivering features and trembling lips
were all so eloquent that I almost heard her say, 'Oh, you are
a mother! Can you understand my anguish? *You* would
have stolen; your children's hunger would have given you
the courage! You know what strength I needed to act as I
did. Thank you for understanding me.'

That woman has engraved the name of Newgate forever in my memory.[5]

The wing in which the men are lodged is larger and if anything even gloomier than the women's quarters. All the faces I saw there were hideous.

The children are divided into two categories: one for first offenders and one for habitual offenders. These young prisoners display an effrontery which it is difficult to imagine unless one realises how quickly children learn to dare anything, fear nothing and bear everything. The average number entering prison each month is *forty*: while there, they are taught to read and count.[6]

In one of the prison yards I saw eight of those unfortunate Canadian soldiers of freedom who fell into the hands of the army of the English aristocracy: five of them were wounded.[7] They had been waiting to know their fate for two years. One of them spoke French and he told me that they were forbidden any communication with the outside world and were not allowed to receive letters, newspapers or visits. For two years they had had no news of their families. The English government was empowered by law to sentence them all to death. But the cause of the rulers is no longer the cause of the people, and the government – fearing, no doubt, that to spill the blood of these victims would lead to an outcry against the aristocracy – was allowing these redoubtable patriots to languish and die in prison.

I could not help noticing that these prisoners were treated with something very much like deference. I mention this fact because I consider it a sign of great progress. At last the English are beginning to understand that prisoners of war should be treated as *hostages*, not as *criminals*. Would to God they had thought this way during the war with France! Then they would not have treated our unfortunate soldiers with such infamous cruelty, to the eternal shame of Pitt and the Tories. On that subject I have heard the most terrifying stories.[8]

I was told that there were two murderers in Newgate – one of the most unregenerate wickedness and the other showing signs of repentance. The latter was lodged in a cell on the ground floor. I entered and saw a slight young man of about twenty, very thin and very pale. He was sitting in the darkest corner as if to escape observation, and I noticed that he was weeping. I did not like his face; his expression was insincere and he seemed to be begging for sympathy. His crime was that in a fit of jealous rage he had murdered his father's maidservant, who was also his mistress.

From the precautions which were taken before I was allowed to set foot inside the cell of the other murderer, you would have thought him as ferocious as a hyena and given to falling upon visitors and tearing them to pieces. At first the governor tried to persuade me not to see him, then yielding to my insistence, he sent two of his officers into the cell and ordered two more to accompany me.[9] All these precautions sent my imagination racing and as I climbed the narrow twisting stair I fancied that I was about to see the most fearful monster; shades of Shylock and fantastic vampires were impressed upon my brain. I went in and – what a surprise! – I saw a young soldier of between twenty-two and twenty-four, sitting at a table reading the Bible, with the most agreeable countenance imaginable: a small round face, fresh rosy mouth, a little aquiline nose, dark blue eyes sparkling with mischief, a noble brow, a mass of naturally curling hair, and a complexion of lilies and roses. This was the *monster* they were all afraid to approach! The moment he saw me, he blushed like a girl and hastily began to button his tunic, straighten his collar and adopt a more military air; then he gave me a timid glance and I read, in his eyes rather than on his lips, a smile which said, 'Forgive me, Madame, I was not expecting visitors, so you find me rather carelessly dressed.' Poor young man! How naïve was his confusion and how sad the contrast between his youth and his cruel fate! I was very interested in him and longed to be able to speak to him, but I refrained from asking any questions for fear of embarrassing him; nevertheless my face expressed all the sorrow and compassion I felt for his plight.

No sooner was I outside than I demanded what signs of ferocity this soldier had shown to justify keeping such a close watch on him. 'Ah, he is a monster,' one of the prison officers told me, 'it is not just that he does not repent of his crime, but he tells everybody who will listen that he would do it again if he could; he laughs and sings all day long, and never stops joking for a moment with anyone who comes to visit him; in short, he is the most shameless murderer we have ever had here!' I confess I did not find all these reproaches threw much light on the ferocity of the young soldier.

I was going on my way, still unconvinced, when at the foot of the staircase I came across Dr Elliotson whom I had already met several times at the house of one of my friends who was also a doctor. This Dr Elliotson is a zealous disciple of Gall and Spurzheim[10] and is always to be seen in prisons and madhouses examining prisoners' heads for convex protuberances and predicting where the concave ones will be found. He speaks perfect French, so I lost no time in telling him how perplexed I was by the case of the young murderer.

'What do you expect,' said the doctor with a faintly disdainful smile, 'the governor of Newgate is an excellent man full of human kindness, and the warders treat the prisoners well enough, but they know absolutely nothing about science, without whose divine light they will never understand why one man steals and another man murders.'

I asked the divinely inspired doctor, who could so infallibly discern the cause of human actions, why the young soldier had murdered one of his officers.

'Why, because he has two extremely well-developed protuberances, one of pride and the other of vengeance.'

'I see, but have you spoken to him, doctor, and do you know his *reasons* for acting as he did?'

'Yes, of course. I have been studying him for two months; a charming lad, with a good heart and an amiable disposition.'

'Then why . . . ?'

'Let me tell you his story; he is twenty-three years old and was lately serving in — Regiment, stationed in Cornwall, when one day a new officer arrived. It seems that this officer spoke in a feeble nasal voice and had a peculiar accent. The poor lad, who had not long left home and was not yet accustomed to army discipline, thought it was quite in order to make fun of the officer's comical voice, and one day on parade he unfortunately confided to his neighbour one of those apt and witty asides that make you laugh in spite of yourself. The furious officer fell upon them both, struck them brutally in the face, made them surrender their rifles and had them locked up in the cells. The other soldier accepted his punishment, but our friend's bumps of *pride* and *vengeance* were too pronounced for him to be able to do the same; he vowed to kill the man who had publicly assaulted him. As soon as he was released he began to look for his opportunity, and three weeks later he shot the officer dead at point blank range. Had this young man had the opportunity to develop his talents, he might have done supremely well; but he was certainly not cut out to serve in the English army, where the discipline allows officers to beat men like mules.'

Poor boy! So because he had asserted his human dignity, because he had revolted against cruel injustice, because he had had the courage to obey the voice of his conscience and punish his persecutor, he was doomed to end his life upon the scaffold. But God is great; from the blood of martyrs new martyrs are born, and this brave soldier will not die in vain, because every day other men will arise who prefer death to slavery and are willing to lay down their lives for their brothers. The time will come when English soldiers will no longer submit to the orders of gentlemen officers who *purchase the right* to flog them. If the English people ever dare to be free, they will not allow their army to be composed of slaves.

I confess I felt a lively satisfaction. In England, it is true, such examples of pride are rare, but they are sufficient to prove that although the aristocracy imposes on the people a heavier and more oppressive yoke than any other nation on earth has to bear, they still retain the divine imprint. The sacred flame is not yet extinct in their hearts, and even if today they are crushed beneath an intolerable burden, the day will come when they will arise and reclaim the equal rights which God gave us all at our birth. Then the aristocracy will pay dearly for the long years of oppression, violence and hypocrisy.

I had spent more than an hour locked inside Newgate, and the feeling of horror which seized me when I entered the arsenal and beheld the instruments of torture increased as I penetrated deeper into that den of infamy where misfortune is treated as a vice, hunger as theft and nobility of conscience as murder, so that now I suffered so intensely I could hardly breathe. However I had still to visit the chapel, the yard where the condemned are prepared for execution and the window by which they leave the prison for the scaffold and end their sad lives of worry, vice, crime, poverty and misfortune. As for the sentence of death, it is an ignominy to which base souls are insensitive and which great souls transcend.

The chapel is very sensibly arranged; there is an upper gallery reserved for women and a lower one for men, with curtains all round to prevent the two sexes from seeing each other.

The condemned pew[11] occupies a central position on the floor of the chapel with its back against the wall. This Anglican ritual of the pew, a ludicrous parody of Catholicism, plumbs the very depths of inhumanity. What good is served by torturing an unhappy wretch in this way, making him brood on his death for a whole day and night? What moral usefulness has it for society? The Catholic priest finds in the faith of the condemned man the power to reconcile him to death and even to embrace it with joy, by absolving him of all sin; therefore there is some justification for his presence. But for a Protestant preacher to mediate on behalf of a man

122

who believes in sin but not in the power of his fellow man to grant him absolution, seems to me to be an exercise in futility.

At three o'clock on the eve of the day fixed for the execution, the condemned man is taken to the chapel where he must undergo the ritual of the pew. This pew is round and looks like a miniature pulpit; it contains a bench and a prayer-desk. It is draped in black for the ceremony and the condemned man too is enveloped in a black shroud; he sits upon the bench with the prayer-book open before him. The chapel is dark, lit only by one sepulchral lamp; all the prisoners are present and follow the chaplain in low tones as he recites the prayers for the dead.

The pew resembles a half-open tomb from which emerges only the head of the condemned man framed in black and looking as if it was already separated from his body. His pallor, his haggard look, his restless gaze, his hair standing on end and the incessant agitation of his funereal drapery: all bear witness to his extreme fear and are dreadful to behold, like the convulsions of a human being buried alive, the sound of the death rattle coming from the tomb. The mournful solemnity of the infernal ritual affects the congregation so strongly that many are unable to bear it and the chapel resounds with their cries as they fall fainting to the ground. It is rare for the condemned man to endure this trial to the end; often he has to be supported and is finally carried from the pew unconscious. When he recovers his senses it is to be told that as a favour he is to be allowed a lamp so that he may spend his last night on earth reading the Bible. What an absurd and cruel jest! As if at such a moment the poor wretch can understand the import of what he reads! The chosen few who are undismayed at the approach of death, however it may come, are very rare. How is it possible to hope that the condemned man has sufficient strength of mind to meditate on the lofty sentiments of the Bible when every quarter of an hour the chimes of St Paul's clock make him count his remaining minutes and fill his fevered brain with images of his impending execution? If at dawn the unhappy victim, overcome with weariness, manages to close his eyes in sleep, he is aroused at five by the sound of horses' hooves and the wheels of the ponderous and fatal machine as it is drawn from the neighbouring yard in readiness for his punishment. What a dread awakening! From that moment onwards every sound he hears heralds his approaching doom. At six o'clock they come to take him to the last yard where he is prepared for execution. He is stripped of his clothes and dressed in trousers and a shirt of grey cloth and his hair is cropped short. All this while the chaplain exhorts him to resignation. When the preparations are complete the Sheriff himself binds the condemned man's arms. Then the Sheriff, his deputy, the chaplain and the prisoner go up in procession to the platform of the scaffold which is just outside the window; here the executioner and his assistants take hold of the prisoner, stand him upon the moveable plank, place the rope about his neck, lower a sack over his head and put a handkerchief in his hand. When he lets the handkerchief fall, the plank is removed from under his feet, and then, as the English say, he is 'launched into eternity'.[12]

As Newgate was originally intended to house only prisoners awaiting trial, rules are not as strict as in other prisons. The rule of silence is not rigorously enforced; the men and women officers maintain order, prevent disputes and tolerate the occasional remark but cut short any attempt at conversation. Nobody from outside is allowed in to sell food, but any prisoner with sufficient means may have food prepared for him in the prison kitchens.

The prisoners are given nothing to occupy their time but have to endure the corrupting effect of idleness. If this is intended as a punishment (and it is a severe one) how can the English legislators reconcile this penalty − imposed before sentence − with the principle, universally accepted on the continent, that the detained suspect is presumed innocent until he is proved guilty, and that until that time, society has the right only to keep him in custody?

One of the improvements introduced into Newgate which has had the most salutary influence is in the selection of the men and women officers responsible for guarding the prisoners. When one reflects on the qualities necessary to control a shameless and profoundly vicious population and exact obedience without frequent recourse to punishment; when one considers the degree of composure, self-control and firmness needed to perform these duties properly, one can only be agreeably surprised at the composition of the staff at Newgate. Never do any of them address prisoners without cause, use abusive language or treat them harshly; they exhort and command, are heard in silence and obeyed promptly, otherwise punishment follows.

I cannot leave Newgate without mentioning the estimable Mrs Fry, whose love of humanity has brought about notable improvements in the prison, especially by the introduction of work for women prisoners; she is also responsible for the distribution of a considerable number of Bibles among them.[13]

It is well known that the various English sects make it their sacred duty to spread the Bible all over the globe; they are so convinced that they alone understand the true meaning of this very complex book that there is not one sect which does not believe that, by distributing the Bible, it is propagating its own doctrines. But the man who is not blinded by fanaticism will question whether the improvement of the human race is an infallible consequence of reading the Bible, and whether up to now the results can justify such confidence; he will ask himself whether the ideas and diverse precepts the Bible contains form a consistent whole which the person of ordinary intelligence can understand, and whether the conglomeration of good and bad examples it provides add up to an unmixed blessing.

Nobody can deny that the books which make up the Bible are of too elevated a nature for even the most learned men to understand their significance, except after profound study. The preaching of the Gospel does very little to increase most people's understanding of the Bible; besides, in Europe religion no longer exercises more than a superficial influence. It may affect external appearances, but it is no longer the guiding force behind men's actions. Everybody wishes to rise in the world and make a fortune; men trust to the infallibility of their own reason to bring them success. When such a philosophy is universal, what place is there for religion? Will religion teach the poor man resignation if he is convinced that by exerting all his energies he will gain riches? Will religion make the rich man humble if he is convinced that he owes his wealth to his good works – or will he not prefer to believe that he is superior to his fellow men because they are poor? When men praise or blame human conduct according to its results, how can they be willing to abjure their self-love and own themselves the blind instruments of God?

Whether good luck or misfortune befalls him, the Mohammedan cries, 'It is the will of Allah!', because he does not presume to see beyond the immediate consequences of his actions; he is not sufficiently arrogant to believe that he alone is responsible for what he does, or that he can ordain the future. For good or ill he accepts his fate, with joy or grief no doubt, but without boasting or complaining.

If like the Mohammedans we would commit ourselves to Providence and be content to live from the fruit of our labours, if like them we had no other aim in life but to fulfil the duties prescribed by the law of our religion, and recognised no evil save the violation of that law, then I would believe that religion had the power to reform the guilty. But when I see that in our society civil laws often run counter to the teachings of the Gospel, that in England they reject the spirit of equity, establish inheritance by right of primogeniture, create an army of privileged classes and make the poor contribute three-quarters of the taxes, I do not believe that any Christian teachings have the power to reform men who have offended against a society which has placed itself outside Christian law. Among the peoples of Europe, religion is no longer considered essential, for society functions without it; civil laws alone wield any authority, and religious laws are observed only when there is nothing to be gained from flouting them.

In support of this opinion I shall quote those persons who have written about prisons. All observe that religious instruction is a failure. It wearies the prisoners, exasperates them, and gives them an aversion to religion and to its ministers, while the ministers themselves, whether they are monks, Quakers, priests, evangelists or chaplains, all find that the only fruit of their labours is the scorn and contempt of those to whom their preaching is addressed. [14]

What magic words could all these well-paid preachers borrow from the Bible to reconcile to his fate the wretched prisoner lying on rotting straw in his cell, without fresh air, light, water, clothes to cover him, warmth for his frozen body and numb limbs – without even a crust of coarse black bread to stay his hunger? Will he not cry aloud like Job, 'There is no God!'

Resignation! But will the man who cannot find sufficient strength in his soul to withstand physical and moral suffering be persuaded by Biblical texts to accept his lot without a murmur? I know that friendly words and sympathetic tears have power to calm even the greatest grief; but preaching sermons to comfort the torments of the soul has always seemed to me the ultimate absurdity.

What has Mrs Fry to say to those unfortunate girls who have been forced to abandon themselves to prostitution and trade their bodies for a morsel of bread – through lack of work, seduction, prejudice, or any of the thousand and one evils that abound in our society? Will she find words of consolation for their misery in the Bible? No; for the prostitute, goaded beyond endurance, will see only their literal meaning; 'An eye for an eye, a tooth for a tooth!' she will cry, in the words of the terrible Mosaic law. The pauper is spurned by the rich man, yet sees himself condemned to poverty and contempt in order to swell the luxury and pride of men who call themselves his masters; will he not also echo the prostitute's cry? And what of those proud spirits, conscious of their worth, who refuse to submit to the yoke of privilege, the tyranny of prejudice and the dominion of money; when they rise in revolt against an oppressive social system, will not they too take up the cry: 'An eye for an eye, a tooth for a tooth'?[15]

But what sort of instruction should prisoners be given? I shall be asked. First, a training in several trades, so that if there is no employment to be had in one, they may find it in another; next, they should be instructed in the virtues of order, thrift, sobriety and toil; they should be shown that unless they practise these virtues, they cannot expect any improvement in their lot, and that it is the most arrant folly for the individual or the group to set themselves up against society. In a word, since they have violated society's laws, they must now be led to hope for a share in its benefits, as a reward for their efforts; at the same time they must learn that a return to vice and crime will inevitably lead them to perish in prison, in the galleys, or on the scaffold. I think this would have considerably more influence on them than the prospect of the joys of Paradise or the torments of Hell.

The painful memory of my long visit to Newgate was still fresh when I went to Coldbath Fields. The high walls which surround the prison are visible from a long way off, yet the severe and simple entrance is not in the least frightening. The building is forty years old and very well maintained; it was built according to the principles of the philanthropist Howard, and is spacious, airy and light, with a plentiful supply of water and two acres of grounds. But the vanity of the architect prevailed over the plans of the philanthropist. Howard had wished to improve on the penitentiaries of Pennsylvania, but the builder completely disregarded his wishes, thereby demonstrating his ignorance, lack of taste, and complete absence of intelligence. Given a magnificent site, all he could think of was to build thick walls. The yards are too small, the staircases too narrow, the interior arrangements leave much to be desired, and there are not as many individual cells as were originally planned. Nevertheless, in spite of its shortcomings, this prison is a veritable country mansion compared with the sombre and terrible Newgate! Coldbath Fields is at the same time a prison and a reformatory.[16]

The governor, Mr Chesterton, is a very distinguished man; he speaks Spanish and French with equal facility, has travelled widely and is well-informed on all the countries he has visited. Everything about him proclaims the man dedicated to the service of his fellowmen: he does not utter a single word which does not show how deeply his soul is steeped in the universal charity preached by Jesus; his philanthropy is enhanced by an amiable manner and extreme courtesy.

Mr Chesterton was good enough to accompany me and show me all round the prison in the greatest detail. It is clearly the mainspring of his life and he regards the prisoners as his family; he knows nearly all of them by their first names. He has been here for ten years and with such a man as governor one can imagine the quality of the prison officers. If I had been impressed by the warders at Newgate, I was lost in admiration for those at Coldbath Fields. Nearly all are chosen by the governor and have a pleasant appearance in perfect harmony with their quiet voice and gentle manner. What a salutary effect habitual contact with such people must have on the prisoners! There can be no doubt that mild and humane manners have the power to change men whose hearts are poisoned against society.

At Coldbath Mr Chesterton has carried the classification of prisoners to its limit. The recidivists are in five categories; if condemned for the sixth time they are sent to Millbank Penitentiary or transported to Botany Bay. The other prisoners are classed according to the nature of their crimes.

The governor enforces the rules of his prison with scrupulous firmness. I must say these rules seemed very harsh to me; they prescribe perpetual silence and idleness, with solitary confinement for the slightest infraction.

Under no pretext may the prisoner address either his fellows or the warders. If a visitor asks him a question he must on no account reply; only when he is ill is he permitted to speak, to ask if he may see the doctor. Then he is immediately taken to the infirmary and examined, given a comfortable bed, and treated with every attention and kindness.

Any prisoner who breaks the silence is severely punished.[17]

We visited the men's wing first, and there I found all the old Newgate faces, but what a change had come over them! The men who before being sentenced had had defiance and wickedness written all over them now went about with heads bent and eyes lowered in total submission. Constrained by the severity of the régime, not one even dreamed of resisting it. They were very clean and tidy, with clean hands, combed hair and neat beards (for they are shaved twice a week).[18]

Their clothing consists of thin cloth trousers in summer and heavier ones in winter, a long jacket of the same material, a woollen cap, a coloured shirt, woollen stockings, shoes, waistcoat, cravat and pocket handkerchief. They change their shirts and stockings every Sunday, and all their clothing is clean and in good condition.

Next I went into the children's division. There were so many there that it was quite frightening: out of 1,120 prisoners confined at Coldbath at the time of my visit, three hundred were children between the ages of nine and seventeen. What drove these children to crime? Poverty, lack of a trade and the corruption in which they were brought up. Nothing could be more distressing than the sight of these pale, thin little creatures probably destined for transportation or the gibbet. The most serious offenders are condemned to spend so many hours each day on the treadwheel; the rest do nothing at all. So these children who are driven to vagabondage, theft and crime because they have no profession or occupation will leave this so-called house of correction after anything from two to five years of detention without having learned any trade which would enable them to make a living.

I can see no evidence of *correction* here, only a system of punishment. Instead of reforming the criminal, these institutions serve only to corrupt him further; the errant but not yet vicious child will find no good example here but will acquire slack and slothful habits and easily succumb to every kind of vice.

I could not hide from Mr Chesterton my astonishment that children should be abandoned to idleness in this way instead of being engaged in productive work. He replied that in England the workers were so numerous that the government was not disposed to take work away from them and give it to prisoners.

'But is England so rich that she can afford to turn her prisons into refuges where the inmates will be well-housed, well-dressed and well-fed and do nothing in return? If that is her intention, before twenty years are out half the population will give up struggling against poverty and flock into the prisons.'[19]

At Coldbath there are five hundred and twenty cells. They are allotted to children for preference so that at least during the night they are isolated from the rest. All the cells are kept *extremely clean*: the bed has a good mattress, a pillow and two blankets, and a shelf fixed to the wall serves as a table. Each cell has plenty of fresh air, but through the fault of the architect several are rather dark. All the walls and stairways are whitewashed twice a year. There are no offensive smells here such as you would find in a French prison.

The women and children find it very difficult to observe the rule of silence, and I saw a number of unhappy little creatures locked in solitary confinement as a punishment. In every one of their cells I saw a copy of the Bible.[20]

While I was there the master responsible for teaching the children came to hold his class. I greeted this venerable old man with the greatest respect; he has been teaching in the prison for fifteen years. What devotion it must take to live among children doomed to ignominy, vice and suffering! The goodness of his heart is plainly written on his countenance: his voice is gentle and he speaks to the children with a benevolence and solicitude that reassures them and banishes all fear from their hearts.

After visiting several further wards where I observed the same cleanliness, the same order and the same expression on all the faces, I came to the wing where the fifth-grade recidivists are confined.

There I was expecting to encounter some of those hideous faces on which the marks of crime are as if cast in bronze – faces furrowed by uncontrolled passions in which shamelessness, cunning, audacity and the constant workings of the criminal mind all display their repulsive traits. Of course these features were present, but what astonished me was the complete apathy expressed on every countenance. Not one man turned his eyes towards us. They were equally indifferent to our arrival and departure; they seemed sunk in a lethargic slumber. These men living the life of automata, their passions spent, their souls empty, their faces still bearing traces of their crimes – the stamp of the outcast, the profound despair – were a sight to inspire terror!

There were far more prisoners in this section than in the others. They were older too, and I thought they seemed more ailing and morose, more slovenly in their habits and less cleanly in their persons. Struck by this difference, I wanted to know the reason for it and asked the governor; he told me that these prisoners gave more trouble than all the rest: not that they were refractory, but their excessive apathy, the extreme difficulty in getting them to wash themselves, comb their hair and brush their clothes, meant that they required constant supervision. Several would not take exercise; sometimes they refused to eat; then again they were nearly always ailing, and it was this division that filled the infirmary.

'And to what do you attribute this behaviour, which seems so contrary to the turbulent character one would expect them to have?'

'To boredom; it is very rare for recidivists to adapt to life in prison.'

This is understandable; the monotony of their idle silent existence must make them apathetic, and from then on, life is just a burden of intolerable weight. For men like these, life means action: they love to take risks, they love the excitement of crime and cannot accustom themselves to their crippled existence. The soul has never exercised any power over them and its qualities have remained undeveloped; for them repose and the quiet mind are the greatest torments. They look back with bitter regret upon their former lives full of adventure, danger and privation, a time when their intelligence, imagination, courage and skill were in constant use. Alas! It must be admitted that such men *need* to struggle fiercely against poverty and against society; men who feel a savage exaltation in defying prison, the galleys and the scaffold cannot endure the gloomy inactivity and sepulchral silence of Coldbath; it drains their strength and they find it the worst punishment of all.

The number of recidivists demonstrates only too well that punishment does not reform the criminal. He must be educated, for only orderly and industrious habits have the power to transform a life of vice and crime.

But whatever penal system a nation chooses to adopt, it seems to me that when the recidivist is living proof that the means of correction is ineffective and the criminal is incorrigible, it is absurd to put him back into society when you have not succeeded in adapting him to its ways. If the penitentiary system has not been successful in reforming the criminal, society must deport him, send him to work in the mines, or at least put him where he can do no harm. In all English prisons there is a very great number of recidivists[21]; and the men in this category are noticeable for their taciturnity. It is almost unnecessary to impose the rule of silence on them, for they often refuse to reply when the warders ask them a question.

The infirmary at Coldbath is a haven of peace and comfort. On the whole there are very few sick prisoners. In two large rooms I saw only twelve or fifteen men and they did not seem to be very ill; some were drinking tea, others were lying down, listlessly reading the Bible; some were walking up and down, others quietly chatting; you would have thought they were free men. The comfortable atmosphere in this infirmary is enough to show that in every sick prisoner the governor sees a suffering human being, an unfortunate brother whom his duty commands him to succour.

I saw there a young man of twenty-six condemned to death for having killed a friend in a quarrel. He belonged to one of the best families in the aristocracy and had a private income of six thousand pounds; had he been a penniless son of the people his neck would assuredly have felt the embrace of the hangman's noose, but thanks to the circumstances of his birth and even more to the sacrifice of part of his fortune, his sentence was commuted to six years' imprisonment at Coldbath. There too the fascination of noble rank exerts its influence. This young man stays in the infirmary although he is perfectly well; when it is fine he walks in the garden, and he spends his time learning French as he intends to make his home in France when he has completed his sentence.

Apart from this one exception, which one can easily understand in a country which worships wealth and still believes in the superiority of the nobility, there are no privileges at Coldbath. The former practice of paying for special food has been rigorously suppressed and everybody eats the same diet without favour or exception. I saw the prisoners at dinner; each division has its own refectory. The fine wooden tables, polished to enhance their whiteness, are meticulously brushed and washed so that there is not the slightest mark to spoil their gleaming surface. The prisoners eat out of pewter dishes which are rubbed and polished until they shine like silver. The food is wholesome and abundant but of a tedious monotony: a bowl of gruel in the morning, vegetable soup for dinner (with meat twice a week), and more gruel in the evening. The bread is excellent: each prisoner receives with his dinner a little loaf shaped in the English style, nicely baked with a golden crust and an appetising smell. I cut off a piece and tasted it; inside it is as white as the best Paris bread and far better than anything I have had in London; you may be sure that in Ireland even the better class of farmer has never eaten anything to match it, even on his wedding day. The bread at Newgate is not nearly as good.

After dinner everybody resumed work: those on duty began to clean the refectories and yards, others went off to the schoolroom; many busied themselves making tow out of old rope, while those condemned to the tread-wheel climbed onto the instrument of torture.[22]

From the comparative lack of movement of the prisoner on the tread-wheel and the slowness of his tread which seems to call for no great effort, the visitor passes by unaware that the man who operates it is suffering the greatest agony. I would never have suspected the refinement of cruelty produced by the inventor of this infernal machine had not the governor explained to me how it works. It is the excessive slowness with which the great drum turns that is the precise cause of the torture. It revolves only twenty-eight or thirty times a minute, because the treads are set very far apart. This makes the prisoner's step slow, arduous and painful; he has to stretch his limbs to their utmost in order to reach the step, so that one of his legs is always in mid-air and takes the whole of his weight when it lands on the step. During this horrible exercise his body remains completely motionless. The very slowness of the movement is enough to make his head spin, numb his limbs and strain the muscles of his stomach. Sometimes he loses consciousness and falls from the top of the wheel, breaking his bones or even killing himself. The punishment upsets his nervous system, causes hernias and chronic illnesses, and often cripples its victims. I watched men and children as they came off the treadmill at Coldbath, and not one of them had the slightest trace of sweat upon his brow; on the contrary, they all appeared to be cold, for they were all pale, some of them almost blue. Their muscles were racked, their eyes dead. They looked as if they had reached the very limits of physical suffering. Some were yawning, others were stretching their legs and arms. Women, young people and especially children suffer far more from this punishment than men in their prime and even old men, which would seem to prove that it makes far greater demands on the nervous system than it does on the strength.

Is it by means such as these that men lay claim to reform the luckless youth driven to break the laws of society? Is it by upsetting a nervous system already prone to disorder, destroying his health, crippling him for life, and weakening his mind and body that they hope to restore him to the straight and narrow path? It is quite impossible to understand how a country held up as a model of rectitude and justice could ever adopt so barbarous a torture as the treadwheel for punishment, or enforce the silence of the grave and idleness as a means of correction.

The effect of excessive punishment is to corrupt, never to correct. Even if it does not result in death, prolonged physical suffering disorders and brutalises the organism. In this state, men are useless, and it would be better to kill them outright rather than sentence them to transportation at the fifth or sixth offence. But men who have had no previous conviction prior to transportation are less liable to be corrupted, and sometimes even manage to reform.[23]

At Coldbath there were two prisoners who particularly engaged my attention. One was a Jew, the biggest rogue in England, according to Mr Chesterton: this was the ninth or tenth time he had been arrested on charges of forgery. I was curious to see what the biggest rogue in England looked like; his window overlooked a little passage and I stopped there to examine him. He was sitting at a table studying a pile of papers covered with figures and he must have been completely engrossed in his calculations for he did not appear to notice my shadow darken his cell. His face could have come straight out of a painting by Rembrandt. I have never seen a countenance of such black wickedness or such brazen hypocrisy. Although he must have been at least sixty years old the fire that flashed from his little grey eyes revealed an infinitely fertile imagination, a tenacious will and boundless avarice.[24]

It was easy to read on the depraved features of the other criminal the revolting nature of the crime he had committed. Four months after his marriage to a beautiful, wealthy young heiress of seventeen, he had brutally raped his wife's sister, a child of twelve, who had died as a result of his savage attack. This man had the grotesque body of a faun: an enormous belly, shoulders like Hercules, the head of a pig and very short legs. His lascivious gaze, thick pursed lips and blotchy nose – in short, everything about him – recalled the satyr as it is represented in paintings. What kind of mother could have so little judgment of physiognomy, so little womanly instinct, as to give her daughter to such a vampire?

At Coldbath the convicts have nothing to do with prisoners awaiting trial.

We proceeded to the women's wing which is separated from the men's by a garden. Here too order and cleanliness reign, as well as the same silence and the same strict observance of the prison regulations. The women have more to occupy them than the men: they sew, mend and launder all the linen used throughout the prison. They also make all their own clothes, which consist of a blue cotton skirt in summer and a woollen one in winter, long jackets of the same material buttoning up to the neck and white cotton caps. They are much cleaner than the men. Every week they are issued with two blouses, two petticoats, two handkerchiefs, two caps and two pairs of stockings, with a clean skirt and jacket every fortnight; their shoes are so well polished that they look like new. Their cells are better furnished than the men's: they have sheets on their beds, a towel, a washbasin and a glass. They are given the same food as the men, except that the washerwomen and ironers have meat every day, with beer and tea to drink.

The prison has a superb laundry, a big drying-yard and a fine linen-room. There is more activity in the women's wing than in the men's. The women cook, wash and iron, they hang out the clothes, they sew in the linen-room; there are always dozens of them busy sweeping and scrubbing the floors of rooms, cells, passages and staircases; even the out-side yards are swept and scrubbed. You could make a tour of the whole prison in white satin slippers and a muslin gown without getting a speck of dust or a drop of water on them. It is all quite admirable.

In spite of all their activity the women appear no happier than the men. To see their sad lack-lustre eyes and impassive faces you would think them both blind and deaf. Before entering some of the work-rooms, I stopped and listened outside the door, but all was silent as the grave. Whenever they have to speak about their work, they do so in a whisper and the wardress replies in the same tone. It is like being in a sickroom.

Apart from a very few exceptions, these women are all prostitutes hardened by the shameless life of drunkenness and debauchery which they flaunted in the streets of London. Nevertheless, under the prison régime they become sober, humble, diligent and submissive; they all made me the *servile curtsey* that seems to be the rule in all establishments of this kind, as I had remarked at Newgate. This display of hypocrisy seems immoral to me; it must humiliate the women and cannot have any salutary effect. Out of the two hundred and eight women I saw, not one was pretty; only three were even passable. The rest were hide-ous, although they all had a fresh and healthy look that one rarely encounters in London women.

I noticed fewer Bibles in the women's wing than in the men's.

In the infirmary I saw a remarkably beautiful little girl of seventeen months; the poor child had been born in prison. In the same room there was a woman who had only recently given birth, and she was suckling her child. In the last yard I saw a child of three, a frail little thing who looked sickly and of low intelligence. As soon as she saw the governor her face brightened, she stretched her little arm through the railings and said in an impatient and wheedling tone, 'Please sir, I want to go into the garden, I'm bored here, I haven't been out for three days.'

Mr Chesterton took her hand and had the gate unlocked for her, but as soon as she was let out she ran after him, crying uncontrollably as if she were having a fit.

This poor little girl was in Coldbath with her mother, who normally worked in the garden and had the child with her; but she had committed the double offence of breaking the silence and of asking a fellow-prisoner why she was in prison. The penalty for asking this question is a fortnight in solitary confinement, so the unfortunate child was being punished as well as her mother.

The number of children in women's prisons is clear evidence that there are no special institutions for them. Education begins in the cradle; so what sort of influence must life in prison have on these tender creatures? However it is run, a prison will always be a school of cunning, deceit and every kind of vice. You might well say that in England the children of thieves are fated to follow the *profession* of their parents.

Mr Chesterton showed me round the garden which is very well tended. Working in the garden is a reward given only for good conduct. I went into one workshop with fine iron roofing which the prisoners had made themselves. It is here that workers in different trades make everything used in the prison. Tailors, shoemakers, locksmiths, carpenters and masons spend all their time working on the maintenance of the various buildings: this is how the prison is kept in such an admirable state of repair, but none of the work done here ever finds its way outside.[25]

Before I left I said to Mr Chesterton, 'I think it would be impossible to find a better run prison than yours anywhere in England, sir, but I find a good deal to criticise in the way you leave your prisoners idle; in my opinion it is a deplorable system which must certainly foster the seeds of crime in their hearts.'

'Madame, not everybody would agree with you there. Last year, when Marshal Soult did me the honour of visiting Coldbath, what he most admired is what you most dislike. "Good," he said, "I see you are going about things the right way here; you are not taking work out of the hands of men with families to maintain and giving it to convicts, as we are foolish enough to do in France, so that honest workers are facing ruin in their attempt to compete with prison labour." '[26]

Anyone would think Marshal Soult was ignorant of the fact that in France the prisoner's wage is lower than the worker's because the state which maintains him also monopolises his labour. The objection he raised would be avoided if instead of having the state act as entrepreneur we were to follow the example of the United States penitentiaries and set up outside agencies for selling whatever the prisoners make. They open an account for each prisoner, debit him the cost of his keep and the raw materials he uses, and credit him with any money made from the sale of his work; the sum to his credit is not given him until his release, and if by the end of his term he has not paid for his stay in prison with his labour, he remains there until he has balanced his account. The prisoner is then working on the same terms as the free worker and cannot be accused of competing with him and thereby giving him just cause for complaint. But in our system the prisoner is maintained at state expense and it is rare for a man to leave prison at the expiry of his sentence with earnings which bear any relation to the time he has spent in confinement. By way of compensation the contractors make a fortune at the expense of the state and the sweated labour of the prisoner!

This system is not only a burden on the state: it is also essentially immoral. What! you punish the prisoner for violating the laws of property, then you violate *his* rights by making him work for a quarter, or even less, of the value of his labour! Be just towards him, then, or he will come to believe that all is subject to the *law of brute force* and cunning, and his heart will rejoice in his evil deeds. In America, convicts have the most powerful motives for doing well, and they generally become excellent workers. If we suppose that food, clothing, heating and light cost about the same there as they do in the Hôtel des Invalides (say about a shilling a day) several prisoners would return to society after serving from eight to ten years with sufficient capital to set themselves up in the trade they had acquired in prison. I cannot believe that there would be very many recidivists among them!

If when he visited England Marshal Soult felt so strongly about the wrongs inflicted on the free worker by prison labour, why, in his capacity as Minister of War, does he continue to put prison labour out to contract in our military prisons? Could it be that he is only paying lip-service to the notion of reform? But it does not surprise me to hear such opinions in the mouth of Marshal Soult. Did he not refuse to allow our soldiers to undertake any work of public utility? Do not expect an old soldier of the Empire to have any understanding of social science; all he can think of is military glory, which counted for everything *then* and counts for nothing today.

The impression Coldbath had made on me was quite effaced when I went to Millbank Penitentiary,[27] the model prison which has adopted the system of separate cells, although this does not seem to have been particularly beneficial.[28] If Coldbath was a mansion after Newgate, Millbank was a sumptuous palace after Coldbath! This time I was received, not by the governor, but by two gentlemen, one from the House of Lords, the other from the Commons: both members of the Commission on Prisons. From the beginning to the end of my visit, these strictly polite, cool and reserved gentlemen behaved like *Englishmen* in every sense of the term. I presume they understood perfectly well the significance of the figures submitted to their attention by the prison authorities, but I could see that they were completely ignorant of any details concerning the prisoners themselves. How different from Mr Chesterton, who made a special study of each prisoner in his care!

I went into a long wide gallery on the first floor which contains forty-two cells; it is lit by large windows that are nearly always open to let in air, light and sunshine. The floor is made of narrow deal planks, the same wood as the tables at Coldbath; they are so smooth and clean that you could draw on them. Each cell has two doors: the first, of wood, is always open; the second, an iron grille, is always closed. The back wall contains a small window which lights the cell and ensures a constant flow of fresh air as it is opposite the large window in the corridor. The furniture is not limited to bare necessities; it is decorative as well as useful: an inviting bed with very white sheets, a cupboard, a little table and a shelf on which various toilet articles are displayed. Everything, like its surroundings, is polished and shining as if it were new.

I cannot speak of the male prisoners because my two guides thought it *improper* for a woman to visit the men's quarters. This did not surprise me: banning women visitors from men's prisons and refusing them entry to the Houses of Parliament are typical examples of their mental attitude. For ridiculous scruples and rigid etiquette the English aristocracy will never be surpassed. . . .

The women prisoners were even better dressed than the women at Coldbath: they were busy sewing, each sitting on a chair with a foot-stool before her. Every time we stopped at a door, they rose to their feet as they had done in all the other prisons and made us the *eternal curtsey*. I could not help noticing on every table not just one Bible but sometimes two and even *three*; I had seen them at Newgate and

Coldbath as well, in the hands of criminals and recidivists, and now I could not control my indignation. 'Ah!' I cried, 'English prisons are the graveyard of sacred books!' But beyond a doubt the most monumental stupidity of all is the existence of a flourishing Society with the aim of distributing the Bible to all and sundry. If you take the trouble to examine any ten, hundred, or thousand people who claim to have read it, you will very soon realise that most of the Bible is too difficult for ordinary folk to understand; however, the subscribers to this Society are convinced that the wholesale distribution of the Bible is the most meritorious cause to which anybody could give his money. If they had understood this holy book, they would have realised that *preliminary instruction is indispensable* if the reader is to be improved and not corrupted. I would go further and state that in the Bible criminals can find good reasons for persisting in their life of crime. It has been affirmed that these voracious readers of the Bible are hardened criminals who are constantly being re-arrested for fresh outrages against society. From the religious point of view, is it not profane to entrust the revelations which God made to his elect into the hands of a horde of ruffians? I am convinced that no good can ever come of such odious sacrilege.

The prisoners at Millbank enjoy all the amenities their condition permits: wholesome food in abundance and very little work.[29] The extreme cleanliness of their surroundings makes their life as comfortable as possible on the material side. On all their faces was the expression I had already observed at Coldbath: no sign of suffering, only total apathy.

The prison is very large and can hold twelve hundred prisoners: there were eight hundred there at the time of my visit. In its construction every effort seems to have been made to ensure the material comfort of the prisoners while making it impossible for them ever to escape. However, it is hard to credit that an institution intended to accommodate so many people should have been built on such an unhealthy site: it is on marshy ground on the bank of the Thames, surrounded by factories constantly belching out plumes of smoke and giving off evil-smelling fumes.

NOTES

1(TN).   Louis-Mathurin MOREAU-CHRISTOPHE (1799–1881) was an authority on crime and the penitentiary system, appointed Chief Inspector of Prisons in 1837. His great work is *Rapport sur les prisons de l'Angleterre, de l'Ecosse, de la Hollande, de la Belgique et de la Suisse* (1839).

2(FT).   'The number of thefts that go unpunished in England is estimated to amount to the sum of £700,000 per annum.

'Yet there is a law called the Warrant Act relating to suspected persons which empowers local authorities to arrest at their discretion "every suspected Person or reputed Thief frequenting any River, Canal or navigable Stream, Dock or Basin, or any Quay, Wharf or Warehouse near or adjoining thereto, or any Street, Highway or Avenue leading thereto, or any Place of public Resort, or any Avenue leading thereto, or any Street, Highway or Place adjacent, with Intent to commit felony."

'And the Commissioners report that by virtue of this act, a large number of mayors make a clean sweep of all the disreputable characters in their parishes and put them under lock and key on the eve of fairs, public holidays and horse-races, and release them when the holiday is over.

'And when you ask any of them what law authorises him to act in this way, he replies, "I take all that upon myself." '

Moreau-Christophe, op. cit.

(Moreau-Christophe is citing Section 4 of the Vagrancy Act, 1824, known today as the 'sus' laws, and due to be amended in the course of 1981–1982: TN.)

3(FT).   'The average population of Giltspur Street Compter is a hundred and fifty prisoners a day, and five thousand three hundred a year.

'There is another prison in London (Mill Lane, Tooley Street) which serves as a police station for those arrested in the borough of Southwark. This prison is under the direction of the Lord Mayor and the Court of Aldermen of the City of London and under the superintendence of the High Bailiff of the Borough of Southwark: it is called Borough Compter. The average population is fifty prisoners a day and fifteen hundred a year. The way every class of prisoner is allowed to associate, the laxity in the separation of the sexes, the extortion of fees from prisoners, the almost constant presence of numerous visitors, who are for the most part either thieves or prostitutes, the drunkenness due to the ease of obtaining alcoholic liquor, the profanation of the holy Sabbath, etc.: these, according to the prison inspectors, are the principal abuses in the administration of this prison and Giltspur Street Compter; and their report is in no way exaggerated.

'The average population of Clerkenwell Prison is a hundred and fifty on any one day, and six thousand in a year, men and women together. This prison has the same vices as Giltspur Street and Borough Compter.'

Moreau-Christophe, op. cit.

4(FT). 'The builders of Old Newgate seem to have regarded in their plan nothing but the single article of keeping prisoners in safe custody. . . . I was told by those who attended them that criminals who had affected an air of boldness during their trial, and appeared quite unconcerned at the pronouncing sentence upon them, were struck with horror and shed tears when brought to these darksome solitary abodes.'

John Howard,
State of the Prisons in England and Wales, 1777

(Several prisons in succession were built on this ancient site, and the one Howard refers to as 'Old Newgate' was not the prison that struck terror into Flora's heart in 1839, but the dreaded eighteenth-century Newgate, demolished and rebuilt only to be destroyed by fire in 1780 during the Gordon Riots. It was rebuilt yet again by 1783 and stood as a grim landmark to Londoners all through the nineteenth century. It was demolished in 1902 and some of its stones were used in the construction of the Old Bailey which now stands upon the site: TN.)

5(TN).   Charlotte Brontë reacted in a similar way when she visited Newgate in 1853 with her publisher, George Smith: 'At Newgate she rapidly fixed her attention on an individual prisoner. This was a poor girl with an interesting face, and an expression of the deepest misery. She had, I believe, killed her illegitimate child. Miss Brontë walked up to her, took her hand, and began to talk to her. She was, of course, quickly interrupted by the prison warder with the formula, "Visitors are not allowed to speak to prisoners." '

George Smith, quoted by Winifred Gerin,
Charlotte Brontë (Oxford, 1967; p. 521).

6(FT).   'A child of seven may be a felon and therefore liable to be hanged. Blackstone reports that in his time children of eight were condemned to death and the sentence carried out; I myself have seen children of that age sentenced to transportation!'

Moreau-Christophe, op. cit.

7(TN).   These men were settlers from Upper Canada who in 1837 had taken part in the rebellion led by Mackenzie and Papineau against the British, which was savagely put down.

8(FT).   This is what Marshal Pillet, who was a prisoner of war, has to say: 'Hunger knew no bounds: men would keep corpses hidden for five or six days without reporting them, in order to obtain their rations: this was called living off the dead; Lord Cordower, colonel of the Carmarthen Regiment on duty at Porchester Prison, visited the prison one day and left his horse tied up to one of the gates; within ten minutes it was cut up and eaten. When Milord came to get it, a search was made and he was informed what had happened; he refused to believe it unless he was given proof in the shape of the animal's remains. It was easy to satisfy him: they took him to see the hide and entrails, and a poor starving wretch devoured the last morsel of raw flesh in his presence. A large butcher's dog – in fact, all the dogs that entered the prison – suffered the same fate.'

Pillet, op. cit.

9(FT).   In England anybody with any kind of official post is called an officer.

10(TN). John ELLIOTSON (1791–1868) was a somewhat eccentric disciple of Franz Joseph GALL (1758–1828) and Jean Gaspard SPURZHEIM (1776–1832), the founders of the pseudo-science of phrenology, which affirmed that man's character and faculties depended on the development of his brain and could be deduced from the shape of his skull.

11(FT). The pews in English churches are separate enclosed benches, like little pulpits.

12(TN). Charles Dickens visited Newgate a few years before Flora, and he, too, was moved to reflect on the last hours of a man in the condemned cell. His account of his visit appears in *Sketches by Boz* (1836).

13(TN). Elizabeth FRY (1780–1845), a Quaker, devoted a great part of her life to prison reform. For Newgate she advocated strict segregation of the sexes, classification of prisoners, supervision of women prisoners by women officers, provision of religious and secular instruction, and employment. While Flora was observing conditions in English prisons in 1839, Mrs Fry was doing the same in France.

14(FT). 'The Bishop of London said that his clergy would never raise the moral standards of the masses by preaching to them; and in my opinion what he said was very true. He added that to make ordinary people better, it was necessary to speak to them as individuals.'

Moreau-Christophe, op. cit.

'I do not know what part our ministers of religion could play in reforming prisoners. I only know that in the French prison system, they play no part at all. The attempts made in Paris recently by a young priest with nothing but his zeal to commend him, prove my point, whatever the newspapers may have said to the contrary. The religious books he distributed to the inmates of Bicêtre and Sainte-Pélagie were all sold to pay for gambling and brandy. My pen refuses to describe the blasphemous scenes which take place at night in prison cells as a direct consequence of allowing all manner of persons to go and preach inside Paris prisons. Nevertheless, while admitting that what goes by the name of religious ideas serves only to alienate us, the good religion can do must not be ignored; what matters is to take the right kind of precautions. It is contrary to reason and experience to imagine that in order to turn a pack of ruffians into honest men it is sufficient to plunge them straight into the doctrines of religion, when religious ideas, more than any others, need to be presented in such a way that they will have the greatest possible influence on the hearts and conduct of men. And if you observe our prisons closely you will soon realise that the only hope of preventing prisoners from corrupting one another is to house them decently, separate them more rigorously, make them sleep alone in separate cells at night and work regular hours by day, dispel the profound ignorance in which the majority are sunk, and temper severity with justice and humanity; in short, they must be placed in a situation which offers them a motive for reform and an alternative to corruption. This is the way to open the heart of the criminal to morality. I repeat, it is only after these precautions are taken that religion may be introduced. If you want religious teaching to bring the guilty to repentance and make them virtuous, you must begin by destroying every obstacle in their way, otherwise you are exhorting the poor wretches to struggle out of the abyss, yet you do not see that all the time you are pushing them back again. I have put particular emphasis on this point, because at the inaugural meeting of the Royal Society for the Improvement of Prisons, it was announced that the chief concern of the Society was to be the religious instruction of prisoners. This decision was predictable: one reason for it is that it was made by people who have very little knowledge of prisons or the circumstances of prisoners' lives.'

Villermé, *Des prisons telles qu'elles sont et telles qu'elles devraient être* (Paris, 1820)

(Louis-Réné VILLERMÉ (1782 – 1863) made an exhaustive study of prison conditions in France which he published in 1820. Later in life he turned his attention to conditions for the working classes in the world outside prison: TN.)

15(FT).   In any case the books prisoners are given to read are not very suitable for achieving the moral purpose intended. As the writers of a well-known review say: 'If education is to be continued in jails, and tracts are to be dispersed, we cannot help lamenting that the tracts, though full of good principles, are so

intolerably stupid – and all apparently constructed on the sup-
position that a thief or errant ploughman are inferior in commonsense to a boy of five years. The story generally is that a labourer
with six children has nothing to live on but mouldy bread and
dirty water; yet nothing can exceed his cheerfulness and content
– no murmurs, no discontent; of mutton he has scarcely heard –
of bacon he never dreams; black bread and the water of the pool
constitute his food, establish his felicity and excite his warmest
gratitude. The squire or parson of the parish always happen to be
walking by, and overhear him praying for the King and the
Members for the county, and for all in authority; and it generally
ends with their offering him a shilling, which this excellent man
declares he does not want and will not accept! These are the
pamphlets which Goodies and Noodles are dispersing with
unwearied diligence. It would be a great blessing if some genius
would arise who had a talent for writing for the poor.'

Edinburgh Review, vol. XXXVI, p. 363, February 1822

(Had Flora read the whole of this article, she would have found
that most of the opinions expressed in it were completely at vari-
ance with her own. The writer insists that the aim of imprisonment must be to punish and not to reform. Prison life had become
too soft; prisons should not be converted into schools and workshops. The writer favours the tread-wheel, the capstan, 'a great
deal of solitude; coarse food; a dress of shame; hard, incessant,
irksome, eternal labour; a planned and regulated and unrelenting
exclusion of happiness and comfort.': TN.)

16(TN). Prisons were divided into four categories: common
jails, which were detention centres like Newgate, where nearly all
the prisoners were awaiting trial; houses of correction for convicts,
like Coldbath Fields; penitentiaries like Millbank, only one of
which existed in 1839; and the old debtors' prisons, like the
Marshalsea, which was closed in 1842. Coldbath Fields, situated
to the east of Grays Inn Road, was administered by the Middlesex
Justices. It was rebuilt in 1794 and when Flora visited it, the
authorities were trying out the American innovations of separate
cells and the rule of silence – a complete break with the chaotic
conditions of the previous century. The Governor, Captain
George Laval Chesterton (whose mother was French) had served
in the Peninsular campaign and later fought under Bolivar in

South America, which must have made Flora's heart warm to him, considering her own connections with Bolivar and the revolutionary struggles in Peru. When Chesterton left the army, he applied for the post of governor of Coldbath, where he remained for thirty years.

17(FT).   'It is difficult to believe that this silence could ever be enforced, but it is, and strictly, too. It is such torture that several prisoners declare that they would prefer death.'

Villermé, op. cit.

18(FT).   In London the coal-smoke makes everything so black that prisoners have to be given soap to get their faces and hands clean.

19(FT).   'A poor chimney-sweep, sixteen years old, ragged, barefoot, his legs red and chapped from the cold, was put in prison for some minor misdemeanour. The hot bath he was made to take upon entering delighted him; but what caused him most amazement was when he heard that he was to put on shoes and stockings. "Am I really to wear this? and this? and this as well?" he asked as each fresh article was placed in his hands. His joy reached its height when he found himself in his cell; he kept turning back the coverlet of his bed in rapture, as if he dared not believe in so much happiness; and timidly he asked if it could really be true that he was to sleep in a bed. The next day when the Governor asked him what he thought of his situation, he cried, "What do I think of it? Well, I'll be damned if ever I work again in my life!" He was as good as his word: later on he was transported.'

Moreau-Christophe, op. cit. (quoting from the Report of the Royal Commission on Prisons, 1835)

20(FT).   Moreau-Christophe gives the following table of punishments at Coldbath Fields for one year:

Lash	9
Irons	4
Solitary confinement	3,232
Other punishments	8,760

21(FT).   'Out of 109,495 individuals in the various English

Above left: A drawing by an unknown artist of Flora Tristan in Arequipa in 1833. *Above right*: Flora Tristan, first published in the *Galerie de la Presse* in 1839.

Overleaf: London at the time of Flora Tristan's visits.

Left: A medallion of Flora Tristan was designed by Alfred Baron in 1840. This drawing of it by Perassini was published in *L'Artiste* in 1844.

Above left: Flora Tristan in the 1830s.

Above right: Aline Chazal-Tristan, Flora's daughter. This inspired Gauguin's painting below.

Right: Paul Gauguin's painting 'The Artist's Mother' was done from a reproduction of the above in Tahiti in 1893.

A LA MÉMOIRE
DE MADAME FLORA TRISTAN
Auteur de l'Union Ouvrière
Les Travailleurs reconnaissants.

LIBERTÉ — ÉGALITÉ — FRATERNITÉ

SOLIDARITÉ

FLORA TRISTAN
Née à Paris le 7 avril 1803,
Morte à Bordeaux le 14 *novembre* 1844

SOLIDARITÉ.

Flora's monument in the cemetery of Bordeaux, erected by the workers of that city and inaugurated by 8,000 of them on 22 October 1848.

Above: Chartist Procession of 1842.

Interior of the House of Commons in 1833.

The Gas Works in Horseferry Road, 1842.

Newgate Prison in 1831.

Ascot Races – Arrival of the Illustrious Visitors', 1844.

The Upper Classes: 'A Scene in Kensington Gardens – or – Fashions and Frights of 1829' by George Cruikshank.

The Brook Street Ragged and Industrial School, 1853 – little changed since Flora's day.

The Reform Club, 1841.

prisons in 1837, there were reckoned to be 24,876 habitual offenders, and of these 12,920 were imprisoned for the second time, 5,190 for the third, 2,312 for the fourth, and 4,454 for the fifth or more. The number unrecorded must be far greater.'

Moreau-Christophe, op. cit.

22(FT). The cost of constructing a tread-wheel is estimated at between £15 and £20 per prisoner. The tread-wheel at Coldbath Fields is said to have cost more than £12,000, or 300,000 francs.'

Moreau-Christophe, op. cit.

That is rather expensive for an instrument of torture!

23(FT). 'England's penal colonies prove that the man who is removed from civilisation and sinks into barbarism passes beyond every imaginable state of human degradation. Just as Ireland is the absolute example of human misery, so the English penal colonies are the perfect example of the immorality of man. Here, in an abridged version of the hideous original, is some idea of the depths of depravity to which man can sink.

'Dr Ullathorne, the vicar-general of Australia, says in the work he published on that unhappy country, "The eye of God looks down upon a people such as, since the deluge, there has not been. Where they marry in haste, without affection; where each one lives for his senses alone. A community without the feelings of community, whose men are very wicked, whose women are very shameless, and whose children are very irreverent. . . . The naked savage who wanders through those endless forests, knew of nothing monstrous in crime except cannibalism, until England schooled him in horrors through her prisoners. The removal of such a plague from the earth concerns the whole human race."

'The Report of the Committee on Transportation, presented to Parliament in 1838, informs us that in 1835 the number of summary convictions in New South Wales amounted to 22,000, although the number of *convicts* was only 25,000! But of all the penal settlements, Norfolk Island is the worst. To quote Dr Ullathorne: "It is as perverted as the cities God visited with fire from Heaven; so corrupt was the most ordinary language as incessantly to present the imagination with the absent object of the passions as though present – so perverse, that in their dialect, *evil* was literally called *good*, and *good, evil* – the well-disposed man was branded *wicked*, whilst the leader in monstrous vice was styled *virtuous.*''

' ''So indifferent had even life become,'' says the Report on Transportation, ''that murders were committed in cold blood; the murderer afterwards declaring that he had no ill-feeling against his victim, but that his sole object was to obtain his own release. Lots were then cast; the man on whom it fell committed the deed, his comrades being witnesses, with the sole view of being taken for a time from the scenes of their daily miseries to appear in the court at Sydney.'' '

Buret, op. cit.

(Dr Ullathorne was the Roman Catholic Bishop of Birmingham, who went to Australia as vicar-general of the Vicar Apostolic of New Holland and Van Dieman's Land (Tasmania). He visited the terrible penal settlement of Norfolk Island where he converted many convicts to his faith. The quotation is taken from his book *The Catholic Mission in Australasia* (3rd ed., 1838). The government report quoted is the Molesworth Report. Transportation to New South Wales was abandoned in 1840: TN.)

24(TN).   This was almost certainly Emmanuel Moses, known as 'Money Moses', notorious for one of the most sensational robberies of the day, the gold-dust robbery. He was condemned to death, and his sentence was commuted to transportation.

25(FT).   'Nowhere in English prisons are there any workshops run on the same lines as those in French prisons; free industry would be terrified of such a thing.'

Moreau-Christophe, op. cit.

26(TN).   Marshal SOULT (1769–1851) was a distinguished veteran of the Grand Army and held high office under Louis-Philippe. He was in London in 1838 to represent France at the coronation of Queen Victoria.

27(FT).   'This prison cost the staggering sum of £788,000, that is 19,700,000 francs in our money!'

Lessons of Dr Julius, vol. II, p. 47

(I have been unable to discover the source of this quotation. Millbank Penitentiary represents the first attempt to put into practice the 'panopticon' scheme devised by the Utilitarian Jeremy Bentham. The layout was intended to ensure that every part of the prison was under constant surveillance. It consisted of a chapel and administrative offices in the centre with six pentagonal blocks radiating from it, the whole surrounded by an octagonal wall. Prisoners worked and slept in their cells, and the only reading matter permitted was the Bible, religious books and tracts. It was found that unrelieved isolation affected their mental balance, so a certain measure of communal work and exercise was introduced, but this of course led to clandestine communication between prisoners, so when the next model prison was built at Pentonville, prisoners were made to wear masks whenever they left their cells so that they would not be recognised by their fellows. Millbank, unlike other London prisons at the time, was under the direct control of the Home Office. It was demolished before the end of the century, and the site is now occupied by the Tate Gallery: TN.)

28(FT). 'But prisoners in the same category meet twice a day in the yard allotted them for exercise; this takes place in silence, and consists in marching up an down one behind the other under the surveillance of a warder.

'As we have seen, they also meet in chapel.

'They meet in the school, too, and at the pump, in the corridors, the washroom, and so on.

'These encounters, though momentary and subject to the rules of a severe régime, none the less result in the establishment of dangerous contacts between prisoners, if not during their term of imprisonment, certainly when they are once more at liberty. This is why I feel sure that the fact that this institution [Millbank] has so far produced such disappointing results must be largely attributed to the vices it shares with ordinary houses of correction.'

Moreau-Christophe, op. cit.

29(FT). 'The amount spent on each prisoner [at Millbank] was about £26.10s, or 665 francs in our money. . . .

'In 1837, the revenue from prisoners' labour in all English prisons amounted to only £6,601, and the cost of maintaining and guarding the same prisons came to the enormous sum of £243,988. The income of the prisons, including the prisoners' labour mentioned above, was £21,711; from which it follows that the total cost of English prisons for the year 1837 was £222,277, not counting the expenditure on prison buildings. The cost of keeping each prisoner varies, according to the régime followed in each prison, between 1s. and 2s. per head per day.'

Moreau-Christophe, op. cit.

❦ X ❧

St Giles Parish

I have seen the Indian in his forests and the negro in
his chains, and as I looked upon their pitiable state I
thought that this was the ultimate in human misery;
but then I did not know the fate of poor Ireland. . . .

Irish poverty is a thing apart; it has no model or
parallel anywhere in the world; once you have seen it
you know that in theory the wretchedness of man has
no limits. . . .

When I see a nation which has had the misfortune
to fall beneath the yoke and remain in servitude, I do
not ask what vices it has, but rather what vices it lacks
and what virtues it can possibly possess.

Gustave de Beaumont,
Ireland, its Society, Politics and Religion (1839)

There are more than two hundred thousand members of the
Irish proletariat living in different parts of the metropolis;
they work as porters, men who are given the heaviest tasks
because they will work for the lowest wages. That they are
poor, Heaven knows, but at least they are employed; they
do not give a true picture of Irish poverty, covered in rags
and disputing with stray dogs for potato peelings in the
streets.[1] The Irish poverty that M de Beaumont describes in
his book is found in the very heart of one of London's
wealthiest districts, and that is where we must go to see in all
its horror the misery that exists in a rich and fertile country
when it is governed by the aristocracy for the benefit of its
members.

At its starting-point, the elegant, long thoroughfare of
Oxford Street, with its throng of carriages, its wide pave-
ments and splendid shops, is joined almost at right angles

by Tottenham Court Road; just off this street, facing Oxford Street, there is a narrow alley nearly always obstructed by an enormous cart loaded with coal, which leaves hardly enough room for you to pass, even if you flatten yourself against the wall. This little alley, Bainbridge Street, is the entrance to the Irish quarter.[2]

Before I left Paris a Spanish gentleman told me of three parts of London he thought I would find it instructive to visit; the Irish quarter, the Jewish quarter, and the place where stolen silk scarves and handkerchiefs are sold.

In England patriotism is nothing but the spirit of competition; it consists not in the love of one's fellow men, but in the desire to emulate all other nations. This absurd vanity, which I shall have occasion to mention more than once, makes every Englishman conspire to *conceal the poverty of his country* – an odd kind of patriotism, to suppress evils which can be remedied only by the greatest publicity, by bringing them to the notice of everybody who has a voice to speak or a pen to write so that the ruling classes are forced to blush for shame!

I sought in vain for anybody who could direct me to the Irish quarter, as everybody I approached seemed ignorant of its existence, but at last I met a Frenchman who offered to escort me to all three places I wished to observe.

It is not without fear that the visitor ventures into the dark, narrow alley known as Bainbridge Street. Hardly have you gone ten paces when you are almost suffocated by the poisonous smell. The alley, completely blocked by the huge coal-yard, is impassable. We turned off to the right into another unpaved muddy alley with evil-smelling soapy water and other household slops even more fetid lying everywhere in stagnant pools. I had to struggle against my revulsion and summon up all my courage to go on through this veritable cesspool. In St Giles, the atmosphere is stifling; there is no fresh air to breathe nor daylight to guide your steps. The wretched inhabitants wash their tattered garments themselves and hang them on poles across the street, shutting out all pure air and sunshine.[3] The slimy mud beneath your feet gives off all manner of noxious vapours, while the wretched rags above you drip their dirty rain upon your head. The fantasies of a fevered imagination could never match the horrifying reality! When I reached the end of the alley, which was not very long, my resolution faltered; my body is never quite as strong as my will, and now I felt my stomach heave, while a fierce pain gripped my head. I was wondering whether I could bear to go any further when it struck me that I was in the midst of human beings, my fellow men, my brothers and sisters who had mutely suffered for centuries the pains I had endured for barely ten minutes. I overcame my suffering; the inspiration of my soul came to my aid and I felt within me an energy equal to the task I had set myself – to examine one by one every sign of destitution. Then an indefinable compassion surged through my heart, and at the same time a sombre terror took possession of me.

Picture, if you can, barefoot men, women and children picking their way through the foul morass; some huddled against the wall for want of anywhere to sit, others squatting on the ground, children wallowing in the mud like pigs. But unless you have seen it for yourself, it is impossible to imagine such extreme poverty, such total degradation. I saw children *without a stitch of clothing*, barefoot girls and women with babies at their breast, wearing nothing but a torn shirt that revealed almost the whole of their bodies; I saw old men cowering on dunghills, young men covered in rags.

Inside and out, the tumbledown hovels are entirely in keeping with the ragged population who inhabit them. In most of them the doors and windows lack fastenings and the floor is unpaved; the only furniture is a rough old oak table, a wooden bench, a stool, a few tin plates and a sort of *kennel* where father, mother, sons, daughters, and friends all sleep together regardless; such is the 'comfort' of the Irish quarter![4] All this is horrifying enough, but it is nothing compared with the expressions of the people's faces. They are all fearfully thin, emaciated and sickly; their faces, necks and hands are covered with sores; their skin is so filthy and their hair so matted and dishevelled that they look like negroes; their sunken eyes express a stupid animal ferocity, but if you look at them with assurance they cringe and whine. I recognised in them the self same faces and expressions that I had observed when I visited the prisons. It must be a red-letter day for them when they enter Coldbath Fields; at least in prison they will have fresh linen, comfortable clothes, clean beds and pure air.

How do they all live? By prostitution and theft. From the age of nine or ten the boys begin to steal; at eleven or twelve the girls are sold to brothels. The adults of both sexes are all professional thieves and their sole passion is drinking.[5] If I had seen this quarter before I visited Newgate I would not have been so surprised to learn that the prison takes in fifty or sixty children a month and as many prostitutes. Theft is the only logical consequence when people live in such destitution as this.

In great distress I asked myself what remedy there could be for such evils; then I thought of the doctrines propounded by our friends the English economists, and their maxims seemed to be written in blood. . . .

'If the people suffer, they should reflect that the cause of their suffering can be attributed only to themselves; likewise the remedy depends on them alone and on nobody else; society can do nothing for them; when the worker's wage is insufficient to maintain his family, it follows that the country has no need of new citizens or the king of new subjects.'

These are the views of Malthus and they are shared by Ricardo and the entire school of English economists.[6] Lord Brougham, one of the most bloodthirsty of these *modern cannibals*, delivered the following words in the House of Lords with the coolness of a mathematician demonstrating a proof:

'Since it is impossible to increase supplies to the level of the needs of the population, the population must decrease to the level of available supplies.'

It follows that in England the moralists and statesmen whose words carry the most authority can suggest no other means of saving the people from destitution than to prescribe *fasting*, prohibit *marriage* and cast all new-born babies into the gutter. According to them only people in easy circumstances should be allowed to marry, and all institutions for abandoned children should be abolished. . . .

I fled from the spot in horror.[7]

'My God!' I exclaimed. 'What false, pretentious hypocrites the English are in everything they say and do!'

'Not as false as you think,' replied my friend, who had known England for many years. 'Their affirmations of probity, altruism and humanity deceive none but the foreigners for whom they are intended; very few people here are taken in by them.'

'So you think they are false and hypocritical only in order to hoodwink foreigners; perhaps you are right. But as I have not been initiated into the mysteries of their politics I cannot conceive why they make such a parade of their religion, philanthropy and generosity.'

'Quite simply in order to evade any obligation to the humane and just.'

'After what I have just seen I am inclined to believe you; still I confess that sometimes I too have almost been deceived by their speeches in Parliament, and when I observe how their deeds contradict their words, I find it difficult to believe they are based on the same principle. How, for instance, can you reconcile the slavery of millions in Ireland, England and Scotland, who receive a wage far short of their needs in return for work which exceeds their strength and shortens their life? How *can* you reconcile this appalling oppression with the abolition of the slave trade and the emancipation of the negroes?'

'My dear lady, there is not a single merchant in the City who could not answer your questions. You are no doubt

159

aware that it is through the products of their colonies and their factories that the enterprising British are able to extort money from so many nations. In order to guarantee them a favourable price in the European market for goods from India and their colonies in the New World they must prevent the development of any other tropical regions, and the only way to achieve this is to prohibit the slave trade and hunt down any ship engaged in it. The huge population of India and the English colonies in America provide them with all the workers they need.'[8]

'I can understand their motives but I still cannot fathom why they freed their slaves.'

'Perhaps you imagine that they freed their slaves in the same way that the Christian countries freed their serfs, by allowing them to settle on the land? Oh no! The Jamaican negroes are less wretched than the English factory worker or the Irish peasant because the fruits of their labour are more valuable, but they are not more *free*; they have been turned into proletarians on the English model; they are forbidden to own land; they are forced to pay an exorbitant rent for the cabins they live in; they contribute to the upkeep of the roads by forced labour and taxes. White officials punish them for stealing a banana in the same way that the English Justices of the Peace punish men for stealing a handful of potatoes – with the lash. You may depend on English ingenuity to invent so many *duties* and *taxes* that the negro is obliged to work just as hard now as he did for the master before emancipation. The abolition of arbitrary punishment has unquestionably improved the slave's lot; but this improvement which will bring about an increase in the population, is calculated to serve the interests of the landed proprietors as well.'

'I see that this form of emancipation is one of those acts of apparent generosity which turn out entirely to the advantage of their authors – but do not forget that the government devoted the sum of twenty million pounds to this measure.'

'The Government ministers who advocated this form of emancipation were assured of the support of English commercial interests because the colonial landowners were indebted to London financiers to the tune of two-thirds of the value of their properties and the only way they could afford to free their slaves was if the government paid them compensation. A much more economical – and beneficial – system was suggested whereby the slaves would be freed gradually, and their freedom paid for with the labour of those waiting to be freed; this would also have ensured that the emancipated slaves received moral instruction and a period of apprenticeship. But the Government could never have got this system accepted, because only by liberating all the slaves simultaneously and paying compensation could it guarantee that the English creditors would recover their money.'

So the great act of *humanity* that the English have boasted about for thirty years was nothing but a carefully calculated *financial transaction* – and for thirty years the whole of Europe has been deceived! The fraudulence of the honourable members of the English Parliament has persuaded us to put our trust in the philanthropy and altruism of a pack of *traders!* In the face of deception on such a scale one is tempted to believe that it is possible for Europe, or even the whole human race, to be temporarily overcome by stupor, or struck down by paralysis or madness, just as individuals are. However, the veneer of hypocrisy that masks all their actions is not intended only to deceive foreigners; they also want the countless millions of workers whom they bleed white, starve of their bread and subject to every kind of oppression – these slaves, who bend beneath their heavy load – *to believe that they are free* – what cruel irony! – and to honour and respect their masters. That is why they make so many grandiloquent speeches about liberty, philanthropy and religion.[9] But the ruling classes are not taken in by all these high-flown professions of altruism, although it suits them to pretend to drink in every word. Self-interest alone

161

dictates all their opinions and actions, down to the societies they join and the company they keep; self-interest makes them smile at the friend they meet in the street, makes them vote for peace or war, for the enslavement of the Indian or the emancipation of the negro.

In London there are hundreds of societies whose pretentious titles are deliberately designed to attract a certain kind of patron; several claim to serve philanthropic ends. One poses as the protector of *all God's creatures*; its object is to prevent cruelty to horses, donkeys, dogs and other animals. People who are deceived by its title and prospectus might easily believe that the members of this Society were universal benefactors. Fancy considering the welfare of horses, donkeys and dogs! Think how generous they must be towards their fellow men! . . . Just another piece of humbug; this Society consists of members of the riding, hunting, horse-dealing and carriage-owning confraternity, whose aim is to keep a *closer watch* on the menials employed to tend their precious animals – for as our French proverb says –

'He who would travel far takes good care of his mount!'

NOTES

1(FT). 'The ordinary potato has become a luxury to which the Irish no longer aspire. The substitution of a smaller variety for the ordinary, better quality potato is a fact of profound economic significance which we shall return to later. . . .

The social and economic conditions of this unhappy country [Ireland] are such that if the people could obtain nourishment from the mud of its bogs, the landowners, with the connivance of the middlemen, would raise the price of land so high that the Irish would still be faced with death by starvation!'

Eugène Buret,
De la misère des classes laborieuses en Angleterre et en France
(1840)

2(TN). The Irish quarter in St Giles, Holborn occupied roughly the area bounded by Charing Cross Road, New Oxford Street and Shaftesbury Avenue, but in Flora's time the two last-named streets did not exist; slum clearance began a few years after her 1839 visit. According to the census of 1831 the population of this district – commonly known as Little Dublin – was a staggering 36,432. The 1841 census registered 82,291 Irish-born residents in London (3% of the population) but this did not include children born in England of Irish parents. By 1851 the number had increased to 109,000 (4.6%) largely because of the influx of Irish after the terrible potato famines in Ireland. Professor Lynn Lees has calculated that if children and relatives were added, the figure would have risen to 156,000, but even this is still short of the inflated figure of 200,000 that Flora gives for 1839.

3(FT). 'In every part of London, Manchester and Liverpool, we found streets completely obstructed from top to bottom by clothes and coverlets left hanging out to dry and dripping on passers-by. We were often obliged to lift these damp rags at every step to clear a way through the streets, which were quite impassable to traffic and had been abandoned to poverty alone.'

Buret, op. cit.

4(FT). 'An English gentleman who has travelled all over Europe to seek distraction and parade his boredom has probably never set foot in those parts of London to which the poverty-stricken inhabitants of this opulent city are consigned; his curiosity is unlikely to have taken him more than once or twice to see the classic horrors of St Giles (the two parishes of St Giles and Cripplegate had a population of 13,134 in 1831), the home of vagabonds, prostitutes and thieves; yet today the notorious district of St Giles is a paradise compared with parts of north-east and south-east London, for this is where the worst poverty is found. . . .

'Perhaps no city in the world presents more desolate a spectacle than the parishes of Bethnal Green and Shoreditch, which together contain 70,000 people. A large part of the land here has retained its original name of *gardens*, where landlords and speculators have raised a multitude of wooden shacks, mostly of one storey, for housing poor families. The appearance of these *gardens* is indescribable: there are no streets or drains running between the miserable hovels surrounded by their rotting wooden fences; the ground has not even been levelled; in some places there are mounds of earth and piles of rubbish, in others there are hollows full of stagnant water; heaps of pig manure lie in front of the hovels; there is nothing but filth, stench and decay everywhere. These abominable quarters are abandoned without protection or surveillance. The civil authorities do not reach this far: in fact they are nowhere in evidence. The hovels are crumbling and rotting away; there is no drainage, no lighting, no regular collection of rubbish – in short, not a sign of urban civilisation. It is the supreme example of *laissez faire*! This quarter is totally outside the law, outside humanity; none of the rules and regulations of civilised society apply here!'

Buret, op. cit.

(In his first paragraph Buret is referring to St Giles, Holborn, the Irish quarter, population 36,432, but he confuses it with St Giles, Cripplegate, population 13,134: TN.)

5(FT). See the description M Buret gives in his section on London.

6(TN). Thomas Robert MALTHUS (1766 – 1834) held that poverty and suffering are unavoidable because population increases by a geometrical ratio while the means of subsistence increase by an arithmetical ratio. The quotation is a condensation of a passage from his *Essay on the Principle of Population* (1798; 2nd edition, 1803: Book IV, Ch. III).

7(FT). The *Little Ireland* in English and Scottish cities matches the parent country in every respect.

'Now every city in England has its *Little Ireland*, which day by day swallows up larger populations; and what is even sadder, some cities on the continent, French cities, as we shall see, have their own *Little Ireland* as well. Not content with taking revenge on England by poisoning her with its poverty, Ireland is also threatening to cross the sea and conquer for her empire of famine and corruption the working classes of every civilised country!'

Buret, op. cit.

8(FT). This is how Marshal Pillet, writing in 1815, judged

English philanthropy as regards the abolition of the slave trade. His prophecy struck me as interesting, which is why I quote it:

'The West Indies are not intended to recover; they are marked down for destruction. England has pronounced a curse on them, and she is strong enough today for her wish to be accomplished.

'It is from the vast rich regions of Hindustan, a land capable of producing in the greatest abundance all the choice foods that Europeans have uprooted from their Asian soil and transplanted to the West Indies, that Europe will, a few years hence, be able to obtain all the sugar and coffee she needs at prices much lower than any the West Indies can offer. In India they cost little more to produce than do our most common garden vegetables, because the cost of labour is nothing, absolutely nothing, compared with costs in Europe, and even less compared with costs in the West Indies, where the plantation owner must cover himself against the value of his land, his buildings, the slaves he has purchased, the risk of their falling ill and dying; the plantation owner who employs free native labour in a country where the cost of land and buildings is negligible does not have to bother with such calculations.

'We are about to see trade take a turn which will permit Europe to enjoy the products of India only after they have passed through England and through English hands. She will fix prices and the cost of transport and impose whatever monopolies she pleases. It is only a matter of time before Indian production is firmly established on lines which the English have laid down. Then the West Indies will be destroyed.

'According to England's diabolical plans, the black population of the West Indies is fated to fulfil a destiny which the whole world will be powerless to escape.

'As allies of England, receiving from her hands food, ships and munitions, this black population – which does not lack courage and is ready for action, which hates work and will tackle it only under duress – will form a chain of pirates which will infest all the seas around America, posing a constant and universal threat to the prosperity of the whole continent. This is how England has resolved to revenge herself upon the American Union, the rebellious daughter for whom Great Britain has sworn an implacable hatred.'

Pillet, op. cit.

9(FT).   The reader should remember that it was in 1839 that I visited London and that I wrote these reflections in the first few months of 1840. Since then, poverty in England has reached colossal proportions. The people are being starved by the aristocracy; every day workers die in their thousands and people no longer believe in the philanthropy of the British Parliament. After the session of 16 June this year (1842) who in Europe would be simple enough to believe that it is Christian charity which makes Sir Robert Peel, Lords Stanley and Brougham, the leading members of Parliament and the majority in both Houses advocate the emancipation of the negroes with such enthusiasm? How could the tortures inflicted on a slave by a cruel master ever equal the tortures of hunger? And it is only to increase their revenues by a few pence that these honourable gentlemen condemn *thousands of their fellow countrymen* to die in unspeakable agony! Listen, you who are still taken in by English hypocrisy, listen to the selfish reasons the Prime Minister gave for rejecting Mr Ferrand's motion; see for yourselves how callously and remorselessly this monstrous assembly VOTED FOR THE DEATH OF THE ENGLISH PROLETARIAT!

'*Mr Ferrand* moved that on the 1st of July, the House should form itself into a Committee for the purpose of presenting an address to the Queen, beseeching her that a sum of money not exceeding one million pounds should be used immediately for the temporary relief of the distress and destitution of the working classes in the manufacturing districts. Twenty million pounds sterling, said the Honourable Member, had been voted for the emancipation of the slaves in the West Indies. Could so small a sum be refused to a suffering people?

'*Sir Robert Peel*: "I would not have taken the floor had I not feared to seem indifferent to the distress of the people. I regard the motion before the House as dangerous. It is a precedent which would not fail to be invoked later, and which would infallibly result in an enormous increase in taxation. The government is labouring silently but effectively to alleviate the sufferings of the working classes."

'*Mr Duncombe* supported the motion: "I could never cite enough examples to illustrate the intensity of the distress. For my part, I would be quite prepared to support a vote of five million pounds sterling rather than one, but the House, sceptical as ever, will never be convinced of the people's distress until it sees

400,000 or 500,000 men dying of hunger bringing the frightful spectacle of their destitution to London.''

'The House proceeded to the vote: Mr Ferrand's motion was defeated by 106 votes to 6.'

(In 1842 England was in the grip of the worst economic depression since the beginning of the century. Flora refers to the parliamentary debate, 'On the Distress of the Country' which took place on 16 June 1842. The motion was put by William Ferrand, the Member for Knaresborough, and he asked the House to form itself into a Committee on 21 June, just five days later (not 1 July). Richard Cobden, the champion of the Anti-Corn Law movement, also supported the motion. Flora gives a fair summary of the argument advanced by Sir Robert Peel but does not convey the force of Duncombe's actual words: 'The people will never obtain redress till some 400,000 or 500,000 men from the manufacturing districts come to the metropolis to demand it'. (See Hansard, 3rd series, vol. LXIII). This was hardly her fault, as she was not quoting directly from Hansard, but (presumably) from a French report of the debate. Duncombe was the Radical member for Finsbury, who had presented the second People's Charter to Parliament in May 1842, one month before this debate: TN.)

CRE XI SD

The Jewish Quarter

Children of Israel, when other nations are advancing,
why do you alone stand still, as if you were guarding
the tombs of your forefathers? . . . Children of Israel,
become the children of Jesus: learn to understand us,
love us and be our brothers.

Adolphe-Louis Constant

Eighteen hundred years have passed since Titus captured Jerusalem and the Jews dispersed; and the Jewish people, with their religion, their customs and their laws, have preserved themselves among the nations. The Romans, and the destroyers of the Romans, have passed away, but the Jewish nation is still standing! When we compare Moses with the other law-givers, we are filled with astonishment at the prodigious longevity of the institutions he founded; but if we examine the circumstances which produced this phenomenon, and if we reflect on the nature of Man, the miracle vanishes. Man's very ignorance is enough to guarantee that any form of religious belief or superstition will endure for ever, and when ignorance is combined with persecution, religious fervour becomes incandescent and religious faith takes on a new lease of life. Since the Diaspora, the Jews have been persecuted by Christians and Muslims alike, and their devotion to their faith has always been directly related to the persecution brought against them. Man is not as selfish, materialistic or as dominated by his appetites as he is represented; the idea of infinity, a feeling of dissatisfaction with sensual pleasures, and a sense of his independence are always present in him, and when his will is sustained by the religious faith in which he was raised, he is ready to brave torture and accept death. Moreover, a life of tribulation

168

spent in isolation from the rest of society gives us a conviction of superiority, and whatever the nature of the religious belief, political principle or personal opinion for which we are persecuted, the more we have to suffer for the right to hold it, the more conscious we are of our moral stature. This feeling may reach such a pitch of exaltation that our suffering is transformed into joy; then how disdainfully we look down on the vulgar herd who only live by their senses!

Elementary education and the printing press, which bring instruction and books within the reach of all, provide mankind with an extra sense. But toleration and free thought very soon weaken the ties of religion; the Jews are now no more zealous in their beliefs than the Catholics, and unless the king of Prussia quickly comes to the rescue of Judaism with a little persecution, the Jewish religion will lose its hold over its adherents in Europe just as other religions have done!

Treated everywhere as PARIAHS, spurned everywhere by society, the Jews have evolved a society of their own; this has given them the inestimable advantage of not being inhibited in their choice of a way of life by any kind of prejudice or concession. At the same time, the persecution they have suffered leads them to help and succour one another, while their trust in Providence and their expectation of the Messiah give their miserable existence a divine ideal, and enable them to endure hardship with pious resignation.

Wealthy Jews are very charitable towards other members of their faith, and live together in a spirit of brotherly love which is rarely found in the various Christian sects.[1]

In London there is a considerable Jewish population in every part of the city, but it is so concentrated in the parish of St Giles that this neighbourhood is known as the Jewish quarter. If I had visited this part of Holborn before I set eyes on the Irish quarter, I might have felt that nobody could live in more extreme degradation than the people of Moses, but in comparison with the Irish, the Jews seemed to me to enjoy a flourishing existence.[2]

Jews in general are more adept at buying and selling than any other nation, but the price they offer or demand is always determined, not by the actual value of the merchandise, but by their knowledge of their customers, and that is why they are so often taken for rogues. It must be admitted that very few traders do not do the same whenever they get the chance – unless they happen to find it more profitable to attract customers by selling their goods cheap! The Jews are very able, industrious and energetic. In the parish of St Giles most of them are either cobblers or dealers in second-hand clothes.

Monmouth Street and St Giles High Street are full of shops displaying worn-out shoes, old clothes and rags; tinsmiths and dealers in bric-à-brac etc., occupy the rest.[3] To see all these thousands of old shoes and such enormous piles of assorted rags and rubbish the object of such a vast trade gives a truer picture of the poverty of the monster city than any number of written reports and memoranda. It makes you shudder and you are so upset that you wonder who can possibly buy such miserable rags! Who indeed? Have you forgotten that the people of Ireland have nothing to cover them – that they have never put on a pair of shoes nor even a shirt? Good Heavens, what misery! How can one bear to dwell on it?

As nearly all the decrepit old hovels in this quarter serve as shops, the wretched owners live in cellars which they reach by means of ladders that are so nearly perpendicular that I have never seen anything like them, even on board the worst sort of merchant vessel. When you go along the narrow streets the sight of all these ladders makes you dizzy. The cellars are little more than kennels where the unhappy children of Israel are crowded together pell-mell; in every one you see seven or eight pale, thin, dirty urchins sprawling among the old shoes and disgusting rags, or crawling up and down the ladders like so many slugs. It is a miracle these children do not break their necks, the way they go up and down a hundred times a day. Poor creatures! There are thousands of them living underground, English subjects, speaking English, yet nobody pays them the slightest attention save to make contemptuous remarks about them because they are *Jews*. How convenient for the English that they can cloak their cruelty in religious prejudice!

But however poor, dirty and depressing this district may be, it is nothing in comparison with Petticoat Lane, the real heart of the Jewish quarter, where the old clothes market is held. I remember that when we were looking for Petticoat Lane we approached a policeman who said in great alarm, 'Don't you go anywhere near that place; the police never set foot in it, so if anybody should attack you, there would be nobody to help you.' I have never forgotten the anxious face of that honest policeman when he saw that nothing he said could deter us from visiting Petticoat Lane.

We went through four or five streets which were completely unpaved and full of mud; most of them were so narrow that a carriage could not pass. But this part of London is quite different from the Irish quarter; there it is empty, sad and silent, whereas here the crowd is so dense that you can hardly move. There is no fresh air and you feel you are suffocating; everybody is constantly on the move – men, women and children, all with an air of active cupidity. They all speak at once, one to vaunt the goods he wants to sell, the other to denigrate the goods he wants to buy, so what with all the shouting, arguments and coarse insults, you cannot hear yourself speak.

We had never seen such *mountains* of old clothes! They gave off such a powerful stench that we were seized with nausea, and we were all retching as we emerged from that den of filth.

However, I suffered less here than in the Irish quarter. The Jews may look extremely poor, but their poverty does not make so painful an impression on the visitor, because their dirty rags have no effect on their morale. The Jew loves money *for its own sake*, not as a means of showing off his luxurious possessions; it matters little to him that he is badly clothed, badly housed and badly nourished, as long as he knows that he has *a little nest-egg* safely hidden away beyond the reach of bankruptcy and revolution; therein lies his secret satisfaction. What makes him happy is not so much to be *thought* rich as to *know* that he is so; that is why the Jews, however wretched they may appear, are full of energy and courage, and content with their lot.

Not far from Petticoat Lane is the street where the Jewish prostitutes live; its appearance is so hideous and disgusting that however much I may be upbraided for my weakness, I must confess that I did not have the courage to venture inside. At the windows I noticed five or six nearly naked women . . . it was too repulsive for words!

Not a single policeman is ever to be seen in this quarter; the poor pariahs are left to themselves, so thefts and murders are very common.

NOTES

1(FT). The widow of Mr Nathan Rothschild displays an admirable charity towards her fellow Jews: she has set up a school in London where five hundred children between the ages of six and eleven receive an education appropriate to their station in life; she clothes them and pays for them to be apprenticed to masters in various trades; she also provides layettes and other assistance for pregnant women, and ministers to the needs of the sick and infirm. In addition to this, other members of the large Rothschild family are well known for their generous acts of charity and the discrimination with which they are made.

2(TN). Whitechapel was the centre of the Jewish community in London – which was neither as numerous nor as widespread as Flora suggests. By the middle of the century the Jews still numbered only about twenty thousand; the great Jewish influx came in the 1880s. The part of St Giles Parish, Holborn occupied by the Jews was often referred to as the Holy Land. This is where Flora went first, then she proceeded to Whitechapel.

3(TN). Dickens describes a visit to the old-clothes shops of Monmouth Street in *Sketches by Boz* (1836). The old Monmouth Street was very near the part of Shaftesbury Avenue that lies between St Giles High Street and Charing Cross Road.

Stolen Silk Handkerchiefs

It is understandable that in a country where the desire to make money is paramount, where even the government profits from the ignorance of other governments by making them subscribe to unequal commercial treaties and resorts to violence against weaker powers in order to extort ruinous concessions from them, the pangs of conscience will rarely make men reject profits when these are to be had at no risk to themselves, and even *scriptural education* will not be strong enough to resist the attractions of gain. There, money dominates everything: consciences are bought and sold, and the desire to strike a good bargain or realise a fat profit is a universal and constant preoccupation, so few people scruple to take advantage of ignorance, carelessness, passion, vice or crime. Respectable capitalists share with the public treasury the profits made from the sale of gin and the encouragement of drunkenness; opulent gambling-houses purchase the protection they enjoy, send out invitations and throw open to gamblers their salons where *trente-et-quarante*,[1] roulette and other games are played. There are some speculators who purchase young girls from their parents in order to traffic in their charms, while others offer to high-class prostitution discreet havens furnished with every luxury.

It is well known that in England the office of Public Prosecutor does not exist, so it is hardly surprising that in a country where immunity can nearly always be purchased – by buying off the plaintiff, providing substantial security, or some other form of corruption – the fruits of crime find ready buyers everywhere, and the traffic in stolen goods and similar industries enjoy the freedom of the city. In London – unlike Paris – the pawnbroking business is not a state monopoly, so it is one of the most lucrative industries; the police have no control over its transactions. The pawnbroker is not in the least concerned to establish whether you are the rightful owner of any article you bring him; he merely states what it is worth to him, and if in the course of a year, you pay him neither capital nor interest, your pledge belongs to him and you have no claim to any further advances on it. Stolen jewels and a variety of other objects are brought to these shops.[2] As dealing in stolen goods is tolerated, theft becomes a regular industry; thus a multitude of people – men, women and children, rich and poor – make a profession out of stealing silk handkerchiefs, and their harvest is so abundant that the resale of these articles constitutes a special branch of the trade of *honest shopkeepers*!

Quite close to Newgate, in a little alley off Holborn Hill called Field Lane, which is too narrow for vehicles to use, there is absolutely nothing to be seen but dealers in second-hand silk handkerchiefs.[3] I am sure I do not need to warn any curious traveller who might be tempted to follow in my footsteps, to leave at home his watch, purse *and* handkerchief before he ventures into Field Lane, for he may be sure that the gentlemen who frequent the spot are all light-fingered! It is particularly interesting to go there in the evening, as it is then thronged with people – which is easy to understand: buyers and sellers alike are anxious to preserve their anonymity for, after his purse, nothing is more precious to anyone in business than the mask of respectability he has been at such pains to acquire.

The shops are in fact stalls which project into the street, and this is where the handkerchiefs are displayed: they hang on rails so that intending purchasers can recognise at a glance the property they have had stolen from them! The men and women dealers, whose looks are in perfect harmony with their trade, stand in their doorways and hector the customers who come under cover of the night to buy *dirt cheap* the spoils of the day. There is a bustle of activity in the street as prostitutes, children, and rogues of every age and condition come to sell their handkerchiefs. They are taken into the back of the shop to haggle over the price, then the handkerchiefs are given to a servant whose sole and constant occupation is to unpick any identifying marks and then to wash them. On the pretext of searching for two handkerchiefs we had had stolen, and by which we claimed to set great store, we went into four or five shops where we were shown all the handkerchiefs brought in over the past five days – a total of over a thousand! Now, as there are more than twenty shops in Field Lane, one may safely conclude that between four and five thousand handkerchiefs are brought each week to this repository of stolen goods. There I saw really superb handkerchiefs selling for two or three shillings. The trade in Field Lane is as brisk as any in the City, and it looks as if fortunes are made there.

The only crimes which the police actively try to detect are forgery – because it has a harmful effect on credit – robbery with violence, murder, arson, and other crimes which endanger public safety; as for the perpetrators of swindles and fraud, they are arrested only when caught red-handed. The administration would have too much on its hands if it attempted to contain petty thefts; it is well aware that the law is powerless to deal with the incalculable number of thefts which are a direct result of social conditions, and it turns a blind eye to the traffic in stolen goods for fear of exposing an unmanageable number of offenders. If the law were administered here as it is in France, England would not have enough prisons to contain its thieves and receivers, or enough ships to transport them to Australia!

NOTES

1(TN). *Trente-et-quarante* is a card game dating from the seventeenth century, in which players bet on the sum of the pip values turned up by the banker. Thirty and forty are the winning and the losing numbers respectively.

2(FT).   Some pawnbrokers buy stolen gold or silver articles and melt them down straight away.

3(TN).   This makes one think of Oliver Twist. Field Lane, which linked Holborn Hill and Saffron Hill, disappeared with the construction of Holborn Viaduct in 1863 – 1869.

The Races at Ascot Heath

Horses are ordinarily 4′ 9″ to 4′ 10″ in height. Their legs are slender, but the development of their hocks and the prominence of their joints are indicative of their great strength and explain their capacity for speed; their bodies are extremely slim and elongated; the muscles and even the veins stand out in great detail beneath the delicate skin and short smooth coat. The racehorse is given very little to eat; the stomach, and consequently the bone structure, particularly of the body, develop hardly at all. The activity of the muscles, stimulated by the effort involved in training and racing, endows the muscular structure with a prominence which is enhanced by the complete absence of fat.

To bring jockeys down to the required weight, they are given a diet high in nourishment and low in bulk, dosed frequently with purges, made to take exercise in heavy clothing to induce perspiration, and subjected to a host of similar precautions.

Baron d'Haussez, *Great Britain in 1833*

In France, and any country which prides itself on being civilised, the most honoured of living creatures is woman. In England, it is the horse; in these fortunate islands, the horse is king, and takes precedence not only over woman, but over man as well.

The most famous racecourses are at Newmarket, Epsom and Ascot Heath; I am acquainted only with the last of these three. In England the races are great occasions which have all the character of a solemn ceremony in the eyes of the spectators. Ascot races are held in the last three days of May, and for the people of London and its environs they are what the august rites of Holy Week in Rome represent for Catholics, or the last three days of carnival for Parisians.

This great holiday has a universal attraction for the English whatever their age, sex or rank. To cut a worthy figure during these three days, everybody goes to some expense. Aristocratic ladies send to Paris for elegant gowns in the latest fashion; noble lords, financiers, dandies and wealthy men-about-town order fine carriages, buy new horses, and fit out all their servants in fresh livery. City merchants shut up shop, hire a cab and abandon business for the races. Ladies of easy virtue put on all their finery and relax in smart broughams drawn by four horses and driven by two coachmen distinguished by the colour of their coats – red, yellow, green, blue, etc. – but all wearing the prescribed white buckskin breeches, top-boots and little hunting-cap. There is no woman down to the lowest prostitute – even if she has to pawn her only shift – who does not find the means to buy new shoes, new gloves, a new gown and a new hat for the occasion, and even the thrifty housewife who has gone without every conceivable necessity all through the winter will spend her entire savings with cheerful abandon just to go to the races!

Fashionable society ladies in Paris perhaps imagine that the races at Ascot are just like ours at Longchamp, where the road is sprinkled with water so that their fresh pretty dresses are not spoiled by the dust; and that all the English ladies have to do is sit back and let themselves be admired. But no! this is not how things are done in London.

Ascot is about thirty miles from London, and as the first race usually starts at midday, patrons must set out at four, five, or six o'clock in the morning to arrive in time. There is only one road, so between dawn and noon or early afternoon, more than three thousand vehicles of every description pass along it. For most of the way it is wide enough, but in some places it is exceedingly narrow; there are several bridges and a number of toll-gates where you have to pay, and then everyone waits in line. The road is sandy, and as it had been raining the day before I went, there were some deep ruts along the way. After we passed Windsor, the wheels stuck in loose sand rather like ashes, but what I found quite admirable was that despite the difficulties of the route and the number of vehicles on it, the most perfect order was maintained every moment of the journey, *and I did not hear of a single carriage being overturned*!

It must be admitted that the English have a special genius for managing horses; besides, they are accustomed to respect the *order of precedence* when they are out in force, and observe it with the precision of a Prussian regiment on parade. This discipline, which is found in no other people, is due to the system of government, for in this country everything is managed on the hierarchical principle, even down to the vehicles on the public highway! Carriages with armorial bearings have undisputed right of way; middle-class conveyances with four horses rank higher than those with only two; then come gigs and tilburys, followed by hired landaus, stage-coaches, omnibuses, cabs, and so on right down to the horse-drawn cart which goes before a hand-cart. Therein lies the secret of this admirable system – everybody knows his place!

Now, would you like to know what all these people from every walk of life were saying and doing in their three thousand vehicles? If this were France we would expect them to be enjoying themselves – talking, singing, launching into animated and probably witty arguments like the fairgoers at Saint-Cloud; but there was nothing like that. The high-born ladies in their splendid clothes lay languidly back in the depths of their carriages and seemed perfectly indifferent to everything around them: some were even reading novels. The young dandies smoked cigars, the financiers had small tables set up in their carriages and drank champagne; the respectable citizens, packed inside and outside stage-coaches and other public conveyances, sat cheek by jowl without exchanging a word with their neighbours; the common people, crammed anyhow into huge covered wagons, played cards and drank beer; and the farmers and small-holders, in their gigs, tilburys and carts concentrated on their driving; so throughout this great concourse of people, horses and vehicles, silence reigned.

However, from time to time coachmen would be heard swearing at each other for their bad driving or their effrontery in trying to get ahead of the rest, but these mutual reproaches, devoid of passion or anger, were delivered in such flat, toneless voices as to lose all their meaning. I was amazed; I could not help reflecting that if this were France, three companies of mounted gendarmes would not be enough to keep three thousand vehicles in order! Think of all the arguments and quarrels there would be – fights among the coachmen, horses injured and carriages over-turned! Think of all the singing, shouting and wild laughter there would be if from forty to fifty thousand of my turbu-lent compatriots were to go from Paris to Pontoise between dawn and noon! Yes, but this same facility for passionate enthusiasm sometimes transforms Parisians into heroes; the men and women who made a revolution in three days are not the sort to let anyone start weighing out their daily bread without a struggle.[1] Yet in England the workers endure poverty and hunger while the aristocracy peacefully enjoy their country mansions, fine carriages and racehorses. . . .

The English climate makes any country outing, if not impossible, at least a very painful experience. When we left in the morning it was foggy, damp and cold, but towards eleven o'clock the sun broke through, and it was soon so bright that it blinded the multitude of passengers perched on top of stage-coaches (myself among them) and quickly absorbed the moisture on the ground. Then from that sandy road trampled by thousands of horses there arose a cloud of dust so thick that it was impossible to see ten paces ahead, and as we left Windsor Great Park it enveloped us completely. I had never seen anything like it, and I was appalled.

We reached Ascot at half past twelve, and found an

enormous number of vehicles already assembled in a semi-circle around the course in the same scrupulous order as before. Every ten paces policemen were stationed to see that the horses were unharnessed without delay and the vehicles placed according to rank, in such a way as to take up as little room as possible.

The site of the racecourse and fairground is very spacious; it is on high ground, and from this vantage point there is a magnificent view.

The space reserved for the horses – the heroes of the day – was roped off, but between races the public was allowed to promenade inside. There must have been fifty or sixty thousand people there, perhaps even more, for they were spread over so large an area that it was difficult to judge their numbers.

This crowd had nothing in common with our Parisian crowds in the Champs Elysées or the Champ de Mars. Silence reigned: there was no music or dancing, no travelling players or showmen with their big bass drums, no monsters or freaks to be inspected by connoisseurs for a few sous, no booths selling cakes or toys, no children blowing tin whistles: nothing, in short, that one would see at our fairs. Instead I saw in one part of that vast heath twenty-five or thirty tents on which was written in big red letters: 'Roulette played here'.[2] And every twenty paces or so I came across an itinerant banker conducting games of chance, with a little folding table about a foot square on which were placed three thimbles and a pea. There was always a crowd gathered round them, and they were playing for high stakes: I saw one young peasant wager as much as six pounds on a single bet. Although gambling is strictly prohibited, it takes place quite openly through the connivance and corruption of those responsible for maintaining the law. I sometimes wonder whether it might not be better to treat the people as we treat the Chinese and *sell them poison*[3] rather than encourage them in a passion which turns them against honest work and disposes them to commit crimes against society.

All the same, as things stand at present, gambling – as long as it is confined to the wealthy classes – is a useful means of dispersing the riches that human activity constantly accumulates. Not only do I regard the ruin of men who live in idleness and luxury, on money they have not earned, as a positive blessing to society, but I cannot even imagine a single instance where the accumulation of wealth in the hands of one man could ever be to society's advantage. There is nothing to prevent men from joining forces and combining their capital in some great enterprise, but accumulated wealth which frees a man from the need to work inevitably corrupts him and constitutes the greatest social evil.

But look! The horses are off – six abreast! On every side voices are raised in exclamation: 'Oh! What speedy racer! Prodigious rapidity indeed! Astonishing! Astonishing! Wonderful! Wonderful!'

Here I expect to find myself in opposition to accepted opinion, but at the risk of appearing an out-and-out barbarian to all lovers of racing and unworthy ever to set foot inside a stable, I must be honest and say that I find the English horse supremely unattractive.

The horse is indisputably one of the finest animals in creation, but domesticity has as good as destroyed the beauty of its line, and it is the English more than any other people who are responsible for interfering with its natural grace. Take note, gentlemen. I speak as an artist, a passionate lover of beauty; I am not concerned with the qualities that matter so much to you! Nobody who sees these English racehorses with their long, thin, narrow bodies, their lean flanks, their disproportionately long legs, their outstretched necks and thrusting heads, sniffing the air like great hunting dogs; nobody who sees their habitually sad, dull, stupid expressions, however rudimentary his instinct for harmony and line, can refrain from saying, 'This is a downright *ugly* animal!'

Horses from Arabia, Andalusia and Chile are divine

creatures. They combine elegance with grace, strength with agility, suppleness with boldness, beauty of coat with purity of line, liveliness of expression with fiery eye. To see one of these horses, whether it is at rest, walking or at full gallop, everybody will cry, 'What a superb animal!'

But, I shall be told, the English horse is not meant to look graceful, beautiful or pleasing to the eye; it is bred for either strength or speed – and the purpose of *these* animals is to race. Poor beast! Men have not respected the work of God; you are the work of *their* hands. How badly they have treated you. They have deprived you of your mane and tail, they have distorted your shape, they have destroyed several of your faculties in order to exaggerate others. Now you are nothing but a shadow of your former primitive self. Poor beast! How they have degraded you: they have reduced you to nothing more than a *locomotive machine*, a sort of *roulette wheel* whose speed determines loss or gain. Poor beast; wicked men!

The jockeys are persons of some consequence, as the outcome of the race depends as much on their skill as on the speed of their mount. It is interesting to see how carefully and suspiciously the backers examine horses and jockeys alike, for in this business, trickery is very common, and grooms and jockeys are hand-in-glove.[4] The backers inspect the horses' feet, mouth, stomach and ears; then they turn their attention to the jockeys and question them closely, noting every word they say.

The horses are distinguished by the colours their jockeys wear, and as I saw the enormous sums wagered on the red or the black, I was reminded of the gambling-den, except that this kind of betting was far more immoral, because the lives of men and horses were at stake. It seems to me that it might be better to replace the horses with *velocipedes*, as this would eliminate the risk to the rider but make no difference to the gamblers.

Five races were run, with either eight, six, four or two horses, but the excitement was short-lived: a few minutes at the most, and the race was over.

Now let us return to the crowd. At first everybody made for the pavilion where the Queen and one of the Russian Grand Dukes were installed. The Queen nodded graciously to her subjects, while the Grand Duke surveyed them with a patronising glance. Then, after taking the air for a few moments, the gentry retired to the tents to play roulette, while the common people went to bet on the three thimbles and the pea with the itinerant bankers.

But whatever the delights of gambling at roulette, three thimbles or the horses, the greatest pleasure of all came from eating and drinking. I found it an experience as curious as it was novel to see all these fine ladies in their silk gowns of every colour – pink, blue, yellow, green, etc.[5] – balancing on their knees plates piled high with ham, cold beef, pâté and so on, helping down their food with copious draughts of port, sherry and champagne. The races lasted for three hours or so, and I saw some carriages in which the occupants did nothing but eat and drink the whole time!

I was still waiting for some sign of gaiety, but it never came.[6] I saw women fainting, others fast asleep, tipsy men making coarse advances, others at an even more disgusting stage of drunkenness who could no longer stand up; but it was all as cold as death, tedious and revolting. So much for the wealthy classes. As for the people, they crowded into tents especially erected for the three days of the races. Poor people! They are not a pretty sight in their rags. These tents were very small, dark and airless; the men sat around rough wooden tables eating coarse bread and dripping, drinking beer or gin and smoking vile tobacco. In one or two tents there was dancing, but the women were the lowest kind of prostitutes: in England, the wives and daughters of working-men have no pleasure of any kind.

At Ascot I noticed an enormous number of gipsies telling fortunes with prodigious success – particularly among the ordinary people. This race of nomads is found in every part of the Old World, living on charity, petty theft and its native wit; its survival is even more inexplicable than that of the Jews, since the Jews work, while these Bohemians do not, yet they spring up everywhere, and even more than the Jews, their race has preserved its primitive character intact. I saw whole families, with their dark, swarthy skins, smooth black oily hair, white teeth, and eyes full of a melancholy fire. They wear the costume of their fathers, and speak among themselves the ancient tongue which we are told was common to all the gipsy tribes of Europe, Asia and Africa. One of these women approached me to tell my fortune: she was a lovely girl of seventeen, a perfect Esmeralda, with a voluptuous voice, a fine supple figure, small hands, and tiny feet worthy of a lady from Lima. These women have a reputation for chastity. An Englishman told me that he had offered one of them forty pounds to spend the night with her, but she had refused. The gipsy children were nearly naked.

At last, when it was almost six o'clock, the vehicles started on the way home. I thought there would be the most frightful confusion, but not at all. Everything was done with the same discipline as in the morning; the police had the carriages of the nobility harnessed first, and if they judged any coachman too drunk to drive, he was removed from his seat and replaced. Drunk and incapable passengers were put inside the coaches, while any who were only half-drunk were settled on top between two sober companions so that they would not fall, and off they went in such a cloud of dust that they were soon lost to sight.

We arrived back in London at one o'clock in the morning and we had left more than a third of the other vehicles behind us. It was bitterly cold, the fog was thick and the damp penetrating; we were all chilled to the bone.

It was quite pitiful to see all the ladies who had set out in the morning so fresh and elegant returning covered with dust, dirty and completely unrecognisable.

In England this kind of outing is called a *pleasure jaunt*.

NOTES

1(TN).   This is a reference to the Three Days of July 1830, when Charles X was forced to give up the throne and was succeeded by Louis-Philippe.

2(FT).   The bankers also display on their tents the name of the London club for which they are agents, so that if necessary, gamblers can accept their note-of-hand in lieu of money.

3(TN).   This refers to the Opium Wars (1839–1842) between Britain and China, which arose from Chinese efforts to prevent the large-scale imports of opium by British traders into China.

4(FT).   I am told that they use various means to prevent a horse from running as well as it should: they weaken it by giving it drugs, they tie one of its legs tightly with a silken thread concealed beneath the hair of its coat, or the jockey rides in such a way that he is certain to be overtaken.

5(FT).   English ladies in general are very fond of *loud* colours, and when a large number of them are gathered together it is easy to see how common this taste is among them.

6(TN).   This passage is strikingly similar to another description of the English at play. Dr William Acton (who, like Michael Ryan, wrote a book on prostitution, published in 1857) is describing a visit to Cremorne Pleasure Gardens in Chelsea: '. . . So little pleasure came, that the Britannic solidity waxed solider than ever in a garden full of music and dancing, and so an almost mute procession, not of joyous revellers, but thoughtful, careworn men and women, paced round and round the platform as on a horizontal treadmill. . . .'

Steven Marcus, *The Other Victorians* (London, 1966)

Waterloo and Napoleon

Kings will mourn me!
> Napoleon, on St Helena

The armies of the Republic made war on kings;
Napoleon made war on the people.

The word *Waterloo* appears all over London: bridges, streets, public squares and monuments bear its name; it is given to ships of the Royal Navy and the merchant fleet, the big shops adopt it as their sign, and manufacturers name their latest fabrics after it, so that this one word has become, so to speak, the coat-of-arms of England, its heraldic device, the symbol of its renown. Everybody understands that Waterloo is the greatest feat of arms that England has ever been called upon to accomplish, and that it alone represents her past power and sums up her entire glory.[1]

Resounding events which everybody recognises as supremely important always have immeasurable consequences, but the rulers of the world, blinded by the selfishness, rivalry and prejudice of nations, are incapable of appreciating facts and assessing the true significance of events. Kings and nobles interpreted the battle of Waterloo as confirmation of their power, whereas the people hoped it would bring them liberty; Napoleon alone seems to have had a presentiment of the future, as if by this revelation Providence had wished to soften the blow of his fall: 'Kings will mourn me!'

The events of the French Revolution were so momentous that men were crushed beneath their weight; however exceptional its leaders, they disappeared the moment they became an obstacle to its progress; the spirit of God led it and men were impotent to direct, oppose or betray it; all unwittingly served its cause even when they appeared to be taking a contrary path.

When France was a prey to anarchy she accepted, on the 18ᵉ brumaire (9 November 1799), the sword of Napoleon – on the implicit condition that he was to affirm liberty and achieve peace: for if the country had wished to return to despotism there would have been no point in shedding so much blood.

In the annals of human history certain men are outstanding for the dominion they exercised and the influence their actions had in shaping the course of society. Napoleon more than any other sovereign made the people he conquered feel the full weight of his power; it extended to the peasant in his hovel and the rich man in his palace: nobody could escape it. But what has Napoleon left us that will endure? Which of his institutions has benefited humanity? What has he done of permanent value? His codes, on which men sought to base his claim to personal glory, are, in the judgment of legal opinion, notably inferior to the so-called intermediate legislation which existed when he came to power. He substituted his prejudices and tyrannical instincts for the liberal principles of republican legislation; he transformed marriage into servitude and trade into sharp practice; he attacked equality, established primogeniture, and introduced confiscation; he made the withholding of information a crime; he exempted the actions of his agents from the jurisdiction of the courts; he all but abolished the jury system; he increased the powers of the Council of State, set up provosts' courts, and took away the people's right to nominate magistrates.

He appointed all mayors, deputy-mayors and chief constables, notaries and clerks, judges and counsellors, bishops and archbishops, prefects and kings; all authority proceeded from him, and no profession or enterprise in all his vast empire could function without his consent; his armies of soldiers and public servants were under the surveillance of a secret police force made up of thousands of agents who were found in every regiment, in ministerial palaces, and even at royal tables. The Press was censored and espionage organised on such a vast scale that nothing could escape imperial knowledge.

During his reign there was censorship everywhere. He treated the French like children who had to be taught what they should *say* and *think*, and to this end he created a *Director of Public Opinion*. From this period date all the securities, permits, licences and diplomas necessary for the practice of professions and trades; he even went so far as to limit the number of people permitted to engage in certain occupations. There is no doubt that the old system was a reign of freedom compared with the imperial innovations, and our people still suffer enough from what survives of these deplorable institutions to be able to understand what life must have been like before a single link of the chain had been broken.

In this system nobody enjoyed any independence. Napoleon suppressed by decree a number of the attorneys of Paris. We have seen the Restoration usurp the prefect's functions and make printers destitute by depriving them of their licences. The threat of arbitrary power still hangs over all professions which may be exercised only by permission of the authorities, and to be a broker, butcher, baker etc., it is not enough to comply with the fiscal conditions or any other conditions required of these professions by law; the numbers admitted to them are limited as well, and the administration can withdraw a man's licence whenever it pleases. The government, which cannot give anything *gratis* without being unjust to the masses, still has the option of withdrawing any privilege it has granted, and can always throw open the profession, make it accessible to all and thereby return to the principle of common law, which is violated by the creation of any kind of privilege.

The Revolution had introduced freedom everywhere; Napoleon left hardly any activity in life free. The numerous decrees enacted in administrative matters during his reign nearly always tended to restrict or shackle freedom. He had no more respect for the Constituent Assembly than he had for the National Convention. The commune, the canton, the *arrondissement*, the *département*: all were stripped of their political rights, could no longer administer their own affairs or keep government administrators under surveillance through freely elected assemblies. As a final measure the nation was totally deprived of any effective control over the actions of the government through the suppression of all electoral freedom. Even the Restoration, although it was supported by the armies of its allies, was too ashamed to make use of the electoral colleges and the rest of the electoral system which Napoleon had established. The Restoration looked upon its invitation to a part of the nation to participate in the act of government as a concession of royal power, and had no wish to see this gesture subjected to ridicule or insult.

Napoleon planted the tricolour on the Pyramids and the Kremlin; his sword was victorious, his vision boundless; yet nothing of him remains but deep scars of oppression. He shook Europe to its very foundations but did not sow one seed of liberty or the germ of one useful institution.

The armies of the Republic made war on kings. Napoleon made war on the people! The Republic set up popular governments in Holland, Switzerland and all over Italy; Napoleon established monarchs with powers modelled on his own. After the peace of Amiens he re-imposed slavery in Guadeloupe and Cayenne and mounted a large-scale expedition in an attempt to do the same to the negroes of Santo Domingo. Absolute sovereignty as Napoleon conceived it – that is, as a power affecting every aspect of life, from which no person or thing could escape – could not tolerate any form of freedom, and the fixed purpose the Emperor followed throughout his career was to destroy freedom wherever he could and in whatever form it appeared. This was the essential condition of his existence, for the power he wielded would soon have lost all moral authority if anybody, anywhere, had been able to challenge its validity, and then the spirit of revolt would steadily have grown. Napoleon's dominion over the people was marked by the destruction of all their ancient and traditional rights; with the title of king, the Electors of Germany received absolute power from his hands; towns lost their autonomy and their municipal councils were replaced by delegates appointed by their new monarchs. To crown all, Napoleon proclaimed himself the great protector of royal power in Europe! He organised the Confederation of the Rhine and founded a Protectorate in Switzerland, less in the interests of his military power than to erect a barrier against the spirit of freedom.

Although Napoleon reasoned that the machinery of government and the political organisation he had given Europe were as infallible as a mathematical principle, they could not reassure him that he had halted the march of freedom. Fontanes[2] once remarked that had he had reason to suspect the existence of an underground press, the Emperor would have died of apoplexy; certainly one of his greatest grudges against England was the extreme licence of its newspapers. He feared freedom wherever on earth and in whatever rank of society it showed its head, and his fears must have been very strong indeed for him to have believed for one moment that the aristocratic freedom of England could be sufficiently contagious to justify his banning English newspapers in France! 'Kings will mourn me!' he declared on St Helena, and this sentence sums up the man and the whole of his political life. If you read Las Cases, O'Meara, Bertrand, Antomarchi, etc., you will find this idea repeated over and over again.[3] No sooner did Napoleon hear of the formation of the Holy Alliance than he cried, 'Ah! they have stolen the idea from me!'[4] Such words need no comment – but quotations are superfluous, Napoleon's actions are well known, and they are all linked: there is not one that does not tend to weaken resistance and enforce passive obedience. If you consult police records you will see that this vast network which reached out to touch every point and hold everybody within its grasp was not enough to satisfy its inventor; he already had power to control men's deeds, now he wanted to penetrate their thoughts and *stifle* them before they had a chance to grow. His spies were everywhere: in the administration, the Army, the Church, and the schools, not only in France but abroad as well. This immense espionage system provides the strongest proof of the turmoil in the Emperor's soul, the knowledge that he was powerless to crush the principles of revolution.[5]

The adversary of freedom, the man who was to delay its advance in Europe, is revealed in the days of vendémiaire, in his conduct of the campaign in Italy, and as the conqueror of Egypt. Throughout Napoleon's career his actions reflect his grand design, and this extraordinary being, the supreme personification of despotism, is completely unmasked at St Helena. From the rock where he was chained came these prophetic words: 'Kings will mourn me!'

Yet Napoleon was destined to do more than halt the advance of freedom. There is also the continental system, the great achievement he was called upon to perform, and this alone will survive for many years to come. The Emperor was well aware that the commercial supremacy of England existed only because continental agriculture and industry had not been protected, and that if Europe could manage without colonial imports and copy English industrial methods, the enormous power of England would vanish like a dream. But brute force has no power to create anything. Napoleon wanted to establish the continental system by force and he failed; however, this system was so much in the interests of all the nations concerned that their governments would willingly have supported it had they not feared the despotism of the Emperor more than the rapacity of the English. The exclusion of English trade from continental Europe so rapidly confirmed Napoleon's expectations that had he not embarked on the Russian campaign, which had the effect of re-opening continental ports to English trade,

England would have been completely bankrupt.

The continental system is very important: it encouraged the cultivation of cotton on the shores of the Mediterranean, the establishment of sugar beet refineries in central Europe, and many other industries; necessity produced these miracles of industrial development, but only peace could guarantee their growth, and now they have developed to such an extent that in a few years the continent will no longer be exposed to English pressure and England will no longer be able – by virtue of her great store of wealth – to provoke wars in Europe whenever she pleases.

However, the people who had been conquered by Napoleon and forced to accept the masters he imposed on them were enraged at such a cruel betrayal of their hopes, and it was with hearts full of vengeance that they answered the call to arms of their kings, who felt humiliated by the superiority of an upstart soldier. It was not the Russian débâcle that overthrew Napoleon, but the spirit of freedom seizing its first opportunity to throw off the yoke! If Napoleon had been inspired by revolutionary principles, he would have been able to drive the royal armies back far beyond the Dnieper when they had him pinned down in the Pyrenees. This is proved by the events of our Revolution, which demonstrate the power of the revolutionary principle in action.

Events follow one upon the other in an unbroken chain; but there are some which sum up the past and contain within them the seeds of the future. The French Revolution was the continuation of the struggle for freedom of thought which began in the sixteenth century; the fall of the Bastille was another victory for this holy cause, which still has many battles to win before it attains its end. The fall of the Bastille symbolised the rejection of all absolute power, whether political or religious, and all hereditary privilege. It overthrew the highly organised monarchy of Louis XIV and the principle of papal infallibility. It marked the total destruction of the old order, since the new order proclaimed the principle of majority rule and the freedom of the individual.

There are periods when progress seems to mark time in order to take root in people's hearts and minds, but it can never regress, for it is inconceivable that God should ever repent of His great design. The Empire was the winter of our regeneration, and Napoleon seems to have survived its rigours only to serve as a striking testimony to the principle which had overthrown him. 'Kings will mourn me!': the lessons of a lifetime are contained in those words, incontestable proof of the vanity of human reason.

The unholy wars waged by kings against freedom had been in vain, and they had to submit to the military power which arose from those very wars. What an irony of history that those kings should be forced to recognise the rights of the people and to promise them constitutions in order to induce them to rise against the despotism of Napoleon! Even the English aristocracy, faced with the necessity of enlisting national support for a ruinous war, had to encourage every aspiration of the people: emancipation for the Irish, political rights for dissenters and electoral reform for all; while it held out to merchants, manufacturers and workers alike the prospect of seizing the European markets and thereby realising enormous profits and higher wages.

In 1814 and 1815 the nations were at war with despotism, *not with France*; kings could raise armies only by promising to make every soldier a *free citizen*. In Spain the first act of insurrection had been to assemble the Cortès; in Germany and Italy likewise the people turned their weapons against Napoleon in order to establish their freedom.

In my view, the battle of Waterloo, until this day misunderstood by victor and vanquished alike, was the second triumph of liberty! It is great because of the progress it proclaims, the future it heralds and the results it has already obtained. Waterloo justified and consolidated the victory of the Bastille, and from that day onward, it would have been as impossible for the rulers of Germany to continue to govern their peoples as they had done in 1789 and later under the protection of Napoleon, as it would have been for Louis XVIII to attempt to restore the rule of an absolute monarch.

The Emperor was defeated, but it was he alone who abdicated at Fontainebleau, not his army, and freedom could not have advanced in the presence of these new praetorians; if Napoleon had died on the island of Elba, his army would have become a blind instrument in the service of power, and an absolute government, of which the Restoration had already provided a foretaste, would have been established. But after the battle of Waterloo Louis XVIII had no other forces at his disposal but the allied armies, so he was obliged to base his government on the consent of a sizeable part of the nation; from that time on, the struggle for freedom of thought could begin and the reign of public opinion was assured.

So the victory of Waterloo is essentially the triumph of liberty; this is certainly how the nations of the North understood it, for the petty princelings of Germany were so terrified by the aspirations to which they had given birth that they hastened to grant Charters to their subjects; the Congress of Vienna prudently invested the Diet with considerable jurisdiction over these governments; and later, Austria, Russia and Prussia formed an unholy alliance in order to stifle any attempt at emancipation. But the foundations of freedom had already been laid.

On 20 March 1815 Napoleon evoked memories of national glory, but the name of freedom died on his lips; he knew that freedom could not claim him as its defender so he spoke in ringing tones of his victories and the might of France. But only his veterans were fired with enthusiasm; France was exhausted by long wars and detested the military government which ruled her. In her desire for peace she saw Napoleon as the great obstacle to the realisation of her hopes.

The betrayal of Bourmont and the blunder of Grouchy are examples of the emptiness of human knowledge![6] At

Waterloo Napoleon seems to have deployed all his military genius only to prove that Providence had deserted him and condemned his cause. He fell, and it was neither Blücher nor Wellington who overthrew him: it was the guardian of our liberties!

The Prussian army, made up of volunteers, fought with the enthusiasm of men determined to win; the English troops had only brandy and the fear of the lash to replace the Prussians' love of liberty. Frederick's impetuous soldier[7] relied on his courage: the 'untoward hero'[8] trusted to his reason and – a great man in spite of himself – consistently achieved the very opposite of what he intended; the one thought he had restored the supremacy of Prussian arms, while the other thought the omnipotence of the English aristocracy was assured for ever, and that continental money would now pour into England in exchange for English merchandise. Blind instruments of change! Little did they know that they had just overthrown the enemy of freedom, and the obstacles in the way of revolutionary progress! In England the aristocracy interpreted the battle of Waterloo as the guarantee of its supremacy; to the manufacturer it meant the certainty of breaking into the continental market and to the worker it brought the promise of higher wages. But these results were short-lived; peace and tranquillity at home saw the establishment of many industries in Germany and the formation of the customs union; industry made great strides in France and Russia while England was reduced to suing for favours under the name of commercial treaties, and now sees the power of her aristocracy threatened by the masses of the proletariat who are deprived of work and bread.

Thus the victory of Waterloo is an act of Providence which heralds an era of freedom for the people; its consequences will be the liberation of the Irish peasant and the English factory-worker, while in France, where the proletariat is more intellectually advanced than in any other country, it has made the return of despotism impossible for ever.

However, what false interpretations man's emotions have given the battle of Waterloo over the past twenty-five years! The French press, preoccupied with narrow ideas of national rivalry, and military glory, deplores our *disaster of Waterloo*, as if this event, like the fall of the Bastille and the Three Days of July 1830, had not been to the advantage of France and of the freedom of the whole world!

If Napoleon had triumphed at Waterloo, the people would have remained convinced that they were powerless to throw off the yoke; their age-old servitude would have weighed still heavier upon them and despotism would have been strengthened throughout the continent and in the British Isles.

The victory of Waterloo was such a considerable victory for the people that royal authority, freed from the dominion of Napoleon, found itself without support. The people had gained too much to return to unconditional obedience; besides, monarchs with no large armies behind them were now obliged to make concessions, and in Spain, Naples and Piedmont where they refused to do so, insurrections overthrew royal authority and only with the help of foreign arms was it restored.

It is to the battle of Waterloo that France owes her right to free assembly and the freedom of the press. Could Napoleon ever have tolerated these two organs of public opinion? Would he have tolerated men like Casimir Périer, Benjamin Constant, Foy, or publications which demolished the divine right of kings?[9] Had it not been for the battle of Waterloo and the influence of French freedom, would O'Connell have succeeded in obtaining even a half-measure of justice for his fellow citizens? No. The Irish would still labour beneath the heavy yoke imposed by their aristocracy and would never have dared to hope for deliverance from the Anglican clergy who extorted tithes from them to pay for the maintenance of a religion not their own. Nor would these Irish Catholics ever have gained political rights if continental Europe had remained under imperial rule, that iron administration from whose oppression nothing could escape.

Freedom knows no bounds, it spreads just as widely as religious faiths and in no other period of history have ideas spread so rapidly as today. Therefore if France had been ruled by a despot the English aristocracy would not have encountered any serious opposition from the people. They would have continued to exploit, torture and starve at their pleasure the twenty million workers of the British Isles without endangering their political existence in the slightest degree, for they would have been strong enough to suppress the great associations set up to organise popular resistance, and the Chartists, the Irish Union and the Communists could never have existed.

May the name of Waterloo be blessed by all oppressed peoples! May the terrible sacrament which the people celebrated with their blood, when they swore an oath *to be free or perish*, be forever present in their thoughts . . . and the day of deliverance will dawn!

Meanwhile, every day some event occurs to demonstrate the meaning of the word Waterloo, and even if the principles which triumphed in 1789 and 1830 are not yet being practised anywhere in the world, even if despotism still rears its arrogant head – nevertheless, as he contemplates the victories that ideas have won, the believer feels his trust in God redoubled. He is confident that the freedoms proclaimed by the various assemblies elected by universal suffrage prior to 18ᵉ brumaire will eventually become reality, because thought is an active and indestructible force, whereas the material forces opposed to progress have only a transitory existence; they soon lose their momentum and begin to fall into decay.

After 1815 the peoples of Germany, Italy and Spain, encouraged by the victory of Waterloo, called upon their kings to fulfil the promises they had made, but the kings went back on their word. Then the people embarked upon that struggle against despotism which continues to this day, sometimes openly, sometimes clandestinely, in spite of all efforts to repress it. Under the despot Napoleon, secret societies had sought to revive the old nationalism, for people wished to break with the Revolution which Napoleon had dishonoured, whose leaders he had deceived and whose soldiers he had corrupted. After the battle of Waterloo, when they found that freedom was to be denied them, the secret societies in Italy and Germany braved the most cruel persecution in an attempt to rouse their people, because they saw no other way to win their freedom save through the national unity of their respective countries. So they adopted the names 'Young Italy' and 'Young Germany'. In those days memories of the Empire made them hostile towards France; but these memories of hatred and vengeance were effaced in July 1830, for in this new revolution people saw the old one rehabilitated, and from that time onwards, the secret societies abandoned their narrow parochialism and embraced the idea of a wider union with enthusiasm. They hoisted the standard of liberty which despotism had usurped and which had fallen from its hands on the field of Waterloo.

The attempts made in Italy to obtain political rights, the equally fruitless attempts made in Germany, the disastrous struggle in Poland, all proved that liberty can exist only through the union of all peoples, and that in this respect they must imitate the despots and found a truly *holy alliance*. This truth struck home in both north and south, and the secret societies adopted the unifying title of 'Young Europe'. Their aspirations will be fulfilled; I have as testimonies to my faith three great events born of the same principles and marching towards the same goal: the fall of the Bastille, Waterloo and the three glorious days of July 1830.

The mad enterprise of Charles X demonstrated to the whole of Europe that the triumph of thought over brute force was a reality in France. The Three Days excited even more enthusiasm than the fall of the Bastille, and at no other stage of the revolution had the kings been more afraid, as now they dared not accept the challenge!

The English aristocracy represented the battle of Waterloo to the people as a national victory; but in 1830 the popular demonstrations which the July Revolution provoked in England made the noble lords suspect that the proletarians who were waving the tricolour as a rallying signal might not attach the same meaning to the Famous Victory as they did! Again, the reverberations of the Three Glorious Days on the continent – Poland and Belgium in arms to throw off the foreign yoke, every nation clamouring for liberties promised them by their rulers and threatening to rise in revolt if those promises sealed in the blood of Waterloo were not immediately fulfilled – all this frenzied agitation awoke the less blinkered among the aristocracy from their dreams of grandeur. Then the more intelligent among them deplored the loss of the strong iron hand which had kept the people in check, and in their ears there echoed the cry from St Helena: 'Kings will mourn me!'

It was then that there suddenly arose in England a resounding cry for *electoral reform*. The Duke of Wellington, prince of Waterloo and champion of the aristocracy, wanted to brave the storm, but in vain. The majority, to his great amazement, declared themselves against him; the nation voted him out of office; the people booed him. The mob pelted his carriage with mud, then followed him home, besieged him in his mansion and smashed all his windows with stones.[10]

It is reported that when His Grace next made his appearance in the House, the following words escaped the lips of several lords: 'Untoward hero! Untoward hero!' and several aristocrats were heard to murmur in gloomy tones as they stood before the Waterloo Column: 'Untoward event! Untoward event!'

Napoleon, like his adversary at Waterloo, fulfilled his destiny without being aware of the fact. His downfall is striking proof that henceforth dominion can no longer rely on brute force. A handful of great men have been convinced of this ever since 1789, but in England popular uprisings have up to now been so easily put down that the aristocracy is still blindly convinced of its supremacy, and obstinately persists in its oppressive policies. It fails to see that the masses both in the three kingdoms and in Europe are no longer willing to resign themselves to suffering, that religion no longer has the power to make men resigned to their lot, and that because of the unrest all around them and the poverty they endure, one revolt will be followed by another until God's designs are accomplished.

NOTES

1(FT).   In the first edition I did not really develop my ideas about Waterloo, so I thought I ought to add fresh material to this chapter.

(What Flora has done is to take everything on Napoleon out of her original chapter on foreigners in London (Chapter IV) and amplify it. The result is not entirely satisfactory: the argument seems repetitive and sometimes paragraphs seem to be in the wrong order, due no doubt to hasty revision: but it is no part of the translator's business to re-arrange the text, especially when it contains material which many people – whatever their nationality – may well find contentious. Flora's judgement of the *Code Napoléon*, for instance, seems unduly harsh, when one considers how widely it has been adopted in the non-English-speaking world; it was the work of distinguished legislators, and Napoleon himself, though present at many of their meetings, had little hand in it: TN.)

2(TN).   Louis FONTANES (1757–1821) was a poet and politician whose career was promoted by Napoleon, but in spite of his admiration for the Emperor, he was no toady, and dared to criticise Napoleon for the judicial murder of d'Enghien in 1804. Nor did he make any secret of his support for the principles of monarchy. He was made a marquis in 1817.

3(TN).   The Comte de LAS CASES and General BERTRAND
accompanied Napoleon into exile on the island of St Helena, and
Dr O'MEARA, the ship's doctor on board the *Northumberland*,
volunteered to join the party as there was no doctor on the island.
After a few years, he was replaced by Dr ANTOMARCHI.
O'Meara's memoirs are slight compared with the massive four-
volume *Mémorial de Ste Hélène* which Las Cases published in
1823. This work amounts to a re-writing of Napoleon's career and
contributed enormously to his legend. Las Cases was sent away
when Hudson LOWE became governor of St Helena, but General
Bertrand stayed until Napoleon's death in 1821.

4(TN).   The Holy Alliance was the inspiration of Tsar Alexander
the First; it was formed in 1815 and its members were Russia,
Austria and Prussia. The three rulers undertook to behave and
govern according to Christian principles: in practice the Alliance
consolidated the absolute rule of the monarchy and suppressed
any movement by subject peoples towards greater freedom.

5(FT).   As proof of my argument, I quote here words which must
carry some weight. This is how M le comte Molé expressed himself
in his reply to M de Toqueville's speech welcoming him to
membership of the Académie française in April 1842: 'Do you
know what Napoleon said to me in conversation at a very solemn
moment I shall always remember? "*Après moi la révolution* –
or, rather, after me the ideas that made the Revolution will
resume their course. It will be like taking up a book, opening it at
the place marked, and continuing to read where one had left
off." '

Now, here is the comment of *La Phalange*, 27 April 1842: 'We
are struck by the inconsistency such a remark reveals on
Napoleon's part, considering his actions – those actions which
M Molé, no doubt fascinated by the magical charm of genius,
makes his imperial hero's claim to glory. What! so Napoleon was
resigned to reaping no reward for his colossal labours – pursued
at the cost of so much blood and sweat – beyond having post-
poned, for a few hours, the next instalment of the Revolution!
And that, on his own admission, was the sole insane goal that he
claimed as the prize for so much toil and sacrifice!

'But if this was really Napoleon's conviction, if he truly

believed that the march of the Revolution was decreed by Fate and could be delayed by only an instant at the very most, was it not conscious madness to block its path? If a man tried to dam a river, would his knowledge that it would soon break through the flimsy obstacle in its way and resume its course make him any less absurd? No, in such a man the attempt would be twice as foolish.

'In spite of the admiration for the Emperor which pervades M Molé's speech, he himself provides an unanswerable case against the great man in the following words: "Napoleon found France so close to ruin on 18ᵉ brumaire (9 November 1799) that despotism was the only remedy. It was characteristic of him to appropriate the country, so to speak, and risk, for the sake of what he called his glory, that very society which he had so ably and laboriously rebuilt." '

Finally, let us hear what Napoleon himself had to say about the conspiracy of General Mallet: "When I arrived in Paris, everybody I met told me quite openly the part he had played in events which implicated them all! They all naïvely confessed that they had walked into a trap: that for one moment they thought they had lost me. . . . Not one mentioned having made the slightest resistance, the smallest effort to defend and preserve the *status quo*. Nobody seemed even to have thought of it, being so accustomed to change and revolution: in other words, everybody seemed resigned to yet another upheaval. So they all changed countenance and some of them looked extremely sheepish when I said to them in a severe tone, "Well, gentlemen, so you think you have finished your revolution? You say you believed I was dead. I have nothing to say to that. . . . But what of the King of Rome! . . . The oaths you swore, your principles, your doctrines! . . . You make me tremble for the future!" '

Las Cases, Mémorial de Sainte-Hélène

(Count MOLÉ (1781–1855) was Minister of Justice under Napoleon, later Prime Minister and Foreign Minister under Louis Philippe; General MALLET mounted an unsuccessful conspiracy against Napoleon in 1812, during the Emperor's absence on the Russian campaign; The King of Rome was the title Napoleon bestowed on his long-awaited son born in 1811, the heir, as he fondly imagined, to a vast new Empire. After Napoleon's defeat and exile, his wife Marie-Louise returned to her native Austria with the little boy, who was later given the somewhat less exalted title of Duke of Reichstadt. He was not very robust, and dashed the hopes of the Bonapartists by dying in 1832 at the age of twenty-one. Edmond Rostand wrote a play about him, *L'Aiglon*, in which Sarah Bernhardt created the title role: TN.)

6(TN).   After a chequered career in the service of both Louis XVIII and Napoleon, BOURMONT (1773 – 1846) came back to Napoleon in 1815 when the Emperor returned to France after his short exile on the island of Elba, but deserted him on the first day of the Waterloo campaign. GROUCHY (1766 – 1847) also rejoined Napoleon in 1815, and at Waterloo he was appointed to command the right wing and prevent the Prussians from establishing contact with Wellington, but he failed in this objective and decided to withdraw his forces from the field. He was court-martialled and exiled. In his memoirs Napoleon blamed Grouchy for his defeat.

7(TN).   Frederick (FREDERICK WILLIAM III of Prussia): his 'impetuous soldier' is BLÜCHER (1742 – 1819) who commanded the Prussian troops at Waterloo. He was a fearless patriot whose greatest ambition was to rid his country of French domination.

8(FT).   It is well known that the Duke of Wellington described the victory of Navarino in Parliament as 'an untoward event'. The noble lord is a master of misapprehension; what took place on the occasion of the Reform Bill and the Catholic Emancipation Bill alone would be sufficient to prove it, even if his whole career did not provide a thousand more examples.

(The Battle of Navarino (1827) was an unauthorised naval engagement in which a combined French and English fleet destroyed the Turkish and Egyptian fleets, although there had been no declaration of war. The Allies were supposed to be imposing a blockade on the Turks as a means of putting pressure on them to grant the Greeks their independence, but when they were fired upon, they over-reacted. Public opinion in England was quite rightly sympathetic to the Greek cause, so there was rejoicing at the outcome of the engagement and a disinclination to censure the Allied commander for his action, but Wellington who was Prime Minister, and more concerned with the threat posed by Russia than the plight of the Greeks, was alarmed to see

Turkey so drastically weakened, hence his celebrated comment on the battle of Navarino, which enraged Members on both sides of the House and may well have given rise to the derogatory remarks about the Duke that Flora recounts later in this chapter, though I have been unable to trace their source.

As to the two Bills she mentions; Wellington's political strategy was to retreat in good order when he found his position untenable. He was opposed to Catholic Emancipation at first, but saw that it was inevitable. He gravely misjudged the mood of the country over parliamentary reform, and was voted out of office in 1830 when he refused even to consider it: TN.)

9(TN).   Casimir PÉRIER (1777 – 1832) was elected a deputy in 1817 and defended the freedom of the press in his maiden speech. Later he moved steadily to the Right and in 1831, as Prime Minister, he put down the revolt of the silk weavers in Lyons which Flora mentions in her Dedication at the beginning of the book. Benjamin CONSTANT (1767 – 1830) was a prolific writer and a politician who consistently upheld the freedom of the press. He founded liberal journals, wrote his autobiography in the form of a psychological novel (*Adolphe*, 1815) and for ten years maintained a close but uneasy relationship with the great lady of letters Madame de Staël. Maximilien Sebastien FOY (1775 – 1825) was a general and statesman whose republican principles were outraged by the rise of Napoleon; nevertheless he remained in the Emperor's service and fought at Waterloo. In 1819 he was elected a deputy and consistently upheld the original liberal principles of 1789.

10(FT).   The noble Duke did not judge it prudent to have the glass in his windows replaced. Ever since that day they have been fastened with iron shutters. What a lesson for him!

(Twice in the course of 1831 Wellington had his windows at Apsley House broken by angry crowds, but he had them repaired for the occasion of the King's attendance at the annual Waterloo banquet in 1833; the shutters remained in place until the Duke's death in 1852: TN.)

Bethlem Hospital

What a rich field of meditation for the philosopher who, escaping from the tumult of the world outside, comes to spend some time in a madhouse! He finds there all the same ideas, the same errors, the same passions, the same misfortunes; it is the same world. . . .

Every madhouse has its gods, its priests, its believers, its fanatics; it has its emperors, kings, ministers, courtiers, generals, soldiers and wealthy citizens, and its obedient subjects. One man may believe he is inspired by God and in communication with the heavenly spirit; it is his mission to convert mankind. . . .

The discourse of the madman is full of lies, exaggeration and confusion, like the ideas and emotions he struggles to express.

E. Esquirol, *On Mental Diseases* (1838)[1]

The organic derangement which leads to madness comes about through physical or moral causes. Intense degrees of heat or cold are sufficient, we are told, to disturb certain parts of the cerebral system. Excessive drinking, abuse of mercury,[2] accidents and disease can also result in madness; but it is generally brought on by moral causes. As long as man places all his trust in the power of his reason or in the affections of a few of his fellows and refuses to acknowledge that all things are subject to one universal law, he will continue to be afflicted by disillusion strong enough to destroy the proud intelligence which seeks to usurp the power of Providence and the heart which elects to live apart from God.

It would be interesting to know how many lunatics each country contains in proportion to its population; no doubt statistics would prove that the more a nation's religion and philosophy incline it to resignation, the fewer madmen one would encounter among its people; while the nations which submit their religious beliefs and daily conduct to the dictates of their reason are those where the greatest number of madmen would be found. 'God is great!' the Moslem cries in response to whatever fate decrees; and among those peoples who do not bow to the authority of human reason, madmen are rarely to be found.

It is generally agreed that England harbours the greatest number of lunatics; it is also the country where the greatest excesses of all kinds are perpetrated, where the belief in free will is the strongest and where there is the most analysis and discussion of religious ideas. There are innumerable private establishments in London where lunatics are confined and tended for the cost of their board, and in general they are very well run. I shall describe only the best known public hospital, which is called Bethlem.

I went there in the company of Mr Holm, one of the most celebrated phrenologists in England, and Mrs Wheeler, a socialist who is also a friend of Fourier.[3] These two people are deeply interested in the phenomena associated with insanity, and Mrs Wheeler gave me detailed information on every inmate whose case was in any way remarkable.

Henry VIII was the first monarch to found a hospital for the insane in London. This was in the Priory of St Mary of Bethlehem in Moorfield, and in 1675 a large hospital with a façade copied from the Tuileries was built on the same site. This was demolished in 1812 and replaced by the present hospital, built in 1814 in the very healthy district of Georgefield. The beautiful central façade of this building has a portico adorned with six Doric columns. With its courtyards and gardens it occupies about eighteen acres.[4]

The entrance to the hospital is most pleasing: its fine gates, extensive lawns and flowerbeds combine to give the poor lunatic the impression that he is entering an opulent country mansion and, suspecting nothing, he allows himself to be locked away in the sad abode of madness.

In the vestibule there are two statues by Caius Cibber, representing *Melancholy* and *Raving Madness*; these formerly graced the hall of the old building, but they are so powerfully expressive that it has been found necessary to remove them from the public gaze. The sight of them produced a very painful effect on friends and relatives visiting the hospital, and on several occasions hitherto docile patients were roused to fits of frenzy with disastrous consequences, so in order to avoid such accidents, the statues were draped with a cloth and are now shown only to visitors who are considered strong enough to bear the sight.

The hospital is very large and can accommodate seven hundred patients, but there were at that time only 422 of whom 177 were women; it is extremely clean and the food is excellent, even over-abundant in the opinion of some doctors. But the administration seems unconcerned with the state of the inmates' clothes; they continue to wear whatever they had on when they entered the hospital, and often they go about in rags which nobody troubles to mend.

The places where they take exercise are just like prison yards with no grass or trees to delight the eye or conjure up the sweet repose of the fields; most of them offer no protection against sun or rain. The poor wretch with bitter heart and head seething with gloomy thoughts sees nothing here that does not remind him of his captive state, which in his eyes is a monstrous injustice. Such a system is either lacking in forethought or deliberately cruel.

Among the women there were twenty or thirty criminals lodged in a separate part of the building. I must confess I could not see the *slightest difference* between these women and the criminals I had seen at Newgate, Coldbath Fields and Millbank. All had the same wild eyes, haggard look, sullen silence, intense manner and type of features that mark the person of low intelligence. Several had committed murders, others were guilty of theft.

Next we went to the men's wing and what befell me there

was one of those bizarre and extraordinary encounters which I think happen only to me. One of the gentlemen with us spoke excellent French, and before we entered the first yard, he said to me, 'We have one of your compatriots here; his condition is a rare one; he thinks he is God.'

Not as rare as all that, I thought; after all, where is the hospital large enough to contain all those who think they too are infallible!

'For the whole of the five months he has been here,' continued my guide, 'he has passed abruptly from a state of exaltation approaching frenzy to a state of lucidity when he reasons very well. He is a former sailor who has travelled widely, speaks many languages and seems to have been a man of some consequence.'

'What is his name?' I asked.

'Chabrié.'

Chabrié! The name had an indescribable effect on me and I could not analyse what passed through my mind; was it joy, grief, surprise, anxiety? Whatever it was, I did not hesitate to approach the place where I was to see him again; I awaited the moment with impatience: it seemed to me that God had inspired me to come to London and rescue this unhappy man![5]

I went into the long passage leading to the main yard looking eagerly at everybody as they hurried past to see if the man who had loved me with such purity and devotion was among them. My agitation betrayed the turmoil in my heart: then the attendant said as he pointed out a man sitting all alone on a bench, 'Look, there is Chabrié!' It was not the captain of the *Mexicain*. Then it occurred to me that the French name might have been mispronounced, so I asked the man to write it down for me, and I saw that the only difference was that the name I had just heard had an 'r' at the end.

However I looked with keen solicitude at this second Chabrier; his features, appearance and bearing formed a striking contrast with everybody around him. This man fixed his big shining black eyes upon me, his fine southern countenance became animated, and a smile of joy and happiness passed over it like sunshine in a gloomy valley. He came up to me, greeted me with the effortless courtesy which betokens the man of good breeding and said to me in French, 'Oh mademoiselle, how happy I am to meet a compatriot at last, and a woman at that! We speak the same language and to you I can convey all that I suffer in this abode of misery where the most hateful injustice keeps me confined.'

He followed me into the yard where all the madmen were gathered; but I saw nobody but him. For the space of more than half an hour he spoke to me in a sober and reasonable manner. His observations were so just and his reflections so profound that I did not think it possible that he could be insane. I was obliged to leave him in order to visit the rest of the hospital, but promised to see him again before I left.

As I had already observed in the women's wing, I saw on the faces of the criminally insane the same expressions that the criminals of Newgate wore, apart from three or four exceptions which deserve a special mention.

I saw James Hadfield, the man who had attempted to kill George IV by throwing a stone at his head; he has been in Bethlem for 22 years.[6] I do not know if he has ever been what one understands by the word *mad*; his speech and actions certainly show no sign of it. He lives in a little room and is only too happy to talk to visitors. We spent quite a long time with him; his conversation and behaviour reveal a loving heart, an expansive nature and an overwhelming need of affection; he has had in succession two dogs, three cats, several birds and a squirrel. He loved these animals tenderly and grieved to see them die; he has stuffed them himself and arranged them about his room. These remains of the creatures he loved each have an epitaph in verse as a token of his grief. His squirrel's memorial is surmounted by a coloured likeness of the friend he lost. I must add that out of his affections he has built a modest trade which brings him in a nice little income, as he distributes copies of his epitaphs to visitors in return for a few shillings!

After this good-natured, gregarious and amiable old man we saw the two lovers of the Queen: one is a slight young man of twenty-two who laughs and runs away if anyone asks him if he still loves his betrothed, the other is a man of thirty with the head and neck of a bull – as he is violent we only caught a glimpse of him through the bars of his cell.

While I was paying these visits, poor Chabrier had been growing more and more agitated. He was waiting for me at the gate; his restless movements betrayed the greatest impatience; his eyes flashed, his voice shook and he was trembling all over.

'Oh! my sister,' he exclaimed in a tone of brotherly affection that was truly angelic, 'my sister, it is God who has sent you to this place of desolation, not for my sake, for I must perish here, but for the sake of the message I bring to the world. Listen! Know you, my sister, that *I am sent from your God, I am the Messiah announced by Jesus Christ*. I come to accomplish his work; I come to make an end of every kind of servitude, to deliver woman from man, the poor from the rich, and the soul from sin.'

As I saw it, these were not the words of a madman: Jesus, Saint-Simon and Fourier had all spoken thus. 'Look!' he continued, 'I bear on my breast the sign of my mission,' and unbuttoning his coat he drew from his breast a large cross which he had fashioned from the straw of his mattress and wool unravelled from his coverlet. I was still wondering whether he could really be mad, when he suddenly darted a terrible look at Mrs Wheeler and said with the voice and gestures of one possessed: 'That woman is English; she represents *matter, corruption, sin*; get you hence, evil woman, it is you who killed me! Arrest this woman! Sister, it is she who killed your God! I arrest you!' he cried, rushing upon her. 'I arrest you in the name of the new law!'

Mrs Wheeler fled in the utmost panic; I was far from reassured myself.

'My sister,' he said, 'I am going to give you the token of redemption, because I judge you worthy to receive it.' Next to his heart he had a dozen or so little straw crosses wrapped in black crape and tied with red thread; with the words 'Mourning and Blood' written on them. He took one and gave it to me, saying, 'Take this cross, wear it on your breast and go through the world proclaiming the new law.' He went down on one knee and took my hand in a grip strong enough to crush it, saying meanwhile, 'My sister, dry your tears, for soon the *kingdom of God* will succeed the *kingdom of the devil*!'

The warders were very much alarmed; they wanted to make him release my hand by force, but I was unwilling to have him upset. I felt sure he would do me no harm. I begged him to let go my hand and he obeyed me without a murmur; then he prostrated himself upon the ground, kissed the hem of my gown and said in a voice broken by tears and sobs, 'Oh! Woman is the image of the Virgin sent down to earth! And men spurn her, humiliate her and drag her through the mud!'

I tore myself away from him; I was weeping too. Poor man! How he must suffer when he is restored to reason. When I had to pass that way again, I went up close to the gate to see what he was doing. He was still kneeling on the same spot with his hands clasped and his eyes fixed on his large cross lying before him on the paving. In this attitude he looked so beautiful that I thought of him as a new St John.

Can this man be mad? Everything he said to me revealed a man whose head is full of social, religious and political theories and whose heart is overflowing with love for his fellow men. His soul is in revolt against every sign of baseness, corruption and hypocrisy and he cannot restrain his holy indignation. I saw in him all the signs of exaltation but none of madness. At times he spoke like a man inspired. He was full of hatred against his persecutors, it is true, but his discourse was logical and I found no difficulty in

213

following his train of thought.

What an extraordinary thing that among four hundred madmen confined at Bethlem there should be one Frenchman admitted as a special favour, and that this same Frenchman should believe himself to be the *Messiah*, claim to be *the messenger of God*, and speak *in the name of the new law*!

Everything I have just related is confirmed by reliable witnesses. M Chabrier was untimely in his zeal and too positive in his opinions, but the principle on which they are founded is incontestable. The authority of the Bible was challenged by Christ himself, and from that time onward it was discredited as social and moral law; if this were not so, how would it be possible to account for the success of Christianity, and six centuries later, of Islam?

M Chabrier comes from Marseilles. The governor of Bethlem told me he had written to the mayor of the city and also to Mme Chabrier. It is inexplicable that so far nobody has claimed him. So the unfortunate man is alone in London and abandoned to the mercy of foreigners. Could his family have any special reasons which might justify such cruel behaviour?

NOTES

1(TN). Étienne ESQUIROL (1772–1840) became Director of the asylum at Charenton in 1835 and published his major work, *Des maladies mentales*, a comparative, historical and sociological study of insanity, in 1838.

2(TN). At that time mercury was a major standby of physicians, particularly in the treatment of syphilis.

3(TN). John Diederick HOLM (1772–1840) was, like Dr Elliotson whom Flora encountered at Newgate in search of 'interesting protuberances', a phrenologist and a disciple of Gall and Spurzheim: (see Chapter IX). Anna WHEELER (177? – 185?) was a cosmopolitan pioneer of socialism and feminism who escaped from an unhappy marriage to act as a link between radicals in France and England. It was probably through her that Flora met Robert Owen in Paris in 1837. She made no secret of her atheism (this explains why poor Chabrier was so upset by her presence) and spread the gospel of socialism wherever she went. Her daughter Rosina disapproved of her and attributed her deplorable opinions to the evil influence of Mary Wollstonecraft: (see notes to Chapter XVII).

4(TN).   This building is now the home of the Imperial War Museum.

5(FT).   This passage can be understood only by those who have read my *Peregrinations of a Pariah*. After I wrote that book, M Chabrié embarked once more for Peru on board his vessel *L'Amérique* and was lost at sea; at least, in the absence of any news of him, this was presumably what happened, but it was never confirmed, which explains my fleeting hope, on discovering in Bethlem Hospital a French seafarer bearing the same name, that this was indeed the unhappy Chabrié, captain of the *Mexicain*.

6(TN).   James HADFIELD was a cavalryman who suffered brain damage as the result of a war wound. He became obsessed with the idea that he was the instrument chosen to bring about the reign of the Messiah by killing the king, George III; after his unsuccessful attempt he was condemned to death, but his life was spared and he was committed to Bethlem Hospital, where he lived for forty-nine years. As for the queen's 'lovers' – nobody seems to know who they were.

7(FT).   At Bethlem I learned that before his arrival, M Chabrier was constantly engaged in writing on the loftiest matters; but it was above all on religious doctrines that he expressed his most significant philosophical and social observations. It was a scandalous incident that led to his arrest as a madman.

He was lodging in a small house in the City. One Sunday while everybody else was deep in the study of the Holy Bible, M Chabrier was pacing up and down the parlour; suddenly he stopped in front of the lady of the house and interrupted her pious reading to ask what she did with old brooms when they were too worn to be of any further use. The Englishwoman, surprised at such a question, replied that she used them to light the fire.

'And why don't you keep them?'

'Why, because they would clutter up the house to no purpose.'

'Well, then, woman, do the same with *old laws* as you do with *old brooms*: put them on the fire, and don't let your mind be cluttered up with ideas that were good enough in their time, but are worn out today.'

So saying, he snatched the Bible from her hands and threw it on the fire.

This incident caused a great scandal; there was very nearly a riot in the neighbourhood. The zealots wanted to lay hands on the blasphemer, but the mad prophet quelled them with the power of his look and the strength of his arm; nobody dared touch him.

Infant Schools

Very few mothers are sufficiently enlightened to raise their children in accordance with the best principles of education.

Even fewer have the freedom to devote themselves to the study and application of these principles.

The most affluent and populous cities are the very ones which present the greatest number of obstacles and disadvantages in this respect.

Nowhere in the infant school[1] should the pedagogue and scholar be found; everywhere, on the contrary, there should be a sound and philosophical system of instruction inspired by the devotion and heroism characteristic of maternal love.

As for small children, their physical development alone deserves prolonged and intelligent study. At this age it is essential not only to maintain healthy organs but to *create* them: an abundance of fresh air and almost constant activity are necessary for the cultivation of a constitution which would otherwise perish through inactivity or constraint.

The intelligence should develop gradually through play and not through sustained effort, until pupils reach the age when they are capable of concentration.

Jean-Denis-Marie Cochin,
Manual for Infant Schools (1833)[2]

If the working classes had the means to arouse the interest and respect of our legislators, would not the legislature and that Church which costs so much to maintain occupy themselves with improving the religious, moral and political education of the people, which so far only a few isolated individuals have attempted to do?

A British Review

Great discoveries are always in accordance with the needs of the times: this is a universal historical truth. The hand of God is behind the establishment of Infant Schools and I am convinced that of all recent institutions these are the most promising and best answer the needs of Europe and the whole world. Education may be said to begin with life itself, and the system of instruction followed in the infant school is so superior to any that the child, whatever his class, can obtain at home, and has so great an influence on all who receive it, that a worker's child sent to such a school from the age of two will undoubtedly make better progress than a child from the wealthier classes who continues to be educated at home.

Infant schools inculcate the principle of mutual aid and respect for communal property in the heart of the child. In his eyes all social distinctions are obliterated and he defers only to the monitors who instruct him. He is required to account for what he knows and to teach what he has learned, and this gives him a great facility for expressing his thoughts; he learns to understand the relation between cause and effect, between men and what they know; and in this way he acquires a thoroughly sound judgment. If when he proceeds to primary school his education continues along the same lines, by the time he is sixteen he will be proficient at reading, writing, arithmetic, drawing and geometry, as well as the practice of most of the processes used in the mechanical arts and in agriculture, so that he need not be condemned, as his father was, to continue in the same work for the rest of his life in order to earn a living. The same method may be applied with equal success to every branch of knowledge, for we learn nothing so well as when we are required to teach it to others. If they were brought up in this way, men would work in large associations because they would find it easier and more pleasurable to work together.

If children were sent to public institutions from the age of two, the needs of the household would be less pressing, the education the wife had received would enable her to earn her living as well as the husband, and this would bring us a little nearer to organising society on Phalansterian principles.[3] In 1440 when the first attempts at printing were being made at Strasbourg, any prediction of the power this new invention was to exercise four hundred years later would have been greeted with nothing but incredulity.

When we observe the fate of children in every class of society we can only marvel that infant schools were not invented long ago, and that they are not being set up faster and in greater numbers to meet the needs of the population. People are forced to work hard every day to feed their families, so they cannot look after their children; when they are young, they are locked up inside the house, or somebody has to be paid to look after them, and when they are older they are allowed to run about the streets. Shut up alone in damp, poky rooms with no fresh air or warmth, even if they survive sickness and accidents these children are weak, undersized and sometimes crippled for the rest of their lives. In the streets the dangers threatening their existence are even greater, and they are almost certain to be perverted in the jungle of vice common to all big cities, so they drift into crime before they have been trained to work.

Then again, if we consider the innumerable hazards which threaten the livelihood of the worker: the reduction of wages, the lack of employment, the excessive increase in the cost of living, to say nothing of the possibility of illness and additions to the family, we can only feel that it must take a rare love of work and an uncommon degree of sobriety and thrift, as well as a great deal of luck and considerable strength of character, if a man is never to fall victim to destitution. However, what becomes of the children in the frightful tribulations that beset the working class?

In the evenings the father and mother, weary and bitter, return from their daily toil, their minds tormented with worry. Ah! The scenes of family life that now unfold are of a kind to brutalise even the child with the happiest disposition: often beaten because he has fallen down and torn his clothes or let the dog steal his dinner, the unfortunate child, constantly reviled and abused, becomes lying and deceitful and nurses a sullen hatred for his father and mother. On their side, dire poverty and addiction to various means of deadening their minds to the sufferings they endure extinguish any feelings of affection in their hearts, so that they come to hate the children who add to their privations, and finally abandon the older ones to vagrancy and leave the new-born baby at the foundling hospital.

Only set up infant schools, and as if by magic you transform the child and his home. First of all, the burden of poverty and worry is lightened; the child leaves the family home in the morning to be welcomed into a place where he will be under the guidance of a friendly person genuinely interested in his welfare; he spends his day with companions of his own age in an uninterrupted round of pleasurable activities: first his attention is captured by a variety of interesting things to look at, then he joins in singing and marching in procession, receives instruction from the more advanced pupils, and passes it on to the others less advanced than himself, thus enjoying all the importance of being a member of the school. Every day he learns how to live in a community, exercises his faculties in preparation for a higher role, learns to know himself and to appreciate others, learns to respect others in order to be respected himself. He enjoys good health, for his strength and skill are improved by gymnastics; he becomes clean and modest and can give a reason for everything he does.

When he returns home at the end of the day, his parents are delighted to see him: he has given them no cause for worry, nor has he taken up a moment of their time. They approve of his behaviour, ply him with questions all through supper, and every day they marvel at the progress he has made in judgment and understanding; then, observing his conduct, they are led to examine their own, and not wishing to be despised by their own child or to see him held in greater esteem than themselves, they too seek diligently to change their ways. They come to appreciate the benefits of education and often go to school to share the children's lessons, so the charming spectacle of moral development in the infant school will improve the morals of the parents.

If we now turn our attention to the affluent professional class of society, which is probably more able and better educated than the opulent leisured classes, we shall see that the children of this class have no less need of infant schools than the children of the proletariat.

Most of our moralists have declared themselves in favour of public education because it has been proved that teaching is more effective in action than in precept, that practical lessons which pupils give one another have more influence on their moral and intellectual development than instruction by even the most skilful teachers. If we consider the irresistible and unfailing enthusiasm which mutual instruction generates whenever children are gathered together, and the intense competition which is stimulated by their awareness of their daily progress, and if on the other hand we consider how profound first impressions are and how many corrupting influences surround children in the paternal home, we cannot understand why the middle classes regard infant schools with such marked repugnance that they will not accept this system of instruction for their children, but prefer to cut them off from the social advantages which come from a common education.[4]

Of all the educational systems in vogue in modern times, the only truth to be almost universally accepted is the advantage of public education over private. There is such a wealth of precise observation in Xenophon, Plutarch and Montaigne that it seems inconceivable that it has taken us so long to arrive at the only complete, effective and true method, which takes Nature as its guide and leads man from the cradle to the age of puberty. Rousseau owes his influence solely to the ideas he borrowed from these three thinkers; unfortunately he did not know how to make use of them, for he did nothing to advance the most important of the social sciences. His bizarre system combines the most erroneous prejudices of society with the revelations of Nature; fashion kept it alive for a time, but now it is well and truly dead, and if I were to exhume a few of its pages, it would only be to point out yet again the absurd lengths to which his imagination took him. Since Rousseau, the public has been bombarded with numerous educational systems and new teaching methods, all of which have been summarily accepted or rejected depending on who put the forward. At the present time, small seminaries and convents are in conflict with government institutions, and people concerned with social progress seem to have no firm convictions on this very important question – everybody has his own little system. Ideas on education are still in a state of anarchy, and public opinion, as is its custom, follows wherever it is led.

We live at a time when political theory is a universal preoccupation: philosophy, education, religion, even fashion, are all coloured by it. In any family there are as many points of view as there are individual members, so what becomes of the children in this welter of conflicting ideas, desires, caprices and passions? Today there is so little harmony in the home that married couples seem obsessed by the need to differ on every point. Whatever the father says is invariably contradicted by the mother, then along come the grandparents to fill the child's ears with their outmoded ideas, then come the friends who see everything in terms of social position and press their views as if they alone were right. Finally there are the nurses, maids and servants whose ideas and actions have such a strong influence on children. How are these young minds to extricate themselves from the chaos all around them? Is it not obvious that amidst so many conflicting opinions, their judgment, deprived of solid foundations or guiding principles, is bound to be inconsistent, that they themselves must inevitably grow up contrary and wilful, that their natures must become embittered by frequent submission to the tyranny of others, that, in a word, they cannot have sound ideas about anything, since they do not know what truth is? As everybody around them express different opinions about the same things, they see nothing but the clash of wills, and absorb self-interest through every pore.

It cannot be hoped that a child raised in this fashion can ever be a good citizen; he will be the slave of his passions, of prejudice, of all things and all men. Either he will never rise above mediocrity or he will sink to the depths of villainy because of his uncontrollable vices; for things to turn out otherwise he would have to possess quite extraordinary qualities to surmount all the obstacles to the rational development of his intelligence.

If we now turn our attention to that part of the population which fortune permits to live in luxury, we perceive that there is no child who suffers more and whose mind and body deteriorate faster because of his family life than the child of wealthy parents. Providence may save the child of poor parents from the perils of vagrancy, and sometimes we see men rise from the depths of poverty to be an honour to the human race; middle-class children are nearly always in the company of their parents and receive constant signs of their affection, so that the qualities of the heart may develop in them in spite of the defects of their mind or the vices of their character; but it is quite otherwise in wealthy families. Their children are certain to be corrupted and they have no chance to acquire any good qualities. They are brought up by nurses, tutors and servants: all these slaves strive to humour the little ones whose tears frequently have the power to bring about their instant dismissal; they anticipate all their desires, they yield to them in everything, they even rack their brains to create artificial needs for their charges, and the unfortunate little creatures, cradled in idleness, spoiled by adulation and puffed up with pride, develop the vices of tyrants and the habits of despots. They are imperious, bad-tempered and unable to resist the slightest whim. Their parents rarely see them, and scold them, punish them unreasonably or reward them undeservedly, according to

223

their mood. The servants, fearing the children will tell tales, teach them to lie, and when the little despots are displeased they invent lies of their own and accuse the servants who have offended them of the very misdeeds they fear to be accused of themselves. The very air the rich child breathes is corrupt! Hypocrisy is constantly before his eyes: now it is the mask the servants wear in the presence of his parents, now it is the two different faces his parents assume inside or outside the home. He hears two different languages as well: one of servility, the other of arrogance. To hold his attention his nurse fills his head with fantastic tales. At home the whole world is at his feet: if he is angry or tearful they all bestir themselves immediately in their anxiety to soothe him; outside, everybody greets him with deference, fawns upon him and seems flattered to receive him, so how can he fail to believe himself a person of consequence and to affect the hard, proud manners of his parents? Tender affections are unable to grow in his heart, only vanity has a place there; pride makes him touchy and every day he grows more demanding until finally the imprint of Nature is quite effaced and there is no child left, only a puppet in rich clothes. He is the son of a lord, a man who lives in a palace with an army of servants, never goes out save in a coach, and is greeted very humbly by all the tradesmen in the neighbourhood.

Excess of food and excessive precautions against cold, heat, rain, fresh air and any kind of fatigue, form a régime which makes no demands on the child's constitution, so that when he is old enough to go to college, he has no physical or moral resources. Transported into this new world, he finds it hard to adapt himself to its rules and the spirit of equality among his companions; he complains to his parents who redouble their admonitions to his teachers, and their efforts are not without fruit, for henceforth their child is treated with every indulgence, always excused and never constrained; some poor, intelligent classmate writes his essays and is paid in cakes. Every Sunday he takes home to his parents a good report; sometimes he is at the top of his class and at the end of the year he is sure to gain a prize. After seven or eight years he leaves school as stupid as when he entered it, having acquired nothing but fresh vices.

I have no hesitation in affirming that the rich child needs to be rescued from the characters and the influences around him just as much as the poor child does from the brutality of his parents and the influence of the streets.

In the infant school the education is the same for all. The most intractable and fretful child absorbs the information imparted to him; lack of intelligence is no drawback as everybody starts at the same level and lessons are always based on the progress made by each member of the class. The child receives none but sound ideas and learns to live in a community, to perform happily his share of the common tasks, and to acknowledge as the true aristocracy only the intelligent and gifted; he willingly accepts the poorer child as his leader if the latter happens to be a monitor and stands above him in the intellectual hierarchy.

In the age of tyranny[5] the high valleys of the Vosges sheltered in their inaccessible retreats intrepid Protestants who had chosen to abandon their fields to be plundered rather than give up their freedom of conscience. Their new home could sustain only goats and deer, so they and their descendants led a harsh existence. In 1767, Oberlin, a pastor of the Protestant church, arrived in their midst: he was a man possessed of that powerful energy which betokens a heart full of love for his fellow men. Through his labours he overcame the barrenness of the soil, set up schools and established apprenticeships in various trades, so that prosperity took the place of poverty. As the parents were busy in their fields or at their trades, and were unable to care for their little children, Oberlin had the inspired thought of gathering them all together under one roof and selecting suitable young women to be trained by himself and his wife as teachers; this was the origin of the infant school. Later Oberlin's methods were imitated and perfected in Switzerland.

Robert Owen, convinced that in order to be effective education must start in the cradle and aim to fit children for the society to which they are destined to belong, founded his own infant school in New Lanark, Scotland, in 1816, but it was not until 1827 and 1828, when the system had already taken root in Germany, that France and England thought of adopting it.[6]

What could be more admirable than the accurate observation and sound judgment of the practical philosopher Owen when he founded the infant school? The principles he discovered for the education of children contain a truth plain for all to see. By his study of nature alone, Owen bequeathed to the world a system for the moral development of young children far superior to any previously known – because it contains nothing that cannot be verified by simple observation.

The energy and curiosity which a child displays at every stage of his development are the two forces which Owen controls with benevolence and forbearance, for the infant intelligence recoils from suffering and cruelty just as quickly as the body recoils from physical pain. Owen attributes a good share of the evils of this world to the system of rewards and punishments; he banishes both from his school to prevent the growth of envy, jealousy, vanity and false standards, and to avoid provoking lies and deceit. In his school the natural consequences of good and evil actions are their own reward: the child who behaves well is happy to see the joy his conduct gives to others, while the child who behaves badly finds no allies, and the abuse of force is put down by the intervention of all. Owen has learned from experience what unlimited power love and kindness exert over children: mutual acts of benevolence and generosity are the foundations of his educational system. The gentleness and goodwill of teacher and pupils blend in harmony with the natural energy and curiosity of childhood to form the simple and powerful instrument which Owen discovered as the means of shaping the social character of human beings. He controls their will through the constant exercise of kindly feelings, overcomes their antisocial tendencies through the influence of training in good habits, and wins their unlimited trust through the authority which truth exerts upon us all, for he himself says nothing that is not true, and in all his teachings his disciples recognise the light of truth.

The fundamental law of the Owenist school responds to the need of love, the desire for knowledge and that thirst for truth which reveals the soul. Owen discovered this law through a series of experiments and through careful study of the social behaviour of his workers and children. He found that the influence of custom, affection and truth produced such favourable results that it is hardly surprising that he vented his indignation against the absurdity of persisting in the use of antisocial educational methods which have for centuries been vainly piling 'precept upon precept and line upon line'. The results of conventional education demonstrate only too well the poverty of educational theory, and provide ample proof that the principles of truth and morality can have a lasting influence on us only when they are practised in life. When they are constantly applied to our actions, these principles cannot help but exercise our judgment, motivate our conduct and shape our habits.

This is how Owen puts it: 'Reading and writing are merely instruments by which knowledge, either true or false, may be imparted; and, when given to children, are of little comparative value, unless they are also taught how to make a proper use of them.

'When a child receives a full and fair explanation of the objects and characters around him, and when he is also taught to reason correctly, so that he may learn to distinguish general truths from falsehood, he will be much better instructed, although without the knowledge of one letter or figure, than those are who have been compelled to *believe*, and whose reasoning faculties have been confounded or destroyed by what is most erroneously termed learning.

'It is readily acknowledged that the manner of instructing

children is of importance and deserves all the attention it has lately received; that those who discover or introduce improvements which facilitate the acquirement of knowledge are important benefactors of their fellow-creatures. Yet the *manner* of giving instruction is one thing, the *instruction itself* another; and no two objects can be more distinct. The *worst* manner may be applied to give the *best* instruction, and the *best* manner to give the *worst* instruction. Were the real importance of both to be estimated by numbers, the manner of instruction may be compared to one, and the matter of instruction to millions: the first is the means only; the last, the end to be accomplished by those means.

'If, therefore, in a national system of education for the poor, it be desirable to adopt the best *manner*, it is surely so much the more desirable to adopt also the best *matter*, of instruction.'

Owen has observed the development of human intelligence; he does not speak to children of abstractions or the revelations of the soul, for the simple reason that such ideas are beyond their comprehension. The first things that man learns, as well as all the means of self-preservation, come from the exercise of instinct and the power of intuition on objects submitted to the perception of his senses. Education must therefore begin with learning about the material world; furthermore, the child should take a pencil in his hand before a pen. He should be able to draw objects before he learns the combinations of conventional signs which represent their names, for once he understands the intellectual fiction which connects a collection of different signs with the means of remembering sounds and speech, words and songs, as well as the concepts of size and number, his intelligence has taken a giant step and henceforth the world of ideas is wide open to him.

In the Owenist system children are admitted to school from the age of two; they stay until they are ten, and not until they reach the age of seven or eight do they learn to read. One general rule dominates the entire system: the child is taught nothing that does not follow directly from what he already knows. Owen has too much commonsense to want to tell his little pupils about God before God has revealed Himself to their hearts; he trains them to practise charity, shows them that true self-interest consists in *not* being selfish, and relies on their personal satisfactions and regrets to teach them the meaning of conscience.

In his infant school Owen follows where Nature leads; he adapts his material to the intelligence of his pupils and uses the methods of Lancaster.[7] Step-by-step explanation, exercises in judgment, physical training and an introduction to the methods used in various trades, simultaneously develop the intellectual faculties, a rational love of one's neighbour, manual skills and physical strength. Owen does not permit any formal religious instruction, preferring to base his moral code on the principle of reciprocity: 'Do unto others as you would have them do unto you.' In that sense he was right when he informed me that there was no infant school in London run according to the principles he had followed when he set up his own.

In England when the question arose of following the example of Germany and setting up infant schools, Owen was consulted by Lord Brougham and informed him that in his own school he permitted only such abstract ideas as the child could understand, that is, ideas capable of being explained through material objects; that he did not know of any religious beliefs appropriate to the infant intelligence; that children, like all other living beings, are affected by pleasure and pain and are just as capable as adults of understanding that self-interest obliges them to observe the rules that reciprocity dictates; and that in his view the dogmas of original sin, paradise, hell etc., were of a nature to create false notions of justice and injustice, to make the mind disputatious and to foster hatred against anyone of any other religious persuasion. Lord Brougham objected to Owen's system on the grounds that religious beliefs still exert a considerable influence. The institutions known by the name of National Schools and British and Foreign Schools (which the learned lord has favoured with his patronage) admit children of all persuasions and do not seek to convert them to any particular creed; yet all the same, fanatics have prevailed upon them to prescribe the study of the Bible – and this is for children between the ages of eighteen months and seven years! The converts in Tahiti and New Zealand could not do better than that!

In Switzerland and several of the German kingdoms schools and infant schools had already been flourishing for some years before public opinion in England showed any signs of interest, for in intellectual matters, Germany is far ahead of England. Religious controversy ceased to excite any interest there long ago, and intellectual inquiry has abandoned the countless different interpretations of the Bible to explore the higher realms of thought. The establishment of infant schools and the methods of teaching children have excited neither controversy nor theological objections.

In the Austrian states parents are obliged to send their children to school: this government measure is no more than the fulfilment of its most pressing duty, for it is in society's interest that each one of its members should receive an education in keeping with the way that society is organised.

As I was strongly convinced of the importance of infant schools I was very eager to visit the places where the children of the poor find shelter and instruction. There are still so few real infant schools in London that I asked fifteen or twenty people if they could direct me to one but nobody knew what I meant. In the end I approached the founder of the infant schools himself, the estimable Mr Owen, whom I had the pleasure of meeting during his stay in Paris in 1837.[8] 'Alas!' Owen said to me, 'I do not know of a single infant school in London which is a genuine school for children. There are any number of establishments supported by public charity, but not one founded on my principles.' In the mouth of Owen such words could not help but carry weight, and they frightened me. If there were no infant schools in the monster city, where did children go when their parents worked all day long; where did those poor half-naked, barefoot little children take shelter during a whole long day of cold, rain or fog? Who would teach them reading, arithmetic and drawing; who would instil in them habits of cleanliness, order and co-operation? Who would teach them all those things that children learn through play? *Nobody*. London still does not possess genuine infant schools, and what few schools exist are far from being a substitute. That is why between five and eight o'clock on summer evenings one sees so many children in the streets, especially in densely populated districts.[9] At that hour, when the day's work is over and the streets less thronged with traffic, the poor little creatures are allowed to emerge from their holes and take the air. In London the poor inhabit either the attic or the cellar; often one single room houses father, mother, and seven or eight children whose faces bear witness to the rank foulness of the air inside. Nothing could be more cadaverous and stunted than these little ones; their extreme emaciation and pallor, their vacant eyes, their excessive dirtiness and hideous rags are a sight worthy of the deepest compassion. I have always preferred to live in populous districts, so every evening I found myself in the very midst of all these children swarming from their homes like ants from an ant-hill, and if the streets were narrow I was all too often aware of the foul stench rising from this mass of bodies. In winter there is no hour at which they may be let out, so I cannot imagine where they can go for a breath of fresh air. Oh! all you poor people of no account, the way you are treated is inhuman! The aristocracy can take the air in their magnificent parks, on their vast estates, or anywhere on the continent, where they go to spend the money the people earn for them; the aristocracy have splendid palaces and mansions in the finest parts of London and use them for only a few months in the year, yet they still reserve for their sole use all the squares which enhance the city[10] while the child of poor parents, lacking the space even to breathe, dies like a dog swollen with dropsy, in a damp cellar or miserable attic!

I was on the point of leaving London without having discovered a single infant school when one day as I was loudly complaining of the futility of my search, a Tory who chanced to be present said to me, 'You are mistaken, madam; London possesses several infant schools just like your own, and if you like I will give you the address of one or two.' I accepted with alacrity and set out at once.

One of the addresses was in Palmer's Village, that is, on the very edge of Westminster, more than seven miles from the centre of the city. This school was so little known that we had to provide ourselves with a guide, and although he lived in the neighbourhood, it was only after asking the way twenty times or more that he succeeded in getting us to the house; but we arrived at last. We had to cross a yard of sorts, then we entered a little room with a low ceiling and uneven floor, furnished with an old table and two or three benches; the children there were all very young, about a dozen little waifs so dirty and ragged that it was painful to behold them. From this room we passed into a somewhat larger one containing fifty-two children between the ages of three and six, just as dirty and ragged as the others; the smell pervading the room was so intolerable that we were forced to go outside, but the door was left open so we could observe the class from the yard. It was similar to our infant schools; they were being taught a variety of things, particularly to count. The old woman in charge of the school was most obliging and gave us all the information she could. The place was not maintained by the parish, but a member of the House of Commons, Mr William Smith,[11] bore all the cost himself: he had built the house and set aside an annual sum of thirty pounds plus coal and candles for those responsible for running it – that is to say, the old woman, her husband and their daughter. In addition to what is given by the founder, each child must pay a penny a week; this sum, small though

it is, is often beyond the means of parents with several children to send to school, and if admission is not absolutely
free, these schools can hardly be said to fulfil the purpose for
which they were set up; however, what would be a niggardly
half-measure on the part of an official body appears in a different light when it is the work of an ordinary citizen; then
it becomes a fine act of charity more likely than anything
else to revive the zeal of parish authorities and rekindle the
spirit of charity, if indeed the last spark is not already extinct
in the Church of England, the richest church in Europe.
Unfortunately in England the parishes are independent and
do not have to fear the censure or supervision of a central
administration.[12] In London, as elsewhere, the parish council or vestry is composed of wealthy people who have at their
disposal a garden or square where they can send their children for fresh air and exercise. They show little concern for
the fate of the children of the poor.

The aged superintendent of the infant school told us of
another school which was also the result of private charity,
the benefaction of a much respected lady, Miss Mary Doyle.[13]

With the same guide to lead us we boldly plunged into a
labyrinth of unpaved lanes where at every instant our cab
was in danger of being shaken to pieces; and this was in
London, very near the fashionable districts and elegant
squares! We passed through streets so mean and squalid
that it would be hard to find their equal in any country of
Europe; most of the houses (or rather hovels) have no
windows or floors and outside each one there is a pit where
rubbish, slops and every kind of filth lie rotting, poisoning
the air with their smell.[14]

The faces, dress and language of the inhabitants go very
well with the names of the streets (Hog Lane, Dung Street,
etc.) but they are not all thieves and prostitutes, for most of
them are weavers with large families to keep who come here
because the rents are low. What utter destitution! The sewer
is not more disgusting. How the poor suffer on the very
doorstep of the rich!

At last after many wrong turnings and vain inquiries our guide made us stop at the mouth of an alley even dirtier than the rest. There we had to leave our cab as it could never have got through the way we had to follow: the school was in an interminable lane with several sharp turnings, and every so often we came upon ponds in which rain-water was carefully saved for washing clothes. This lane, a positive sewer, is dangerous enough for a fully grown person and must be even worse for children as they make their way to school. It was only after great care and many tribulations that we reached the house. It had rained that morning and what with the sticky mud and the soapy water we nearly fell into the pond twenty times over.

A young woman of between twenty and twenty-five was in charge of the school: she was of decent appearance, had a soft voice and courteous manner, and seemed well-bred. She was somewhat embarrassed at our visit and no sooner had we entered than she began to tell us how badly the house was situated; the spot was marshy and the laundries all around made it a very unhealthy place to live in. 'The kind lady who founded the school,' she went on, 'is a good friend of the poor, but she is far from wealthy; this house is all she has, and however shabby and inconvenient it may be, her charity is no less admirable for that! What is more, she goes without the barest necessities of life in order to pay me twenty pounds a year to look after the girls, and the same to my father to look after the boys.' I agreed that such generosity was indeed very noble, and I wondered if anywhere in the three kingdoms there was a rich man capable of such an action.

The school consisted of two rooms, each far too small for the number of children (there were eighty in all) and so low-pitched that the windows had to be kept open in all weathers to let in some air. The boys were on the ground floor and the girls above; there was access from one room to the other by means of a wooden ladder, and children of two were climbing up and down holding on to a rope.

This establishment, judged by its situation, accommodation and furnishings was indeed very poor, but such considerations disappeared in the presence of the affectionate and intelligent spirit of charity which guided it. The children were very clean and so were their clothes, with not a hole to be seen. The girls were particularly neat and tidy; the big ones were making clothes for them all; each one was addressed as *mother* and had charge of two little ones whom she washed, combed and instructed in habits of cleanliness and self-control. The young teacher told me that the children had Miss Doyle to thank for their clothes as well; this respectable lady spent her time in going to all the grand houses asking for charity and used the money she was given to buy material for the children's clothes.

These three people, the father, the daughter and Miss Doyle, who devoted all their time, money and energy to relieving the misery of the poor, rose before my eyes in the midst of the arid waste of gilded wealth like palm trees in the desert.

I would have returned to France in the firm belief that the monster city possessed not a single infant school had not a notice about an organisation calling itself the Home and Colonial Infant School Society come into my hands.[15] The third annual general meeting of the society was held in the Hanover Square Assembly Rooms in July 1839. It was a well-attended and extremely respectable company; that is to say, it was composed exclusively of the feudal aristocracy.

After the necessary formality of opening prayers, the Earl of Chichester addressed the meeting on the aims of the Society. From what he said it seemed that its purpose was not to develop the intelligence of poor children to fit them for apprenticeships and entry into the professions, nor to save them from the perils of being abandoned by their parents; not a word was said about that. The sole aim of the Society is *scriptural education*, and the noble lord strongly criticised all those learned men who base their principles for the education of children on the guidance of Nature, and the training establishments, which he claimed turn out none but teachers of blasphemy and insurrection.

Mr J S Reynolds, the secretary of the Society, was next to speak; he described the efforts of the Committee to promote *scriptural education* among the children and said it was their fear that if the government intervened, education would not contain sufficient religion. He therefore besought the noble company, on behalf of the Committee, to exert all its influence to ensure that Parliament confined its activities to the industrial regions, seeing that the Society could not hope that the Chartists in those parts would ever adopt *scriptural education* for *their* children. The secretary rounded off his report with the tidings that the Committee had despatched teachers to Smyrna, Syria and Egypt to spread *scriptural education* among the Ottomans and the Arabs.

Captain Vernon Harcourt, in an oration worthy of a zealot of the sixteenth century, called the attention of the assembly to the considerable number of children roaming about the metropolis with nobody to make them *read the Bible*. He warned that the Catholics were taking advantage of all these abandoned Protestant children by bringing them up free of charge in their own schools; they were even going so far as to provide them with clothes in the hope of making converts, and he knew of entire families who had been converted to Catholicism by these means.

The Reverend James Cumming proposed that the assembly should affirm that the present and eternal well-being of all individuals, the good order of every class in society and the stability of the most precious institutions of the Empire all depended for their existence on *scriptural education*. It amazed him to hear certain persons maintain that the Holy Scriptures were beyond the understanding of children. He stated that the baptism of new-born infants imposed the obligation to initiate them into the doctrines of religion, so that *their very first halting words* were taught them from the Bible. He rejected the contention of Rousseau that a child's religious instruction should not begin before the age of nine or ten. He said that more than 600,000 people in London had no regular place of worship, and more than 900,000 had no knowledge at all of God or of the Holy Scriptures. 'The question,' he cried, 'is not whether children should be brought up in school or at home, but whether they are to receive an education for Heaven or for Hell. If the children of the poor are not given a scriptural education they will be raised in obedience to one of the two great principles which struggle against us: they will fall into the hands of atheists or the priests of Rome!' And the Reverend Cumming, transported by the fanaticism of a Luther or a Calvin, gave free rein to his hatred of Catholicism. 'The children of England,' he cried, 'are exposed to the greatest dangers; they are rushing headlong to their ruin, for popery is invading us on all sides. Catholic priests are roaming the country setting up schools and enticing Protestant children inside them so that they may corrupt and seduce them and make them abandon the Church of England, *the sole guardian of established truth*! And so our unfortunate children will be turned from the path of righteousness by these idolatrous priests; they will be brought up in idolatry, absurdity and all the stupid rituals of Catholicism; they will worship statues and pictures and be taught the blasphemous words, Hail Mary. The risks the Protestant churches run are so great that infant schools should be set up everywhere so that every child that is born will receive a scriptural education. If Ireland had such schools she would be a very different place today. The effect of scriptural education may be seen in Scotland, where they teach the Bible *from the earliest hours of infancy*, whereas in Ireland the Bible, if not totally rejected, is certainly excluded from all instruction.'

The Reverend Cumming spoke for more than two hours, and all through his long discourse his voice was charged with a holy indignation against popery, as he called it. He concluded with these words: 'For my part, I have no desire that men should say I extended the domain of science, instructed my fellow citizens, shone in literature or electrified the masses with my eloquence: I would consider I had worthily fulfilled my task if a simple epitaph engraved on my tomb proclaimed that I had taught a single child to pronounce the name of Jesus!'

This speech was frequently interrupted by bursts of applause.

Mr Labouchere, the current President of the Board of Trade, a man one would have thought either too enlightened to have any dealings with a Society whose avowed aim is to teach the Bible to infants between the ages of two and seven, or too independent to betray his convictions and toady to the aristocracy, was present at the meeting and spoke in much the same strain as the Reverend Cumming. The Reverend J Stratton showed more tolerance and said that he applauded the establishment of *every kind of school* for the education of children, but this laudable spirit of philanthropy did not meet with the support of the noble gathering, and after several further speeches all in favour of scriptural education, the meeting rose.

Surely nowhere but in England can there still be people simple enough to try to make religious propaganda with Bibles and religion out of argumentation. It must be admitted that to propose stopping the advance of Catholicism by distributing the Bible and teaching it to babes and sucklings is quite absurd, a ridiculous idea for such a solemn assembly to entertain!

Apart from the Society I have just described, there are several others supported by the subscriptions of the aristocracy; but despite all these efforts the Church of England has a rough struggle ahead against the Catholic priests, for they are men who understand the need for toleration and are gaining the acceptance of all parties because they are prepared to come to terms with the ideas of the times, something which the stiff-necked puritans cannot bring themselves to do.

1(TN).   The term 'infant schools' applies here to the education of poor children between the ages of two and six. In the early part of the nineteenth century there was no organised system of education for the poor, but all over the country there were charity schools for boys between seven and eleven who were afterwards apprenticed to various trades. There were also Sunday schools, Dame schools (usually run by elderly men and women), Common Day Schools for older children, and schools attached to some factories, but education was not compulsory and many parents preferred their children to start earning a wage as soon as possible.

It was almost universally accepted by the Church of England and the dissenting churches alike that education, whether denominational or not, must be closely linked with religious teaching, and subsequent efforts by the government to introduce legislation on education were bedevilled by church hostility to any kind of state intervention. In 1806, 1820 and 1833, attempts to introduce a system of education financed partly from the rates were a failure.

The dissenters set up the British and Foreign School Society in 1808, followed in 1811 by the Church of England with its National Society for Promoting the Education of the Poor in the Principles of the Established Church. In 1834 it was estimated that there were one million children in England and Wales receiving education in Church of England schools, half of them in union with the National Society. Both Societies relied on voluntary subscriptions and had to provide education as cheaply as possible, which was why they adopted the monitorial system devised by the Quaker Joseph Lancaster and the Anglican Dr Andrew Bell (see note 7). The teacher would teach the lesson to selected older children (monitors) who would each pass it on to a group of between ten and twenty children.

2(TN).   Jean-Denis-Marie COCHIN (1789–1841) was a lawyer and philanthropist. The general theme of his book, *Manuel des salles d'asile* (1833), is that children of the poorer classes were so much at risk from their parents' negligence – as both parents were compelled to work – that it was imperative to remove them from home as soon as possible and place them in an environment where the conditions of the ideal family home could be simulated.

3(TN).   The phalanstery was the basis of Fourier's social theory: a purpose-built community home with land attached, accommodating upwards of a thousand people organised in such a way that their talents and inclinations were fully employed. Everything in Fourier's system was worked out in the smallest detail, and Flora was critical of him for making it too complicated for ordinary mortals to understand.

4(FT).   When the first infant schools were set up·in England, they met with very strong opposition. Here are some of the objections their opponents raised: 'But if the children of the people are raised with such care from the most tender age, they will have too great an advantage over middle-class children who do not receive such attention; the poor child will become too intelligent, too precocious; inevitably he will do better than children from the other classes, and this could seriously upset society.'

Report of the Committee of the Infant Schools Society

5(TN).   Flora presumably means the absolute rule of Louis XIV (1638–1715) and his persecution of the Huguenots. Jean-Frédéric OBERLIN (1740–1826) was a pastor and philanthropist from Alsace who is credited with setting up the very first infant school in 1774 in the village of Waldbach in the Vosges. He became known as 'the saint of the Protestant Church' and Oberlin College in Ohio was founded in 1833 to commemorate his life and work.

6(FT).   In this second edition I do not reproduce the chapter on Robert Owen because it is incomplete, and such important theories cannot be satisfactorily examined and explained within the ordinary limits of a chapter. I have therefore confined myself to taking from it some passages relating to the educational system of the English socialist.

(Robert OWEN (1771–1858) was Welsh, and left school at the age of nine to earn his living in London. By the time he was nineteen he was manager of a cotton factory in Manchester, where he

NOTES

improved the quality of the cotton, and soon became the foremost cotton-spinner in the kingdom. From Manchester he went as part-owner of the New Lanark mills in Scotland, and this was where he developed the theories on factory administration and education which brought visitors from all over Europe to admire his model school and mills. He drafted a Bill to improve conditions in all textile factories, but by the time it was debated in Parliament it was in such an emasculated form that he disowned it, together with any belief in the efficacy of action within Parliament or parliamentary reform. Thereafter he devoted his life to the theory and practice of a new moral order based on co-operative principles, and his ideas had an incalculable influence on a whole generation of men and women workers, whose early efforts to form trade unions were firmly based on co-operation. But they were suppressed by the government, and when the trade union movement eventually got under way, it was as an adjunct of the capitalist system. Flora describes Owen's practical suggestions for the re-organisation of the working population in her chapter on Owen in the first edition of the *London Journal*: they included the establishment of communities between five hundred and three thousand strong all over the kingdom, mainly agricultural in character, but using all the benefits of machinery in the service of the community. This system, he hoped, would gradually and peacefully spread to all classes of society. It was at first looked upon favourably by the ruling classes, but Owen fell from grace when he declared that he was opposed to all received forms of religion.

The section of the text from 'What could be more admirable . . .' to '. . . teach them the meaning of conscience . . .' is all that Flora retained of her chapter on Robert Owen in the 1840 edition of her *London Journal*. The quotation comes from Owen's *A New View of Society* (1814): TN.)

7(TN). Joseph LANCASTER (1776–1838) founded a school for poor children in Southwark in 1803. Under his supervision the older children taught the younger ones, an economical method later adopted by the British and Foreign School Society. The similar rival system evolved by Andrew Bell was adopted by the National Society. Flora's statement that Owen used Lancaster's method is misleading. In fact, he found the monitorial system too

241

rigid: it crammed the child's mind with dubious and useless facts, whereas Owen's methods used all the marvels of nature to appeal to the child's eyes and ears, and gave a high place to dancing, music and physical exercise. He had no prior knowledge of Oberlin's early experiments when he set up his own infant school in 1816. His was undoubtedly the first of its kind in Britain and was so permeated by the personality of its founder that in a sense he was right when he told Flora that there were no other genuine infant schools in London, though there were certainly one or two run on similar lines, one for instance in Westminster, founded in 1818, and one in Spitalfields, founded in 1820; and the formation of the Infant School Society in 1824 led to the establishment of many more. All these early ventures were financed by voluntary subscriptions: the first state grant for the education of the poorer classes was not made until 1833 – twenty thousand pounds to be used for building schools.

8(TN).   At a public meeting addressed by Owen during his visit to Paris in 1837, a supporter of Saint-Simon objected that Owen's doctrine was incomplete because there was no woman by his side, whereupon a lady in the audience sprang to her feet, raised her hand and declared, 'Oh yes, there is!' This was Flora Tristan; Owen bowed graciously in her direction and some of the audience applauded.

9(FT).   'All the English towns we visited presented us with the sad spectacle of bands of dirty children roaming like animals through the districts inhabited by the poor. On Sundays in particular the sight of these streets defies description. It is no exaggeration to say that every little court and square is full of young children, completely abandoned, gathered together in little groups, often lying huddled together on the muddy pavement or dunghill.
　'Now here is what Mr Beaver Wale [*sic*] has to say in his work on young delinquents: "... Thus are their days of childhood spent without religious or any other species of instruction, and so far from being under any restraint, or receiving any moral training, they are left like the "wild asses' colt", to the enjoyment of a liberty unsuitable to their condition in life, and in many other ways injurious to them." '

Buret, op. cit.

10(FT). All these squares are surrounded by railings, and the enjoyment of them is reserved exclusively for the owners of neighbouring houses, in spite of the fact that not one of them ever has time to walk in these privileged groves.

11(TN). Palmer's Village lay just south of St James's Park, near Buckingham Gate. William Smith was a well known philanthropist who died in 1835.

12(FT). Since the passing of the new Poor Law the government has felt it necessary to intervene in this part of parish administration to prevent scandalous abuses, but in every other respect the English parish is as independent as the Swiss canton.

13(TN). Apart from her name, nothing is known of Mary Doyle.

14(FT). See the description of the poor quarters of London in the book by M Buret.

15(TN). The Home and Colonial Infant School Society was founded in 1836 with the aim of training men and women teachers to give children a thorough religious education in the doctrines of the Church of England. The Earl of Chichester, who took the chair at the meeting Flora attended, was for fifty years President of the Church Missionary Society; the Society's secretary, John Stuckley REYNOLDS, founded an infant school in Putney in 1823; Captain Vernon HARCOURT was one of the ten sons of the Archbishop of York, and John CUMMING was Minister of the Presbyterian church at Covent Garden, a man much given to outbursts of anti-Catholic invective. Henry LABOUCHERE was, at the time of the meeting (July 1839), still Under-Secretary of State for War, but in the following month, he was appointed President of the Board of Trade.

English Women

Is there a shadow of justice in the fate that has befallen women? Is not the young girl a piece of merchandise displayed for sale to any man willing to bargain for her possession and sole proprietary rights? Is not her consent to the marriage bond a mockery, forced upon her by the tyranny of the prejudices which beset her from her earliest childhood? Men would have her believe that the chains she wears are forged out of flowers; but she can have no illusions about her degradation, even in countries with an excessive fondness for philosophising, like England, where a man enjoys the right to lead his wife to market with a rope about her neck and deliver her like a beast of burden to anyone willing to pay the price. In this respect, is our public opinion any more advanced today than in those uncouth times when a certain Council of Mâcon, a real Council of Vandals, deliberated whether women had a soul and decided in the affirmative by a majority of only three votes? English law, which moralists praise so highly, grants men other rights no less degrading to women, such as the entitlement of a husband to be awarded damages at the expense of his wife's avowed lover. In France procedures are more civilised, but in essence slavery is always the same.

Charles Fourier,
Theory of the Four Movements (1808)

What a revolting contrast there is in England between the extreme servitude of women and the intellectual superiority of women authors! There is no evil, suffering, disorder, injustice or misery arising from the prejudices of society, from its organisation and its laws, that has escaped their observation. The writings of the English women who cast such a brilliant light upon the intellectual scene are a dazzling phenomenon – especially when one considers the absurd education they have had to undergo and the brutalising influence of the environment in which they have lived.

One has only to live in England for a few months to be struck by the intelligence and sensibility of the women; not to mention their capacity for concentration and for committing facts to memory. With gifts such as these, nothing in the world of the intellect is beyond their grasp. Their manners are noble and gracious, but alas! all these splendid natural qualities are stifled by a system of education based on false premises and by the atmosphere of hypocrisy, prejudice and vice which surrounds them.

English women lead the most arid, monotonous and unhappy existences imaginable. Time has no meaning for them: days, months and years bring no change to the deadening uniformity of their lives. As young girls they are brought up according to the social position of their parents, but whatever rank they must occupy in life, their education is always influenced to a greater or lesser degree by the same prejudices.

It has long been the fashion to extol English liberties, but England is the seat of the most abominable despotism, where laws and prejudices submit women to the most revolting inequality! A woman may inherit only if she has no brothers; she has no civil or political rights, and the law subjects her to her husband in every respect. She is inured to hypocrisy: she alone has to bear the brunt of public censure. Everything that develops her faculties, everything that she has to endure, has the inevitable result of coarsening her tastes, hardening her heart and numbing her soul.

Revolted by the scenes of family life they knew from experience, English novelists invented others which their imagination persuaded them were true; so the closer they are to reality when they portray the ridiculous habits of the typical

English gentleman, or the bigotry and pretensions of the bourgeois, the tyranny of the husband and father, the offensive pride of superiors and the servility of inferiors, then the further they are from reality when they portray a picture of domestic happiness. Happiness without freedom! How can there ever be happiness in a society of masters and slaves?

This is what happens in wealthy families: the children are confined to the third floor with their nurse, maid or governess; the mother asks for them when she wishes to see them, and only then do the children come to pay her a short visit, during which she addresses them in a formal manner.[1] As the poor little girl is starved of affection, her capacity for loving is never awakened and she does not know the sweet feelings of intimacy, trust and frankness that come naturally to every little girl who has a loving mother, while for the father she hardly knows, she has a respect mingled with fear, and for her brother she keeps the consideration and deference she has been obliged to show him from her earliest childhood.

The system followed for the education of young girls seems to me fit to turn the most intelligent child into a blockhead. M Jacotot says, 'In everything there is everything',[2] but English education on the contrary seems to demonstrate that in everything there is *nothing*! It is concerned solely to imprint on these young minds the *words* of all the European languages without the slightest thought for the *ideas*. This extravagant folly is as cruel as it is stupid: a little girl is given a German nurse, a French governess and a Spanish maid, so that from the age of four to five she may learn as many languages. I have seen some of these poor little things whose plight was truly pitiful; they could not make themselves understood by anyone around them; all the pretty tricks of speech were denied them, and as they were unable to communicate in words, they were obliged to have recourse to *signs*, which led to either frustration or apathy according to the nature of the child: some became fractious and noisy, others moody and silent. Forced to over-load her memory with the vocabulary of three or four languages, the child acquires only a confused notion of the meaning these words express; she retains the oral signal but the idea it represents escapes her; she develops an abnormal memory, but the intelligence required to understand concepts is destroyed. No doubt a knowledge of languages is necessary for a people whose greed invades the entire earth, but it is essential first to subordinate every kind of instruction to the development of the child, and only then to consider the usefulness of the language that the child is to be taught. It is rare, if not impossible, to be able to express oneself with facility and elegance in three or four languages. As incorrect and outlandish forms of speech combined with a foreign accent give offence in any country, and as women are rarely if ever called upon to conduct business with foreign powers, I think that on the whole there are more useful things for them to learn.

But whatever is taught, the system followed is the same as for languages. The young girl must learn music whether she has any aptitude or not; she must also be able to dance, draw, and so on. The result is that young ladies know a little of everything but have no talent which is of any use to them even for their amusement. Of course one meets with exceptions, but these are rare.

As for their moral education – it all comes from the Bible. Nobody will dispute that this book is full of good things, but what a number of obscenities, indecent stories and improper descriptions would have to be removed before placing it in the hands of young girls if their imagination were not to be sullied and they were not to think that all the actions society condemns are justified: theft, murder, prostitution etc.; for whatever the reverend gentlemen may say, *scriptural education* is the most antisocial system of all. There are countless paradoxes in English society, but this is among the most shocking. To insist that a young girl should be pure, chaste and innocent, and then to prescribe for her reading a book containing the stories of Lot, David, Absalom, Ruth and the Song of Songs; to allow her to read St Paul's sermons on fornicators and regale her mind with scenes of rape, orgy, adultery and prostitution expressed in the picturesque language of the Bible; and then to tell her that the words breeches, shift, drawers, thigh, bitch etc., must never pass her lips! In this way young girls are instructed in the *appearance* of chastity and innocence and *the reality* of vice, just as, through being exhorted to observe the Sabbath, the people are instructed in the *appearance* of religion and the *reality* of idleness and its consequent disorders. It is a curious fact, but nowhere is there any morality; nobody believes in chastity, probity, or any accepted sense of the word *virtue* any more; nobody is taken in by appearances, yet they still serve to mask the morals of the nation.

Young ladies have very few amusements: as family life is formal, arid, and intolerably boring, they plunge headlong into the world of the novel. Unfortunately these romances revolve around lovers such as England has never known, and their influence gives birth to hopes that can never be fulfilled. The imagination of our young readers takes a romantic turn and they dream of nothing but abductions, but as this is the century of luxury and comfort, every abductor is the son of a nabob or lord and heir to an immense fortune, and every abduction is accomplished in a superb carriage drawn by four horses. Far from fulfilling the desires of which they are the object, wealthy young men have hard hearts and jaded senses; they submit everything to cool unsentimental calculation. The bitter disappointments young ladies suffer would be avoided had they been brought up to live simply, to enjoy the pleasures of the intellect and to disdain the gratifications of vanity. If they had learned the lessons of the Gospels, they would know that great wealth invariably corrupts the heart, and they would not have the least desire to be loved by young men who spend their lives in gambling and getting drunk with prostitutes. But these young ladies, after waiting in vain for the carriage and four horses, reach the age of twenty-eight or thirty and then marry some small merchant, obscure clerk or someone of even less account; many never marry at all.

Of course the fate of the married woman is very much sadder than that of the spinster; at least the unmarried woman enjoys a certain freedom, she can enter society and travel with her family or with friends, whereas once a woman is married, she cannot stir from the house *without the permission of her husband*. The English husband is like the *lord and master* of feudal times; he is sincerely convinced that he has the right to demand of his wife submission, respect and the passive obedience of a slave. He cloisters her in the house, not because he loves her madly or is jealous like the Turk, but because he considers her to be his property, his chattel, an object for his sole use which must always be within his reach; it never enters his head that he should be bound in fidelity to his wife. This manner of looking at things, which leaves his passions a free rein, is attributed by many people to the influence of the Bible.

The English husband sleeps with his servant, casts her out when she is pregnant or after she has given birth, and thinks himself no more guilty than Abraham when he sent Hagar and her son Ishmael forth into the desert.

In England the wife is not mistress of the household as she would be in France. In fact she is almost a stranger in her own home: the husband holds the money and the keys; it is he who controls expenditure, hires or dismisses servants, orders dinner every morning and invites the guests; he alone decides the fate of the children; in short, he has sole charge of everything. Many women do not know the nature of their husband's business or what is to be the profession of their children, and they are generally ignorant of the state of their fortune. The English wife never asks her husband what he does, what company he keeps, how much he spends or how he passes the time. Not one of them would dare to ask such questions. From the extreme dependence of English wives and the respect they show for the wishes of their lord and master, to the easy familiarity and active interest French wives display towards *their* husbands, is as far as the distance between French civilisation today and in the age of St Louis.[3] The English wife has no guarantee that her fortune will be safe; she is robbed of everything without her knowledge. It is quite common for her to remain in ignorance of her husband's bankruptcy, ruin and even suicide, until she reads in the newspaper that he has blown his brains out.

I have already said that it is customary for children to live with their nurse or governess in a room apart. Their mother never sets foot in it; it is not from her that they learn to speak and gradually develop their heart and mind. When the nurse or governess takes them down to her in the drawing-room she looks to see that they are clean and have fresh clothes on; once she has finished her inspection she kisses them, and that is all until the morrow. When they are older the children are sent away to school so their mother rarely sees them, and once they are married, relations between them are almost at an end; they write to each other and that is all. The coldness and indifference of the wife and mother is not only the result of the soul-destroying education she has undergone, it is also the natural consequence of the position she occupies in the conjugal home. What interest can she take in an association which is one-sided and in which her wishes or opinions are of no account? How can a slave be anything but indifferent to the good or bad fortune of her master?

I think I can guess what gives these English ladies the title of *housewives*: it is their sedentary existence. It is almost inconceivable that anybody who stays at home all the time should do absolutely nothing; however, this is exactly what happens. Not only do they do nothing, but they would con-sider themselves little better than servants if they so much as picked up a needle;[4] so time is an intolerable burden to them. They rise very late, dawdle over breakfast, read the newspapers and dress; at two o'clock there is another meal, then they read novels, and write letters often fifteen pages long. Before dinner they make a fresh toilet, and after dinner, towards seven or eight o'clock, they sit a long while over tea. At ten o'clock they take supper, and then they sit alone by the fire.

Nothing reveals the materialism of English society so well as the state of nullity to which men reduce their wives. Are not social duties the responsibility of women as well as men? Yet these gentlemen think they can banish their wives from society and condemn them to live the life of a vegetable! It must be confessed that scriptural education produces the most extraordinary results! These English households must constitute the most bitter satire on the indissoluble bond of marriage; it would be impossible to invent a more convincing example of the absurdity of marriage as an institution. To account for so large a number of talented women in England one can only assume that the Almighty must have granted them more moral strength and intelligence than He gave their masters; otherwise, living under such conditions, they would inevitably have become completely stupid.

The reasons behind all marriages in England are, on the woman's side, the desire to escape from a father's tyranny, to lighten the burden of prejudice which weighs so heavily on unmarried girls, and the hope of enjoying a more important place in the world, for noble souls feel the need to play an active part in society; on the man's side, solely the desire to appropriate his wife's dowry and use it to pay his debts and dabble in speculation, or if the money happens to be a fortune, to fritter away the revenues from it in clubs and finishes or in the company of his mistresses.

It is the woman who gets the worst of the bargain. Prejudice leads her to the altar where greed awaits her to strip her of all she possesses; whereas men lead exactly the same lives as before. The marriage bond, so irksome for the woman, imposes no obligations on *them*, and there is nothing to stop them from living with prostitutes, maidservants or actresses if they so desire. The majority will maintain a mistress in luxurious style in some pretty little house in the suburbs: this is a universal practice as much among wealthy men from the City as among the denizens of the West End. They make a second home and a second family, and whatever affection they may have in their heart goes to this woman they have chosen and the children she bears them. Then the poor legitimate wife, whom they took only as a *money-lender*, becomes in their eyes an uncomfortable and uncongenial companion; the attentions which are her due and the consideration and respect which society obliges husbands to show all become so many irksome duties which they escape by going home as little as possible. What is the fate of the *lawful* wife? She is reduced, alas, to the state of a machine for manufacturing babies, 'and the best twenty-five years of her life are spent in producing *little ones*.'[5]

Isolation gives English ladies a propensity for observation and reflection, and a great number of them are moved to become writers. There are many more women authors in England than in France, because French women lead a more active life and have more freedom to enter society. There are several illustrious women writers in England, and ever since Lady Montagu[6] wrote describing her travels in so pure and elegant a style, many other women have followed her example and launched themselves on a literary career, showing proof of incontestable merit. It is above all in the novel and in the description of domestic life that these ladies excel. Everybody knows the works of Lady Morgan;[7] nobody before her had depicted the Irish character so well or brought Ireland so vividly to life. The novels of Lady Blessington[8] are remarkable for exactness of observation and penetration of thought, and I could cite many other names. Recently a young woman has made an exceptionally brilliant entrance upon the scene; never has a literary career dawned more brightly or promised better things, and Lady Bulwer-Lytton has taken her place in the foremost ranks of literature.[9] This pearl among women is one of the many victims of the indissolubility of marriage; her first book, entitled *Scenes of Real Life*, is one prolonged cry of pain. On cannot display such talent with impunity, and society, unable to deny her gifts, has raised an outcry against the scandal of her revelations. Poor women! They are permitted only to suffer and forbidden even to complain!

But in England women are also concerned with the most serious matters. Miss Martineau has written some very remarkable works on political economy;[10] Mrs Trollope has published a very successful account of her travels in America;[11] Mrs Gore has written a volume of attractive stories based on the history and customs of Poland[12] and Mrs Shilly writes verses full of melody and feeling;[13] many of these ladies contribute to the reviews and journals, but it grieves me deeply to observe that as yet not one of them has dared to embrace the cause of women's liberty, that liberty without which all other freedoms are short-lived and for which it is so peculiarly fitting that women authors should fight. In this respect French women are far ahead of the English. However, one woman's voice was heard in England half a century ago: a voice which found its irresistible strength and boundless energy in the truth which God implanted in our souls; a voice which was not afraid to attack every prejudice and expose the lies and iniquities of which they are made. Mary Wollstonecraft entitled her book *A Vindication of the Rights of Woman*: it appeared in 1792.[14]

The book was suppressed the moment it appeared, but this did not save its author from calumny. Only the first volume was published and now it is extremely rare. I could not buy a copy, and had not a friend been good enough to lend it to me, it would have been impossible for me to procure it. The reputation of this book inspires such fear that if you so much as mention its name, even to so-called 'progressive' women, they will recoil in horror and exclaim, 'Oh, but that is an *evil* book!' Thus calumny often proves too strong for even the best deserved reputation and transmits its hatred from generation to generation without respect for death or glory.

Mary Wollstonecraft dedicated her book to M de Talleyrand-Périgord. Listen to this Englishwoman who was the first to dare proclaim that civil and political rights belong in equal measure to *both* sexes, and who refers to opinions expressed by M de Talleyrand before the Assembly in order to prove to him that it is his *duty* as a statesman to act in accordance with his convictions and ensure their victory by establishing the complete emancipation of women.

Here are some passages from that dedication:

> Contending for the rights of woman, my main argument is built on the simple principle, that if she be not prepared by education to be the companion of man, she will stop the progress of knowledge and virtue; for truth must be common to all, or it will be inefficacious with respect to its influence on general practice. . . . If children are to be educated to understand the true principle of patriotism, their mother must be a patriot; and the love of mankind, from which an orderly train of virtues spring, can only be produced by considering the moral and civil interest of mankind; but the education and situation of woman, at present, shuts her out from such investigations. . . .
>
> Consider – I address you as a legislator – whether, when men contend for their freedom, and to be allowed to judge for themselves respecting their own happiness, it be not inconsistent and unjust to subjugate women, even though you firmly believe that you are acting in the manner best calculated to promote their happiness? Who made man the exclusive judge, if woman partake with him the gift of reason?
>
> In this style argue tyrants of every denomination, from the weak king to the weak father of a family; they are all eager to crush reason, yet always assert that they usurp its throne only to be useful. Do you not act a similar part, when you *force* all women, by denying them civil and political rights, to remain immured in their families groping in the dark? . . .
>
> But if women are to be excluded, without having a voice, from a participation of the natural rights of mankind, prove first, to ward off the charge of injustice and inconsistency, that they want reason – else this flaw in your NEW CON-

STITUTION will ever show that man must, in some shape, act like a tyrant; and tyranny, in whatever part of society it rears its brazen front, will ever undermine morality . . . if women are not permitted to enjoy legitimate rights, they will render both men and themselves vicious, to obtain illicit privileges.

And now, this is how she addresses women:

My own sex, I hope, will excuse me, if I treat them like rational creatures, instead of flattering their *fascinating* graces, and viewing them as if they were in a state of perpetual childhood, unable to stand alone. I earnestly wish to point out in what true dignity and human happiness consists – I wish to persuade women to endeavour to acquire strength, both of mind and body, and to convince them that the soft phrases, susceptibility of heart, delicacy of sentiment, and refinement of taste, are almost synonymous with epithets of weakness, and that those beings who are only the objects of pity and that kind of love which has been termed its sister, will soon become objects of contempt.

Dismissing then, those pretty feminine phrases, which the men condescendingly use to soften our slavish dependence, and despising that weak elegancy of mind, exquisite sensibility, and sweet docility of manners supposed to be the sexual characteristics of the weaker vessel, I wish to show that elegance is inferior to virtue, that the first object of laudable ambition is to obtain a character as a human being, regardless of the distinction of sex; and that secondary views should be brought to this simple touchstone.

Mary Wollstonecraft claims freedom for women as a *right*, in the name of the principle on which human justice and injustice are founded; she claims it because without freedom no kind of moral obligation can exist, because without equality between the sexes morality has no foundation and ceases to be real.

Mary Wollstonecraft says she has an exalted view of women as creatures who, like men, are placed on this earth in order to develop their intellectual faculties. Woman is neither inferior nor superior to man; the two differ in mind and body only to complement one another, and since the moral faculties of one are destined through union to complete those of the other, both must receive the same degree of development. She fiercely criticises writers who regard woman as a subordinate being created for man's pleasure. On this subject she has some sharp words for Rousseau, who insisted that woman must be *weak and passive*, man strong and active; that woman was made *to be subject to man*; finally that she must make herself agreeable and obey her master, for this is the aim of her existence.[15] Mary Wollstonecraft points out that if such principles are followed, women are brought up to be deceitful, perfidious and coquettish, while as their minds are left uncultivated and the excessive stimulation of their emotions leaves them defenceless, they fall victim to every form of oppression. She shows that the inevitable consequence of all this is to turn morality upside down. The pernicious influence of books in which authors insidiously debase women even as they worship their charms cannot be too often exposed or too severely censured.

Mary Wollstonecraft speaks out bravely and vigorously against abuses of every kind. 'From the respect paid to property flow, as from a poisoned fountain, most of the evils and vices which render this world such a dreary scene to the contemplative mind . . . for all are aiming to procure respect on account of their property; and property, once gained, will procure the respect due only to talents and virtue. Men neglect the duties incumbent on man, yet are treated like demi-gods; religion is also separated from morality by a ceremonial veil, yet men wonder that the world is almost, literally speaking, a den of sharpers or oppressors.'

Mary Wollstonecraft was already publishing in 1792 the self-same principles that Saint-Simon was to disseminate later, and which spread so rapidly after the Revolution of 1830. Her criticism is admirable: she reveals in their true colours all the evils arising from the organisation of the family, and her powerful logic is irrefutable. She boldly undermines the mass of prejudices which envelope our society; she demands equal civil and political rights for both sexes, equal admission to employment, professional education for all, and divorce by mutual consent. Without these fundamental principles, she says, any social system which promises universal happiness will only betray its promises.

Mary Wollstonecraft's book is an *imperishable* work: imperishable because the happiness of the human race is bound up with the cause which *A Vindication of the Rights of Woman* defends. Yet this book has been in existence for half a century and nobody has ever heard of it! . . .

NOTES

1(FT). In the upper classes, young ladies remain with their governess until they marry; when their mother wishes to see them, she sends them a note by her footman inviting them to come and take tea with her, and the young ladies make a special toilet to visit their mother's apartment, just as if they were going to visit a stranger.

2(TN). Jean-Joseph JACOTOT (1770–1840) was a French polymath and educationist: Professor of Latin at nineteen, subsequently Professor of Mathematics and of Roman Law, he evolved a system of education which he put into practice when he was appointed to teach the French language at the University of Louvain in Belgium. Jacotot's system was based on three principles:

1. All men have equal intelligence.
2. God has given to all the ability to teach themselves.
3. Everything is in everything.

3(TN). Louis IX (1214–1270) was the ideal of the medieval king, excelling in all the skills of a knight, yet devout and ascetic. At home he tamed the nobles and consolidated his kingdom; abroad he went on two Crusades, in the course of which he acquired various holy relics, including the crown of thorns. On his return to Paris, he built the Sainte-Chapelle to house them. Among his acts of charity he founded a number of hospitals, visited the sick and gave alms to beggars. He died of the plague at Carthage while on the Second Crusade, and was canonised in 1297.

4(FT). I am speaking only of women in comfortable circumstances, for it is well known that the poor woman and the wife of a small tradesman are forced to work; but many prefer to become ladies of the town rather than descend to the level of working women. In England, work is considered degrading.

5(TN). I am unable to identify the source of this quotation. It is not from the other work Flora quotes in this chapter – Mary Wollstonecraft's *Vindication of the Rights of Woman*.

6(TN). Lady Mary Wortley MONTAGU (1689–1762) was one of the great English letter-writers, best known for her *Letters from Turkey*, where she lived when her husband was Ambassador to Constantinople. In her younger days she was a celebrated beauty and wit.

7(TN). Lady Sydney MORGAN (1783–1859) was an Irish novelist who made her reputation with *The Wild Irish Girl* (1806), an impassioned evocation of the beauties of Ireland. She described the life of the poor with sympathy and understanding. Her study of France under the Bourbon Restoration aroused a storm of fury and she was accused of Jacobinism, impiety, falsehood and licentiousness by the *Quarterly Review*.

8(TN). Marguerite, Countess of BLESSINGTON (1789–1849) was another spirited Irish beauty who, like Anna Wheeler, married a drunkard at the age of fifteen and subsequently left him to make a life for herself. (The Earl was her second husband.) For some years she was editor of *The Book of Beauty* and *The Keepsake*, two popular lightweight periodicals of the day, and she published her *Conversations with Lord Byron* in 1834.

9(TN). Rosina Doyle WHEELER (1802–1882) was the daughter

of Anna Wheeler and grew up just as beautiful and imperious as Flora Tristan. She married Edward Bulwer in 1827, before he became famous as a novelist and dramatist, but they separated in 1836, and, like Caroline Norton, Rosina lost her children. In 1839 she published her novel *Cheveley, or the Man of Honour*, in which she bitterly attacked her husband. (She never wrote a book called *Scenes of Real Life*, and it is possible that in her notes Flora confused Rosina with Mary Wollstonecraft, whose *Original Stories from Real Life* appeared in 1791.) Rosina wrote other novels, but played no part in political life; she disapproved of her mother's revolutionary activities. Ironically enough, Rosina's granddaughter was Lady Constance Lytton, the suffragette.

Rosina, though separated from her husband, still bore his name, and as this changed with his rank and fortune, so did her own: from Lytton Bulwer at the time of her marriage, to Bulwer-Lytton to Lytton. At the time of her death she was known as Rosina, Lady Lytton. Her husband is best known as Edward Bulwer-Lytton, author of *The Last Days of Pompeii* and *The Caxtons*. There was a rumour, which Flora repeats in the 1840 edition of her *Journal*, that Rosina was the author of his books, but this is without foundation.

10(TN).   Harriet MARTINEAU (1802–1876) was brought up a Unitarian and began to write religious articles before she was twenty, but she won an immediate reputation, as well as £2,000, with her huge collection of stories dealing in simple language with every important social problem of her day, entitled *Illustrations of Political Economy* (1831). In 1834 she went to America, and while there she boldly supported the Abolitionists, who were then an intensely unpopular minority in the country. Over the years she moved away from the religious beliefs of her youth, though she never openly declared herself an atheist. She valued her political independence too highly to accept a government pension, so her friends purchased an annuity for her and she had a house built in the Lake District, where she cultivated a small farm and helped her poorer neighbours. She had been a sickly child: she became deaf at sixteen, and in middle age she suffered a breakdown which left her a semi-invalid for five years. But her health improved in later life, and when Charlotte Brontë went to stay with her in 1850, Harriet was in the habit of rising at five, taking a cold bath and a walk by star-light, then working until two o'clock, after which she was ready to devote some time to her guests. The household retired at ten, and Harriet wrote letters until midnight! She was personally acquainted with most of the writers of any consequence in her day.

11(TN). Frances Milton TROLLOPE (1780–1863) started writing rather late in life to help retrieve the family fortunes. Her husband was not very practical, and their joint efforts to make money in America by running a fancy-goods store was a failure. But Frances put her experience to good account in her first book, *Domestic Manners of the Americans* (1832), which gave great offence, after which she wrote over fifty novels and books of travel, which enabled her to maintain her family. Anthony Trollope was one of her children.

12(TN). Catherine Grace Frances GORE (1799–1861) started writing in 1824 and produced at least one book a year until her death. Her works were immensely popular in her day and one of them, *Cecil*, was successfully reprinted in 1927.

13(TN). Mrs Shilly can only refer to Mary Shelley, the daughter of Mary Wollstonecraft and William Godwin, who married Percy Bysshe Shelley in 1816. In 1839, seventeen years after his death, she brought out the first complete edition of his poems and this book was probably being advertised when Flora was in England. It looks very much as if Flora has attributed the husband's poems to his wife – but there is no reason why we should expect Flora to be well-read in foreign literature: her taste inclined more to art and architecture. It is unlikely that she had read many of the books she mentions, with the exception, of course, of Mary Wollstonecraft's splendid *Vindication of the Rights of Woman* which she passionately admired.

14(TN). Mary WOLLSTONECRAFT (1759–1797) had an unsettled childhood as her father moved the family around England and Wales in an attempt to make a living at farming. They eventually settled in London and after trying to run a school Mary became a governess, but she was dismissed within a year as her charges loved her better than their mother. Then she took up work as literary adviser and translator before beginning to write herself. Her first book, *Original Stories from Real Life*, appeared in 1791 and her great work, *A Vindication of the Rights of Woman* in 1792. Against the accepted notion of women as decorative and full of guile, she sets a nobler concept of woman as an intelligent, independent and active force. Mary was tremendously inspired by events in France, and in 1793 she went to Paris to observe the progress of the Revolution. She planned to write a historical and moral review of the French Revolution, but only one volume was published. In trying to live according to her belief that a woman should be free to love where she pleased, she was tragically unfortunate in the man on whom she chose to bestow her love. Gilbert Imlay deserted her and her child, as a crowning insult offered her money – which she scornfully refused. She was driven to despair and tried to drown herself; a waterman dragged her from the Thames. It was when she had recovered her will to live that she met William Godwin and inspired in him an unexpected and genuine passion. Mary became pregnant and they decided to marry, but she died in giving birth to her daughter also called Mary and remembered as the author of *Frankenstein* (1818).

15(FT). This precept follows the law of Moses: since then, humanity has come under the law of Jesus.

SKETCHES

∽ I ∾

Clubs

In England material interests are wonderfully quick to bring men together. Every kind of commercial enterprise – the exploitation of mines, the construction of railways, the settling of colonies and so on – soon unites a considerable number of people who need no other motive but the prospect of the benefits they hope to reap; and it is the sheer magnitude of these benefits rather than the political, moral or religious utility of the undertaking which decides them. Thus, without any mutual acquaintance, liking or respect, and without a single political or religious principle in common, they all sign the same register, where names from every party and sect are to be seen, and the love of gain alone is sufficient to ensure harmony in this heterogeneous company. This spirit of co-operation (I will not say community) extends to the smallest details, as is shown by the numerous London clubs: magnificent mansions in which are concentrated all the material advantages that association has to offer.[1]

I visited several clubs in the vicinity of St James's, Pall Mall and Carlton Terrace; it is impossible to imagine anything more comfortable and luxurious. The entrance is fit for a king's palace: spacious vestibules heated by hot-water pipes, superb double staircases adorned with statues, furnished with fine carpets and lit by a hundred gas-lamps; on the ground floor, enormous dining-rooms overlooking splendid gardens; on the first floor, magnificent drawing-rooms up to eighty feet long. In nearly every room French windows open onto terraces which in summer contain tubs full of beautiful flowers. No effort has been spared to make a stay here agreeable: all the mirrors – so costly in England – are of colossal dimensions; the library offers a collection of all the books most generally read, and the club provides all the English newspapers, the latest magazines and sometimes French and other foreign journals as well. Subscriptions are between eight and twenty pounds per annum, and any member is free to lunch there, read the papers or a novel, attend to his correspondence, change his clothes (several have their own rooms), relax by the fire after a day on the Exchange, and finally eat dinner. Now it is well known that for every Englishman his chief concern, not to say the purpose of his existence, is his dinner. There is no reasonably well-appointed club that does not have a French cook in charge of the kitchen. The chef (for the culinary artist retains the grandiose title he has on the other side of the Channel) is the very soul of the establishment, and at the club one invariably dines very well indeed: the cuisine is French, the Sauternes and champagne of the best quality and the prices very reasonable. So much for the great material benefits to be gained from a common interest; now to examine the intellectual results.

What do they do, the two or three hundred members of a club? Do they earnestly seek to be enlightened on important social questions? Do they discuss business, politics, literature, drama or the fine arts? Not at all. They go there to eat well, drink good wine, play cards and escape from the tedium of the home; they come to seek a refuge from the tribulations of the day, not to submit to the fatigue of a prolonged discussion on any subject that may arise. Besides, with whom could they converse? They do not know one another; membership of a club does not entail any obligation to speak to one's fellow members or even to acknowledge their presence. Everybody enters the public rooms with his hat on his head, looks neither to left nor to right and does not greet a soul. There is nothing more comical than the sight of a hundred or so men disposed about the enormous rooms like so much furniture. One sits in an armchair reading a new pamphlet; another writes at a table next to a man he has never spoken to in his life; yet another is stretched out on a sofa fast asleep. Some pace up and down while others, so as not to disturb the sepulchral silence, converse in whispers as if they were in church. What pleasure can they find in such company? I asked myself as I watched them. They all looked so bored. Astonished at such a singular mode of association, I imagined I was looking at a collection of automata. I inquired of the Englishman with me why there was not more contact between the members of a club. 'What!' he exclaimed, 'Would you have me speak to a man I do not know and of whom I know nothing; would you have me risk offending his pride or his opinions without thought of the consequences, when he might be rich or poor, Tory, Whig or Radical? Only the French could behave with such imprudence!'

'But why,' I persisted, 'do you accept people here when you do not know them?'

'Because a club must have a certain number of subscriptions in order to cover its expenses, and we are perfectly satisfied that a man is respectable if he has been proposed by two members of the club and accepted by the committee.'

This reply is a perfect illustration of the English mentality; Englishmen always seek to obtain material advantages from association; but do not ask them to join together for the sake of their ideas, feelings or principles, for they will not understand you. There is something frightening about this spiritual inertia, this social materialism.

English clubs make men more selfish and aloof. They serve as gaming-houses, literary salons and restaurants; if they did not exist men would go into society more often or spend more time in the bosom of the family. Clubs are the cause of many domestic troubles: husbands desert the home, leaving their poor wives to dine alone upon a piece of beef which must last them a week, while these gentlemen go off to their clubs to eat sumptuous dinners, drink expensive wines and lose their money at the gaming-tables. When I left London in 1839 there was talk of setting up clubs for the use of unmarried men, where members could go and live as bachelors. . . .

NOTES

1(TN). It was in the first part of the nineteenth century that the gentlemen's clubs began to move into splendid new premises designed by the foremost architects of their day and acquire their distinctive character. The various Service clubs sprang up at the end of the Napoleonic Wars to cater for the large numbers of officers arriving in the capital. Several distinguished political clubs already existed, of which the two best-known were White's and Brooks's in St James's Street, and they were joined by the Carlton (1831) and the Reform (1834) in Pall Mall, representing respectively the Tory and the Whig interests. Among the literary and artistic clubs the Athenaeum in Waterloo Place, designed by Decimus Burton in 1831, was the most impressive, while a more overtly social club was the Travellers' (1819) which moved into its new home designed by Charles Barry (later to be selected as the architect of the new Houses of Parliament) in 1832. Perhaps this was one of the clubs in Pall Mall that Flora visited. She says that in 1839 there was talk of setting up a club for bachelors only: the Bachelors' Club was established in 1881.

Pockets

I truly believe that it is not necessary to understand the language of a country in order to divine its morals: they are revealed by outward signs, above all by habits of dress.

As opinions, morals, customs and fashions all proceed naturally from original causes and are expressed in actions and in material things, I maintain that there is no aspect of a nation that cannot be understood by close and thoughtful observation, without the help of its written or spoken language. When written evidence is all we have left, everything else — opinions, events, objects — are just as if they had never existed. Consider the Arc de Triomphe, the obelisk of Luxor, the church of the Madeleine, the Chamber of Deputies, the Tuileries, the Champs Elysées, the fountains, the monuments which personify the cities of France, and the whole of the Place de la Concorde: would you not say that they are the expression of a race avid for every kind of glory, lovers of war, poetry and the arts? Do they not tell of the marvels of its history and industry, the discoveries of its scholars, the genius and talents of its artists? Whereas the maze of dirty narrow streets which covers Paris is testimony enough that its people care more for national glory and artistic masterpieces than for the comforts of life.

Matters of dress are not dictated by the climate alone; a host of circumstances, customs and beliefs combine to modify them. If the *burnous* or hooded mantle of the Arabs reflects the nomadic habits of people who live in a hot country, if the uniformity of costume in the East confirms the unchanging nature of oriental thought, belief and custom, so too can the movement of ideas in Europe and the length of their influence be measured by the duration of the fashions that reflect them. In France the abandonment of the sword and the universal adoption of the frock-coat announced the triumph of equality before the principle was acknowledged in our institutions. Every phase of the Revolution, war and peace, successes and reversals, had its particular style of dress, and not only do religious sects, political parties and schools of philosophy proclaim their identity by their costume, but the physical and moral diseases afflicting a country may be recognised by the same sign. In France, the inroads made by cholera doubled the consumption of flannel, while in England, tailors make the pockets of men's coats so that they open from *underneath* the coat-tails; the only country where this is done!

I had not thought of an explanation for so inconvenient a practice, but on noticing the irritation this eccentric fashion was causing one of my English acquaintances, I asked him the reason for it. 'What! can you not guess?' he replied. 'If our back pockets opened on the outside as they do in Paris, we should lose four or five handkerchiefs every day. Our light-fingered friends still manage to rob us of a few, but this precaution saves us a good many.' Then I recalled my visit to Field Lane, and I began to look for a reason why England should have more thieves than any other country in Europe.

The climate, the food and the social atmosphere spread such total apathy that in order to escape it the English take to drink, travel, indulge in every excess, and frequently do the most bizarre things. This need for excitement which so often leads them to hazard their fortunes at cards, expose themselves to danger, make long perilous journeys or go away to sea etc., also makes them defy the law and set themselves against society through their crimes of robbery and violence. Laziness and aversion to the monotony of their daily work lead them to break the law, it is true, but hunger and the desire to gratify their passions are the chief reasons why they commit crimes as well as the chief reasons why they work.

The moralists of antiquity and the Fathers of the Church

all preached the virtues of resignation and disdain for the riches of this world. In England, on the contrary, poverty is not only suspect but is often treated as a crime. Luxury and debauchery abound, and in every profession the ambition is to achieve a position of honour and wealth, no matter how it is come by, so it is hardly surprising if men seek to become wealthy at any price. Under the influence of this sort of morality, a man may as well embrace *the profession of thief* as any other. Nowadays people calculate the chances of being robbed, and it is only a question of time before the robbers and the robbed begin to *take out insurance*: the first against the punishment, the second against the crime!

The Tribulations Of London

> In every age, in every country, it has always been easy
> to establish false reputations, whereas to establish the
> simplest truth is well-nigh impossible.
>
> Rousseau

The English are so boastful and so ready to extol England and its customs wherever they go that it is a foregone conclusion that if you are seeking the comforts of life, England is the only place to stay! This reputation is formally endorsed every day by thousands of respectable gentlemen in every dining-room, in every hostelry and coffee-house throughout France, Germany, Switzerland and Italy. Anybody would think they had left England in order to *mortify the flesh* and not because they were more comfortable on the continent; people who have lived in John Bull's island have a different tale to tell . . . but in the face of so many testimonials, woe betide anyone bold enough to say so!

It is only fitting, in any examination of the advantages and resources a country has to offer, to single out first of all those which cater for intellectual needs, for this is the very barometer by which the progress of a nation is measured.

In England there is no *free* instruction of any kind; the man without money must renounce any hope of cultivating or broadening his mind by acquiring general knowledge.

Access to libraries, museums, churches and scientific collections is very nearly impossible for the working class; the library of the British Museum is to my knowledge the only place where admission is free, and even then it is necessary to produce guarantors, securities, etc. In England every poor man is *ipso facto* a thief. There is no literary institute in

London; foreign newspapers and recent publications are to be found only in the clubs, and there none but members are admitted. It is true that English newspapers may be read in coffee-houses and taverns, but then one has to order food and drink.

There are a number of scientific institutions; however, I know of no free course in any science. The word *gratis* is either a nonsense or it hides a trap for paying twice over, since the clergyman, the professor, the member of Parliament, all make money out of their professions; everything must be paid for, everything is for sale, *gratis* is a *crime*!

The worker is treated like a beast of burden. Hardly anyone spares a thought for his material comfort, to say nothing of his intellectual needs. Nobody even supposes that he might have any; so his sole distraction is drunkenness. For study and the pleasures of the mind, there is not a town in Europe that does not offer its people more resources than London and England.

If we turn to the ordinary comforts of life, we find that here too the country provides them only for people with a well-lined purse. In cities on the continent there are facilities for satisfying all the little needs of social life which are within the reach of those of the slenderest means, but in London the thousand and one little amenities which make life sweeter for everyone, shorten domestic toil, and procure for even the poorest citizen some of the comforts of the rich, thus mitigating the horrors of poverty, are nowhere to be found.

Should you be in a hurry to send a letter and receive a reply, you will not find a commissioner at the nearest street corner to provide you with a messenger for a few pence; should your boots be covered with mud after a long journey, you will not find a single public shoe-black in London; should your affairs detain you in some outlying part of the city, you will find no restaurant where you can lunch or dine, no coffee-house where you can obtain refreshment. The doctor may prescribe baths, but the patient cannot take them in his home, for there are no portable baths in London. In church you must sit through a sermon two hours long upon hard wooden benches; in the boxes at the Italian Opera there are only tiny wooden chairs so uncomfortable and narrow that it would be a veritable penance to have to sit on them for five hours at a stretch. Should you wish to invite the friend you have just met to dinner, the restaurants will have nothing but very ordinary dishes to offer you, and should you express surprise, the proprietor will tell you that if you want a good dinner in London you have to order it the day before. It is the same with everything: in London, unlike Paris, they are never prepared; they need at least twenty-four hours' notice to prepare anything.

And now if I enter an English house in search of domestic comfort, I shall be very disappointed. In England, if a house is fitted out with carpets from hall to attic, if a handsome tea-tray and service adorn the drawing-room table, if the fireplaces all have their sets of shovel and tongs in polished steel, then it is generally agreed that it is fit to show its face to the world and possesses every comfort a well-to-do gentle-man could demand.[1] The drawing-room chairs are awkward, heavy and lumpy; they are uncomfortable to sit upon, as are the chairs in the dining-room. But enough of these two rooms for now: let us go up to the bedroom.

There is no doubt that it is the French, of all people, who have the most refined taste for the comforts of life, and they make the bedroom the prettiest room in the house. How well they understand the sensual delights of solitude, the notion of a place of retreat, of *bueno retiro*! External objects have so much power over us that they often change the whole tenor of our thoughts; pictures, family portraits, a collection of pretty ornaments each with its special memories: all these things awaken in us a host of thoughts and reflections. Whatever one's age, who could not write an entire book under such inspiration? What is more, I am convinced that a dainty bedchamber, prettily furnished and decorated in the manner I have described, makes its owner more sensitive, more appreciative, not to say much tidier. But the English go about things the wrong way; they decorate their drawing-rooms in a style of luxury and harmony while the women sleep in veritable kennels.

An enormous bed occupies the centre of the chamber; a large commode stands in one corner, the table in another, while the dressing-table is set in front of the window, which overlooks a tiny yard (for in London all the bedrooms are at the back of the house and the yards are so narrow that they lack air and light). Five or six chairs piled high with boxes, parcels, shoes etc., stand around the room; gowns, mantles, shawls and hats hang from nails on all four walls in the absence of a clothes-press: this is what an Englishwoman's bedchamber is like! It is difficult to imagine the disorder; a Frenchwoman could not set foot in it without a shudder of disgust. I have travelled a good deal and I may safely say that never have I been more uncomfortable than in an English bedroom.

The English bed sums up to perfection the nature and reality of most things in England. In appearance nothing could be finer! But just lie down on it for a moment and you will think you are lying on a sack of potatoes; that is how soft these feather beds are! And let me conclude with that English cleanliness we hear so much about, for cleanliness certainly counts among the comforts of life. In England one constantly encounters a concern for *outward appearances*: the front door onto the street, the stairs, the fireplace and all its appurtenances, the knives, the dish-covers and everything else on display are all scrubbed and polished until they could not be cleaner. But take care not to set foot in the kitchen or inspect the state of the bedrooms!

Whatever one may hear to the contrary, the arrangement of English houses is very inconvenient. In small households where only one servant is kept, it is impossible to obtain good service because the poor girl is always exhausted; she spends half her days going up and down stairs, for the kitchen is in the basement, the dining-room on the ground floor and the bedrooms on the second or third floor.

But I must stop; I fear I should be accused of exaggeration if I were to enumerate all the trials and tribulations to be found in London. I shall sum up by saying that there is nothing to alleviate the distress of the poor, that the respectable citizen lives a life of constant privation, that even the rich cannot satisfy all their desires – and that the foreigner will search the British metropolis in vain, for he will find no *fried potatoes* or *roast chestnuts*![2]

A TENDENCY TO FRANCOMANIA – However, since 1830 there has been a great change in the people of London. In spite of the efforts of the Tories to revive the ancient hatred for the French, labourers, sailors and working people in general have a great liking for the French and hold them in high esteem.

On my last visit it happened a score of times that I was greeted by a coachman, a servant or a sailor with these words, 'Bond jourre, madame Frenceze': pronounced in the most comical way but always with a friendly smile which clearly showed how glad they were to see me. Whenever they had the opportunity to show me some small courtesy or say something flattering about my nation, I could see that they really meant it. But it is not only the ordinary people who are becoming Francophiles: a number of young people, especially women, judge nothing good or beautiful unless it is French. They learn the French language, read French books and newspapers, dress in French style, have everything sent from Paris, replace their tea with coffee, roast beef with lamb cutlets, beer with wine, feather beds with mattresses; and there are some who even go so far as to transform their bedchamber into a *boudoir à la française*! What is happening is that sensible Englishmen are beginning to realise that up to now the people have been the creatures of the aristocracy, the pack of hounds trained to hunt their prey; now they understand that it is in the interests of the English people to be *united* with a nation whose principles are equality and toleration. In London you no longer hear any of those tall stories which used to be spread among the people to sow seeds of prejudice and revive old scores against us.

The ease and cheapness of communication bring 200,000 English people to France every year: merchants, shopkeepers and workers all come to breathe the fresh air of the continent for a few days and briefly throw off the yoke of servitude that the proud aristocracy imposes upon its servants. In France there is no arrogance to offend them and they become conscious of their human dignity. They learn from their own observations that the French are well-dressed and eat very good meat, and that the women are not ugly and dirty, as Goldsmith claimed in order to please his patrons: a lie that dishonoured both his poverty and his genius.[3]

The railways from Paris to Calais and from Dover to London could enhance the well-being of our two peoples in moral as well as material respects. Oh! the railways, the railways! In them I see the means whereby every base attempt to prevent the growth of union and brotherhood will be utterly confounded. Let people unite and share their thoughts: let them exchange their various talents as they now exchange material goods, and quarrels between nations will become impossible. It is always the leaders who provoke strife. The people, who have to pay the price of war with their blood and sweat, ask only to live in peace!

NOTES

1(FT).   Here I am speaking only of the moderately wealthy, for the rich aristocracy and financiers combine great luxury with all the refinements known to the voluptuary.

2(TN).   There is no reason to accuse Flora of exaggeration, though some of her complaints deserve comment. **Food** and **drink**: what few restaurants there were seem to have been in the

West End and were not suitable for a lady to enter. But particularly during the winter months there was an astonishing variety of hot and cold food and drink for sale in the streets, including roast chestnuts, hot baked potatoes and fried fish, though perhaps no fried potatoes. **The messenger service**: apparently in Paris this was an organised business, whereas in London it was up to the individual to hire a messenger or porter, or entrust a servant with the errand. But there was always the postal system, which had existed since 1680 and was both quick and efficient. Up to 1846 the GPO used bellmen to patrol the streets and collect letters, thus saving people the trouble of taking them to the nearest receiving-house. **Personal cleanliness**: in the 1830s it was not customary to take a bath; only eccentrics – like the Duke of Wellington – took a cold bath every day. Even at the universities and the schools where gentlemen sent their sons, men and boys washed at an outside pump in all weathers. Only the very wealthy had fixed baths in their homes, and it was not until later in the century that middle-class families adopted the habit of trooping down to the back kitchen once a week to take a bath in a zinc tub, or that ladies began to indulge in a warm bath taken before their bedroom fire. The use of soap was a late addition to the ritual: it was certainly not a part of one's ablutions in the 1830s, which explains why Flora makes a point of mentioning the soap given to prisoners in Coldbath (see Chapter IX note 18). Doctors prescribed baths for medical reasons; the practice of 'taking the waters' was centuries old. In Paris, water-sellers carried portable baths with them on their rounds, and over a thousand were duly recorded and licensed in 1838. **Standards of comfort**: people were beginning to display their affluence by filling their houses with solid, pretentious and uncomfortable furniture, a practice which started with the downstairs rooms and gradually spread to the bedrooms. In Regency times, clothes were still kept in a press and stored horizontally; the hanging wardrobe was not in general use until much later in the century, so if you had no clothes-press, you hung your gowns on hooks or nails around the walls as Flora reports. She had very little money and always stayed in run-down neighbourhoods for preference; her very first visit to England had been in the capacity of lady's companion, so what she experienced was probably a fair sample of what people of no account had to accept. Changes were on the way, and later in the century there was a deliberate effort to imitate the French in matters of comfort, cleanliness and cooking, but in 1839 it was early days: Queen Victoria had been on the throne only two years and the Victorian age had hardly begun. **Entertainment**: this was a poor time for the theatre, and Flora devotes a whole chapter to its shortcomings in her edition of 1840. Covent Garden and Drury Lane were the only two theatres licensed to put on serious drama; the numerous other theatres showed melodramas, vaudeville and a variety of hybrid and spectacular attractions. Her Majesty's Theatre (formerly the King's Theatre) in the Haymarket was the home of the Italian Opera, then under the management of a Frenchman, Laporte, and it is interesting to speculate whether Flora, who loved Rossini, might have seen the famous soprano Pauline Viardot make her London début in Rossini's *Otello* in 1839 – an experience which might have compensated for the discomfort of the seating.

3(TN). Goldsmith made his disparaging remarks about the French in one of his *Chinese Letters* published in 1760, purporting to record a Chinese traveller's impressions of English society, and obviously not intended to be taken too seriously. What particularly upset Flora was the insinuation that the French ate no meat and had no shirts to their backs, and that their women were so pale and sickly that they were obliged to wear rouge, which made their skin wrinkled so that they began to look old and faded at twenty-five. Goldsmith was not noted for his powers of observation nor for his veracity, but whatever his motives for writing as he did, he could at least claim some acquaintance with France. As a poor student he had begged his way through the country sometime in the 1750s, thirty years before the French Revolution. Flora's source for Goldsmith's allegation about the French is once again Marshal Pillet.

IV

The Idleness of the Old and the Enforced Activity of the Young

From birth to death Man feels the need to act and to acquire knowledge, the need to exercise his physical, intellectual and moral faculties; to understand what binds him to his fellows and to God. Of course these faculties gradually develop, reach their peak and then decline, but at every stage of his life he suffers when they are not in use. If one excepts his earliest infancy and final decrepitude, man in his normal state always has sufficient strength and intelligence to provide for his needs, and if he becomes a burden on society it is because society has not yet learned how to organise labour.

There are both moral and economic considerations in the employment of persons of every age. From the moral point of view, the idleness of old age is paradoxically enough one of the most active causes of corruption. When an old man is cast aside, when he has nothing to occupy his mind or body and no social obligations to fulfil, his character inevitably deteriorates; for whether we are old or young, we cannot endure a life totally devoid of emotion.

In England men are generally driven out of every profession and trade when they reach the age of forty, and there are many in which nobody over thirty is employed. In France persons of forty and over make up thirty per cent of the population; the figure is lower in England because the English do not live so long, but it has been stated that a fifth of the urban population there is nearly always unemployed *solely on account of age*. If you calculate the enormous loss the country sustains by leaving such a considerable number idle, you will understand one of the principal reasons for the impoverishment of England.

Every age has its qualities: the steadfastness and reliability of maturity are sometimes more valuable than the quickness of youth. Older men are less likely to allow their minds to wander and be distracted from their work, more likely to finish their appointed task on time. At any age, then, a man who is not totally incapacitated could be employed for the good of his country if only he could be found work he was able to perform.

But nowadays we see that far from seeking to solve this problem, employers will engage only young people or even children. In certain occupations this choice is due to the attraction exercised by the young, for nobody wants to have old people waiting on them, and in no household will you encounter any male or female servant over the age of thirty. But in agricultural or factory work, it is much more likely to be cruel calculation that determines the preference for children, for their labour is cheaper than men's, and if he keeps a close watch on them the employer can get more work out of them, considering the paltry sum he pays the parents for the hire of their children.[1] These long unbroken days of toil leave the poor ailing little creatures exhausted, sap their strength, ruin their health and condemn them to an early grave. What does it matter? The employer knows that children are tractable and in no position to argue, so he can maltreat them with impunity. In short, the use of children is profitable for the industrialist and for the nation. So the hypocritical speeches made by certain members of the House and the laws voted in Parliament were not intended to put a stop to the oppression and murder of children, but merely to give an appearance of humanitarianism, for the laws have done nothing to change the state of affairs.[2]

In England children enter counting-houses and shops between the ages of ten and twelve, and factories at five or six.[3] You see young men between sixteen and twenty years of age at the head of commercial establishments transacting important business and responsible for cargoes worth several million pounds. The reason is simple: English trade owes its immense development to the export of huge quantities of goods. In every part of the globe there are English trading-posts, and some firms have such extensive interests that the owner could never hope to manage them all himself. Some merchants own several large factories in the industrial regions while they themselves stay in London or Liverpool and export the products of these factories. The consequence of this commercial system is that England needs a larger number of trustworthy agents than any other country.

Now in England men are too experienced in business to believe that a man of *thirty* could still be *honest*. Hardly a man among them reaches that age without having lost all his scruples. Personal gain soon becomes his only consideration, his unique rule of conduct, and he behaves honourably only when it suits his interests. The way things are going it will soon be impossible to find, even among children of twelve, anyone still innocent of duplicity and fraud, anyone whose conscience has not been silenced by the corrupting example before him. It is obvious how uncertain the prosperity of a country must be when it is exposed not only to the idleness and poverty of a large working class, but also to the rapid growth of corruption practised as a means of government and a sure road to wealth – corruption on such a colossal scale that it starts at the top of the social ladder and descends right down to the lowest classes.

Only young men are to be seen in administrative posts, and already they have few scruples left. Not a man among them does not reckon to double his salary at the very least by exacting charges known as *fees*, a practice which up to now the law has been powerless to prevent. But the same rapacity is found in every class: the verger pursues you in church demanding shillings, the servant holds out his hand as you rise from his master's table after dinner, the lawyer sends you a bill for six shillings for writing a letter of as many lines on your behalf or for replying yes or no to the question you put to him in the street. The bishops, all so richly endowed, *sell* everything that lies within their jurisdiction: nominations to livings, the allotment of church pews, and so on. Every man who holds an official post or sits in one of the two Houses of Parliament and has either a vote or an assent to grant, *sells* it for as high a price as he can. All the people employed by the East India Company, even those with the smallest salaries, return with huge fortunes, thanks to *fees*.

In London you see very few old men from the poorer classes. One day I remarked on this fact to an Englishman and he replied disdainfully, 'We do not like old people here and nobody wants to employ them.'

At the other extreme, children of eight or nine are made to work. It is children between the ages of ten and fourteen who are responsible for the postal service in London; others have the job of inspecting the sewers. The police are all young men: they are not accepted if they are over thirty, and I am told that not one is retained after the age of forty-five.

So when a man has worked from the age of eight to the age of forty-five in London or any other town in England, he is dismissed from every kind of employment and has to retire to the country, find some other job and try to make do on less money. But there too he is often refused work; then he has to fall back on the meagre resources of the parish, and, weakened by poverty and hunger, crushed by despair, he dies with his heart full of hatred for mankind.

The universal English practice of putting children to work from the tenderest age transforms the whole of the working population into *machines*, some for copying out columns of figures and business letters, others for spinning cotton, stitching leather, forging iron, filing metal, and so on. They all perform their task as if the faculty were innate, but outside this speciality their intelligence is totally undeveloped, so they are as ignorant of the rest of life as if they did not belong to the human race. They have never had time to read a book or extend their knowledge, so they cannot discuss any matter beyond their trade. That explains why they all drink so much and why their conversation is so intolerably boring.

NOTES

1(FT).   See M Buret's book for what he has to say about child labour in the factories.

2(FT).   For these different laws, the discussion they aroused in English parliamentary committees, and how they worked in practice, see the report in *Le Moniteur* on the debate on the law concerning child labour in factories, which took place in both French Chambers during the session of 1840.

3(FT).   'Child labour in the English coal-mines'. This is what *La Phalange* of 22 July 1842 had to say about the report which Lord Ashley presented to Parliament on the conditions of coal-miners in England, Scotland and Ireland:

> The work formerly imposed on children in factories is more like play beside the work they have to do in the mines. In Staffordshire they commonly go down the mines at the age of nine, sometimes even between seven and eight. In Shropshire they sometimes start work at the age of six. The report states that some children who had not yet reached that age were seen dragging loads attached to a belt around their waists.
>
> In Warwickshire, Leicestershire, Derbyshire, Yorkshire, Lancashire and Cheshire, they start work at the same age. In Halifax they are roused from their beds between four and five in the morning all year round to go down the mines. In Oldham – who would believe it! – the poor litle creatures have to work in the mines *at the age of four*! (I cannot conceive what sort of work can be got out of such young children!) Dr Mitchell, who stated that in Durham children sometimes start work at the age of five, is convinced that the owners of the large coal-mines there are unaware that such things happen.

To get some idea of the plight of these poor creatures, it must be realised that the tunnels where they are employed, with no regard for the weakness of their age or *their sex*, are often very narrow, airless, and extremely humid; that it is quite normal for

281

these little children to work *with their feet in the water*, while more water drips down upon their heads. Women are employed for the most part in dragging enormous loads of coal over long distances. The report describes how they are harnessed by means of chains to take these loads as far as the place where they can be lifted out of the pit. Old age sets in at thirty for these poor women; the children they bring into the world rarely survive more than a few days; they are subject to spinal diseases and to asthma, which has often started by the time they are eight, and which in many cases causes their death. By the time they are forty, the *majority* of men and women, even the strongest, are quite unfit to continue working. Generally it is at the *lowest levels* of the mine, where the men refuse to go, that women are forced to work. So it is from the *weaker* sex that employers demand the *most*.

(*La Phalange* was the organ of Fourierism (see Chapter I note 5) and was edited by Flora's good friend Victor Considérant. The government report mentioned is Lord Ashley's report of 1842 on the employment of women and children in the mines, which shocked public opinion so deeply that the Mines Act was passed in the same year, prohibiting the employment of women below ground and the employment of boys under the age of ten. (In 1872 the age was raised to twelve, and in 1903 to thirteen.)

Lord Ashley (1801–1885) who became the Earl of Shaftesbury in 1851, was a tireless worker for the reform of conditions in factories and mines, but like Robert Owen, he had the frustrating experience of seeing his proposed measures always rejected, delayed or watered down. It was in 1833 that he introduced the Ten Hours Bill (to reduce working hours) in Parliament, but it was not finally passed until 1847. After Ashley resigned his seat he spent the rest of his life working for the establishment of schools, and for forty years he was president of the Ragged Schools Union. He also founded working men's institutes.

The point about all the attempts to improve conditions for the workers is not that the reformers – inside and outside Parliament – were insincere, but rather that the owners of factories and mines did not implement the reforms, and there were not enough inspectors to see that the new laws were enforced. Besides, even after the horrifying revelations of the 1842 report, there were still many people throughout the country who felt that it was not the business of the government to come between the employer and his workers: TN.)

V

A Word on Art in England

Art[1] can make no progress in any country unless it reaches
every class of society. The artist needs to be inspired by the
enthusiasm aroused by his work, and while it may be true
that some people are born with a love of the arts and the dis-
cernment of the connoisseur, nevertheless almost everybody
is capable of acquiring these gifts. But how can a taste for
great art spread in a country where the individual is judged
by the place where he lives, the servants he keeps and the
money he spends? What inspiration can the artist receive
from the world around him in a country where personal
merit has no value or right to any consideration unless it is
accompanied by great wealth? Let Horace Vernet, Scheffer,
Delacroix, Pradier or Marochetti[2] go to London, take lodgings in one of the little streets in the neighbourhood of
Leicester Square on the second floor of a modest house and
go about on foot or by omnibus, and society may call on
them once but never again. A sometime Venetian courtesan
will be received with perfect politeness if she has an income
of fifty thousand francs, a fine carriage, and servants in rich
livery to support her claim to the title of princess; but if one
of our celebrated artists walks down Regent Street in a
threadbare coat and faded hat, he will be treated to the ultimate discourtesy of having his greeting totally ignored. The
Englishman is brought up to despise poverty, which is why
he has no nobility of soul; his self-esteem is founded solely
on his wealth, and he has a profound horror of anything that
smacks of poverty. Even to show signs of financial straits is a
badge of shame in his eyes. So we can see why England so
rarely produces great artists, for there a man does not begin
by acquiring a talent, as he would in France, for what would
be the good? Talent is not considered important. It is the

means, not the end, and to foster it would be contrary to accepted custom, as good as condemning oneself never to be anything but a hired worker. No, first of all a man must work to acquire a fortune, then he may cultivate art, if he still has the strength to do so. The young Englishmen who become artists without first amassing a fortune to proclaim their worth, are condemning themselves to exercise their talent outside their native land.

How can art develop in a country where such conditions prevail? How can it flourish in a people whose every instinct tends towards material things? Of all the countries in Europe, England is a veritable Siberia as far as art is concerned.

This is the sort of esteem they have for art in England. I quote from the *Quarterly Journal of Agriculture*, which raises Robert Bakewell above Michelangelo:

> Now boast if you like about Michelangelo and the other makers of statues, all those artists who model in bronze and stone; but is not Bakewell also a great sculptor and artist? He sculpts life itself and takes bullocks in place of blocks of stone; he goes further than those who merely create in the image of God, for he *recreates* the work of God itself; he does not handle, as others do, dead inert matter with no reaction or resistance, but active limbs which must be carved from living flesh, modelled in blood, sinews, movement and strength of will.[3]

Bakewell had a rare gift of observation and was responsible for very great progress in rural economy – but only an Englishman could compare his talent with the genius of the artist.

Protestantism has chosen to employ the art of words alone to propagate its doctrines; and in the countries where it has become established, the other faculties God gave us have remained dormant. The use of the imagination to describe impressions and excite the emotions has been restricted to what words alone can express, in the same way as Islam, the great sixth-century manifestation of Protestantism, confined the rich imagination of the Orient to the recording of chronicles and tales; the fine arts disappeared from the countries which had been their cradle, and soon the language of art ceased to be understood and the allegorical significance of the various forms of Greek art became as unintelligible as hieroglyphics.

The monuments of the Middle Ages which still survive in England demonstrate how far the imagination had developed by that time; with the help of the chronicles it is still possible to understand medieval thought, whereas if we turn to modern buildings we encounter borrowings from every period of architecture, a bizarre medley of every style, lacking in harmony and thought alike. The public buildings, all on a colossal scale, answer their purpose well enough, and this is all one can say in their favour; one looks in vain for anything memorable, evocative, graceful – this is the plain garb of the Quakeress, not the elegant costume of the Parisienne.

The churches, theatres and institutes of learning are no more than commercial speculations: England has forgotten the language of art. In her churches there is no music capable of lifting the soul towards God, no paintings to depict the drama and moral eloquence of the Bible, no statues of Moses and Christ, the Virgin Mary and the Magdalen, Ambrose, Augustine or Hildebrand. In the theatres there is not one fresco or bas-relief to illustrate the customs and dress of former centuries or commemorate the gods and heroes of the drama in ancient or in modern times. The academies make no attempt to evoke in their decoration any of the great perennial problems which preoccupy the human mind; their students do not strive to interpret revelations or the expression of the divine will any more than they try to appreciate the pleasures of the theatre. Mathematical reason has prevailed, it has annihilated everything; ideas are expressed in numbers, thoughts in geometrical figures.

The *lingua franca* spoken by the Mediterranean peoples is a patchwork of all idioms, and it gives some idea of the architectural Babel one encounters in London. Let the foreigner with a mind to appreciate English taste and sense of harmony go to Trafalgar Square before visiting any of the national exhibitions; at the sight of all these buildings and monuments piled up in this square he will have a very good idea of the chaos there is in their art!

The Queen's palace is a mean, dull, graceless building, its architecture entirely lacking in originality, so that your first thought is that you must have seen it somewhere before. It is too small for a royal residence, so the big receptions have to be held at the old St James's Palace. The small triumphal arch – erected rather late in the day – completely hides the front of the palace: it is a copy of the one by Carrousel.[4] The collection at the National Gallery in Pall Mall is hardly outstanding, but it contains a few of the great masters: Rembrandt, Leonardo da Vinci, Rubens, Teniers, Sebastiano del Piombino, Van Dyck, Poussin, an admirable Murillo, an apocryphal Raphael, and some truly beautiful Claude Lorrains, as well as the Hogarths, Wilkies, Lawrences, etc.

The rich man feels the emptiness of wealth and envies the artist his fame and his exciting life. Having attained the very height of opulence, the English aristocracy looked back with regret on the spirit of poetry which animated the lives of their ancestors and turned their jealous gaze towards Italy, France and Flanders. Since the beginning of the last century, proud noblemen and *parvenus* have been prepared to pay high prices for European works of art. England contains some of the largest and most valuable collections of antiquities and modern masterpieces, but as they are nearly always inaccessible for artists to study they cannot influence the progress of art in any way.

In the picture galleries of English noblemen one often encounters copies – sometimes very mediocre – of works attributed in the catalogue to such great names as Leonardo, Raphael, Domenichino, Velazquez, Murillo, Le Sueur, Poussin, Rubens, Teniers, etc. The owners stubbornly insist that they are originals and take offence if one dares to question their authenticity. It makes no difference whether they have paid enormous sums for these daubs themselves or whether they have inherited them from their fathers, they seem to feel instinctively that a knowledge of art is an infallible sign of superiority. It is at such moments that the spectacle of wealth and rank combined with ignorance is so painful to behold: one suffers for the reputation of the great masters whose works are locked away, deprived of the homage of the public and unable to excite the enthusiasm and the emulation of the artist. Oh! then one feels contempt for the wealthy who, like veritable gaolers, keep genius imprisoned!

NOTES

1(FT).   In any country, art is so vast a subject that in order to understand its present state, one must trace its history, and this is what I would have done for English art, once I had undertaken to discuss it; but then I would have had to spend a great deal of time in England and devote at least a whole volume to such an important subject; therefore my aim here is merely to indicate some of the moral causes which restrict art in England.

(Later in this sketch Flora mentions the National Gallery in Pall Mall. The National Gallery we know was opened in 1838; before that, the collection was housed at 100 Pall Mall. Once again it seems that Flora is drawing on her experiences of an earlier visit to London, either in 1831 or 1835: TN.)

2(TN).   These were the five most celebrated artists of their day. Delacroix, the leader of the Romantic movement in painting, towers above them all. His were huge canvases in glowing colours and his early paintings of contemporary events in Greece aroused sympathy for the Greek patriots in their struggle for independence from Turkey. Horace Vernet was famous for his battle scenes; Ary Scheffer painted historical subjects; Pradier was the most fashionable sculptor of his day, responsible for the sculptures representing the cities of Lille and Strasbourg in the Place de la Concorde; and Marochetti sculpted the battle of Jemappes on the Arc de Triomphe.

3(FT). 'Having learned from experience that the larger breeds of cattle are not the most suitable for fattening, and that it costs a considerable amount for fodder to fill them out, he set to work to produce a smaller-boned but fleshy animal to answer the stockbreeders' needs: an animal with supple hide, exceedingly small head and frame, slightly cylindrical body, a broad and well-developed space between the haunches, an ample chest to give full scope to the lungs, and short legs. But this is not all: he succeeded in getting the choicest and tastiest parts of the animal to develop to an extraordinary degree, concentrating its intake of nourishment upon those particular parts by means of skilfully applied massage and lotions. In this way he managed to increase the volume of the lumbar and dorsal muscles, which form what we call the chine, or fillet. To sum up, Bakewell's results can be expressed in this way: from a carcase yielding 350 clear kilos of meat, he succeeded in producing 210 kilos of superior roasting quality and only 140 kilos of the inferior cuts, whereas previously these quantities were in inverse proportion. Once he had achieved a fair measure of success in shaping the animal to his liking, Bakewell made up his mind to tackle another problem which seemed more difficult to resolve. He had already recognised that for non-working animals, the horns serve no useful purpose; they represent the means of attack or defence, and often cause appalling accidents. Bakewell therefore wanted to ensure that the descendants of the new breed he had created would be hornless, and eventually he succeeded in solving this challenging problem.'

La Phalange, 15 January 1840

(Robert BAKEWELL (1725–1795), the agriculturist, took over the management of the Dishley estate in Leicestershire in 1760 and set about improving the breed of sheep and cattle. His methods were so successful that he acquired an international reputation as a stockbreeder, and it is clear that the French source that Flora quotes was just as enthusiastic about his achievements as the *Quarterly Journal of Agriculture*: TN.)

NOTES

4(TN).   This was Marble Arch, erected in 1828 and intended as a triumphal gateway. But the state coach was too broad to pass through the centre arch, so the whole monument was moved in 1848 to its present site north of Hyde Park.

A Trip to Brighton

English stage-coaches have good horses, are very light and carry hardly any baggage; in their construction every allowance is made for speed but none whatever for the convenience and comfort, to say nothing of the safety, of the passengers. I do not think that anywhere in the world is there a more disagreeable and tiring mode of travel than the English stage-coach.

These vehicles have four seats inside and twelve or sixteen on top. The inside seats cost double and are no better or worse than those on continental coaches. You climb onto the roof by means of a ladder and once perched aloft you have to endure the heat or cold in all their intensity; you are exposed to wind, fog, rain, hail, sun and dust, not to mention the constant danger of falling off should sleep overcome you at any hour of the day or night. In my view only the back of a camel in the desert could equal the discomfort of these seats.

I have made several journeys in England, but in order not to bore the reader I shall describe only one – for the aspect of the countryside is intolerably monotonous.

It was the end of August 1839; the weather was sultry and stormy with intermittent showers, like a March day in France. Towards eleven o'clock I made my way to Piccadilly with my baggage; all the trunks, bags and boxes were loaded onto the coach, then we took our places. I was in the third seat of the back row with three people facing me; all the front seats were filled. We were praying that the two remaining seats would stay empty all the way to Brighton, for we were very cramped. Two gentlemen came forward, but on seeing how little room there was, they decided not to climb up. We had left London more than a mile behind us when the coach stopped at a pretty little house and two ladies, one of them enormous, took the two empty seats. Then I was really able to appreciate the pleasure of travelling on an English stage-coach!

We were so cramped that the four people occupying the corner seats had to put one leg over the low iron rail at the end of the bench. Then there were the boxes, packages and baskets which hemmed us in on all sides. Every time it rained, four umbrellas went up and contributed a steady trickle of water to add to the calamity. We were no more comfortable when the sun came out; our position was intolerable! However, our companions on the front seats were complaining even more loudly, for the wind was driving the rain full in their faces, and one poor lady who was with child was so affected that she fainted.

I swear that what I am about to relate is true, although it may seem incredible, as much for the inhumanity this story displays as for the excessive respect for the rights of property shown by those involved.

The coach stopped and the driver and some of the passengers helped the sick woman to get down so that they could attend to her. We profited from the occasion to get down ourselves; the poor woman was in an alarming state. The driver told us that there were only two old ladies inside the coach; they had paid for all four places so that their dogs could have two of them, and he thought that perhaps if they were asked they might allow the sick woman to join them. Neither he nor anyone else dared to take the necessary step, so aloof is one person from another in England, and so much does the respect for property outweigh the respect for humanity! One gentleman thought that if I, a foreigner, were to approach the two ladies, I should run less risk of being rebuffed; he was obviously hoping that national pride would prevent them from displaying English egotism in all its nakedness; however, the two ladies, well aware of what was happening, had removed their dogs from view, closed the windows, and were pretending to be asleep. I had been watching them from the beginning of this little scene and had not missed one of their movements. I was quite sure of the response I would receive; nevertheless, I did not hesitate, I went and tapped on the glass; then I knocked hard several times and eventually one window was lowered halfway and a cold voice asked what I wanted.

'Madame,' I said in French, 'I come to beg you to be good enough to do a service to a poor lady who has been taken ill; she is not well enough to stay on top of the coach; permit her to occupy one of your empty seats.'

'Madame,' she replied even more coldly, 'we paid for all four seats because we did not wish to be disturbed, and what you ask is quite impossible.' So saying she brusquely closed the window and sat back in her seat. Everybody was outraged at such inhumanity, but they all said, 'She is within her rights, she has paid.' Miserable creatures! As if the precept of charity did not come before *all rights* and *all laws*! Hearing them speak in this way, I was reminded of the passage in one of the books of Moses: that the man who kills his slave will not be punished, because the slave is his property.[1]

This mishap turned out well for me, as having given up my seat to the sick lady, I found I was more comfortable in hers, although I still suffered from the cold and the wind, but at least I could now stretch my legs and rest my back against a trunk, which had been impossible before. Towards three o'clock the rain stopped, the sky cleared, and I was able to enjoy the superb view.

The English countryside has a rich and fertile aspect; the trees are remarkably beautiful, the hedges thick and vigorous, the meadows wonderfully green. I have never failed to be struck by the number of hedges which surround the fields and from a distance make the whole landscape look like a kitchen garden divided into little plots edged with box; I am aware that the authors of picturesque travel books have waxed eloquent in praise of these verdant walls.

But if you trouble to analyse the effect they produce, you will realise that by their very uniformity they reduce a great kingdom to the dimensions of a flower-bed; what is more, they prevent many acres from being cultivated, and in a country where grain and all the essential foodstuffs are always dear, where so many people die of hunger, and where the parks of the wealthy landowners and the pasture for their thoroughbred horses remove such vast areas from cultivation, the loss of land caused by these hedges seems to me a serious error in rural economy. That is why after I had spent a few moments enjoying the fresh and fragrant country air (small recompense that this is for the dampness of the climate), I could not help thinking of the plight of the people in a country where all the land, with its crop of grain, turnips, potatoes – even the very grass – is shut away behind impenetrable hedges. If the people were not dying of hunger, the fields would be open, and folk could be trusted, as they are in France, not to touch the standing crops, the haystacks and the stores of corn exposed so freely and carelessly to view.[2]

When I first travelled through the English countryside and saw an English village, I thought it must have been newly built, but as I travelled further I saw that all the houses looked just as new and it dawned on me that English peasants must be made to paint and whitewash their cottages every year or two at least. No doubt this cleanliness is all very praiseworthy, and I approve of the care of walls, shutters, doors and gates; but the result is wearisome and monotonous. At the sight of all these 'new' houses you have the impression that you are passing through a country no more than twenty-five years old. You tell yourself that the inhabitants of all these villages cannot have been born there, and if you encounter an old man bent with age, you look about you in vain for any place where that old man could have been born. But the immaculate exterior of the houses is only a façade; the inside is quite a different matter.

We finally reached Brighton at six o'clock in the evening, and considering all I had suffered, I could not help thinking of the discomfort and fatigue that must be endured by those who leave London on the night coach at seven o'clock in the evening and do not reach Brighton until five o'clock the next morning.

NOTES

1(FT).   Exodus, Chapter XXI, verse 21.

2(FT).   In France hedges are hardly ever used, except to enclose gardens, or, in certain places near the sea, to protect fruit trees from the wind.

ᘓᙍ VII ᘜᙍ

The English Puff

The puff[1] is so much a part of English life that one encounters it everywhere; its colours are immediately recognisable. But it is at political processions and in the hurly-burly of elections that it swells to gigantic proportions; then it appears in monstrous and fantastic guise, with brazen looks and lying tongue. Observe Lord Palmerston on the hustings: hear how contemptuously he treats the electors, regaling them with puffs as if he were addressing the House of Commons. Read in the newspapers, which resound with the wrath of the noble lord, of his belligerent ranting, his threats to conquer Syria, Egypt, the Balearic Isles and even the Celestial Kingdom itself! Lord Palmerston, it is true, makes excessive use of the puff, and his language is such as to bring an ironic smile to every face; even so, people in high places have sometimes been taken in by his sort of diplomacy, and for a time his outrageous sayings circulated widely throughout aristocratic drawing-rooms on the continent.

The Englishman, obsessed with the need to appear wealthier than he really is, converses with the foreigner entirely in puffs; it is also to this end that he often spends ten times more than his means permit. But do not suppose that this practice is confined only to financiers, who need to pass as wealthy men so that they can gamble with other people's money. No, the habit is general. Everybody from the shopkeeper to the aristocrat lays claim to a bigger fortune than he possesses and makes up puffs in order to make others believe him. It is the same when Englishmen boast about their national power and wealth. They regard themselves as partners in a company which has fallen on bad times and would be ruined if its credit were to run out, so they may be excused their patriotic puffs when every year

295

they see a decrease in public revenues and a proportional increase in poverty and debt. I have said that in England one encounters the puff everywhere. My readers might perhaps be tempted to make an exception of the Queen. Certainly not! The puff is found in her household just the same as anywhere else. Here I do not intend to allude to the sort of artifice ladies employ in their personal toilet – I did not penetrate that far – but if I am not privy to the secrets of the boudoir, at least I have discovered the secrets of the stables.

I had heard the royal stables praised so highly that I decided to pay them a visit. I found them as mean and shabby as the palace I have already described. Everything one would have expected to be built on a grand scale – yards, stables, saddle-rooms, and so on – are all small and poky. Of course I already knew how cheese-paring the English were, so I was not expecting anything better, but the high reputation England has acquired for training horses[2] and the enormous prices English enthusiasts pay for thoroughbred animals made me hope to find in the Queen's stables the finest collection of horses it was possible to assemble in one place. Alas for my hopes! What I saw, in surroundings of doubtful cleanliness, were eighty perfectly ordinary animals (although two saddle-horses, which only the Queen uses, are quite pretty). Our attention was called to eight light bay horses as representing the very finest in Her Majesty's stables. They are used only in state processions on the very grandest occasions: their colour is good and they are perfectly matched, but the head is hideously ugly (what is known in French stable parlance as a calf's head) and the mouth slack, pale and repulsive in appearance. The groom showed us a richly ornamented bridle designed to *hide* the animal's deformity. To see one of these horses, first with its miraculous bridle, then without, you would not know it was the same animal. The bridle is a puff! Next I admired six truly beautiful black horses; but then, happening to glance in another direction, I caught sight of eight big red, ungainly brutes without tails. I was so shocked by the contrast that I could not repress an exclamation of horror at their extreme ugliness. The groom assured me that if I were to see them harnessed I should find them superb. The gentleman with me understood perfectly and slipped the seductive shilling into the man's hand, whereupon he straightway harnessed one of the horses, fitted it with a luxuriant false tail which swept the ground, added a false mane, and threw over it a saddle-cloth as miraculous for hiding the deformities of *this* horse as the splendid bridle had been for the other. To see these puffs applied to the grooming of the Queen's horses struck me as richly entertaining.

On leaving the stables we went to see the State Coach, which cost us two shillings. I mention this sum only to prove that the servants of Her Majesty are more reasonable than the servants of God, for as everyone knows, it costs anything from twelve to fourteen shillings to be shown over Westminster Abbey or St Paul's. The coach is an enormous, clumsy contraption which cannot weigh less than eight hundred kilos; allegorical figures borrowed from paganism and grouped like grotesques symbolise England's supremacy on land and sea. The whole is covered in gilt and represents the royal puff in all its sublimity! This coach was built for the coronation of George III and is *bullet-proof*, which is still a very precious virtue for a royal conveyance nowadays, although it gives the lie to the official puffs on the devotion of the people to their monarch.

A puff is also the name given to bogus advertisements published as a hoax. *The Times* or some other newspaper announces that Mr or Mrs So-and-So is looking for a clerk, say, or a secretary, tutor, governess or lady companion, and that applicants should call at such and such an address between the hours of two and four. The authors of this notice gather with their friends at the appointed time and watch from the end of the street as the crowd of applicants knock on their victim's door. He is at first mystified and then enraged at being disturbed by a noisy rabble all trying to convince him that he needs their services, and each insisting that he alone is best fitted to fill the vacant place.

Puffs of this kind reveal how callous English society is, and how profoundly indifferent to the fate of the poor. To make sport of the desperate plight of the unemployed in search of work, to find amusement in making them waste their time and money in trying to look presentable and rushing from one end of town to the other – this is nothing short of criminal. For some of these poor people, the loss of a day's work means that they have to go hungry. Suppose they leave an exhausting job in the hope of finding something less demanding, all they succeed in doing is adding to their troubles: they must beg a crust of bread in order to be fit for work on the morrow! To find pleasure in this sort of joke, to enjoy watching people struggle against poverty, to laugh at the tortures of hunger and the agonies of despair, is more than indifference towards one's fellow men, it plumbs the very depths of cruelty. In England a man is *transported* for killing a partridge or a pheasant but he may snatch bread from the mouth of the poor as a joke; and people who want for nothing laugh at this sort of puff!

The puff transforms the financier into a charlatan; we have just seen how it teaches the royal grooms all the tricks of the coquette; it gives anyone with a spare shilling or two for an advertisement the power to harm any number of hard-working people by making them leave their jobs. But if we follow the puff into fashionable society we should have to write volumes to describe the variations of this British phenomenon. We shall confine ourselves to showing it playing a role of comic buffoonery which proves that in this country there is nothing to which people will not stoop in order to ape the nobility and abuse the trust of others.

In the London suburbs there are establishments which I am quite sure exist nowhere else on the surface of the earth, and could only have been conceived by a British brain. The *splashing-houses* I am about to describe illustrate better than anything else the sort of transparent pretence which can take the English in.

A smart young gentleman who possesses neither a grand estate nor a pack of hounds but has some credit with his tailor announces to all his acquaintances that he is going off for a few days' hunting; then he leaves his sumptuous house in the West End, says he will be away for a week or more, and hides himself away in an obscure lodging on the other side of the city. When the time is up, he dresses from head to foot in impeccable hunting-clothes, steps into a cab and is taken to the splashing-house, where for the modest sum of three shillings he has himself *splashed with mud* from head to toe.

These places can provide mud from every county, particularly those renowned for their hunting, and are also equipped with a wooden horse. The servant acting as groom asks in all seriousness whether the gentleman wishes to return from Buckinghamshire, Staffordshire, Derbyshire, Kent, etc. When our young dandy has made his choice he mounts the ingenious mechanical quadruped which raises its legs, paws the ground, trots, and spatters its rider with as much mud as randomly placed as if it were a real horse on a cross-country gallop. At the end of the operation the elegant gentleman parades up and down Bond Street, Regent Street, Piccadilly and Pall Mall with a riding-crop in his hand, so that everybody will believe he has just returned from a superb hunt.[3]

All the extravagant follies the French commit in moments of reckless abandon, the English perform deliberately with a phlegm and gravity that is quite comical; enjoyment is utterly foreign to English recreations, and this feigned revelry is quite simply a calculated performance in which self-interest is nicely balanced with self-esteem. So to see nothing in the characteristic English ritual of the splashing-house but fatuity pushed to the limits of the burlesque would be to fail to understand how great an influence is exerted by the social structure of the country.

In England, the landowners rule the country. Now these

rulers have the ability to spend double their income every year without the slightest risk of ruin, because sinecures and lucrative appointments in India always come to restore their fortunes and ensure that they will endure as long as the Empire itself. This means that tailors, dressmakers, and tradesmen of every kind are eager to extend credit to the landed aristocracy, and cover themselves against risks and losses by putting up their prices and interest rates while they are waiting for their money. Thus it is very important to be able to pass as a member of these ruling classes.

Individual aristocrats with a right to a title are generally so well known that nobody would dare to impersonate them, but their family names are found in every class of society, so if our young rake happens to bear an old Derbyshire name, there are people sufficiently credulous to take the mud so liberally splashed all over him as visible proof that he is indeed a Derbyshire landowner, and in this way he exploits their credulity. He borrows, spends and runs up enormous bills in his town house, marries a rich heiress and obtains a government appointment; or he quits the scene, retires to the country, takes refuge on the continent, or ends up in prison.

NOTES

1(TN). The word 'puff' is defined in the *Shorter Oxford Dictionary* as 'undue or inflated commendation; an extravagantly laudatory advertisement or review of a book, a performer or performance, a tradesman's goods, or the like' (1732). The practice was satirised in Sheridan's play *The Critic* in the person of Mr Puff, who makes a living from writing puffs of every description. Flora uses the word as a blanket term to cover every manifestation of English pretension, hypocrisy and imposture that comes her way.

2(FT).   In England they care far more for the schooling of horses than the schooling of men. For a comparison of the two, see the little English pamphlet *Care (for) Men as well as Horses, and all will thrive*.

3(TN).   I have been unable to discover whether splashing-houses ever in fact existed; perhaps somebody was playing on Flora's credulity.

The Iron Spoon

The fountain reveals the hand of Providence: no other creation in nature evokes such pleasant, graceful flights of fancy;
nowhere else in the leafy grove is poetic and religious inspiration so intense. It sustains the birds of the air and the denizens of the forest. There the shepherd leads his flock to
drink, there the young girl comes to draw water, there she
hears her first words of love, there, too, the old man bends
his faltering step in the hope of alms. At the sight of it the
weary caravan hastens to slake its burning thirst, and as the
water escapes into the stream, it murmurs the name of
Allah!

The Muslim bequeaths gifts to the fountain, the dervish
draws near it to pray. In every land the fountain speaks of
hope and happiness. Why then in England does it bring to
mind only the selfishness of the rich and the misery of the
poor?

I have brought back from London a sound which will ring
in my ears whenever misfortune greets my eyes, a sound
which recalls the wretched English worker, oppressed and
crushed by the rich, the beggar furtively demanding charity
and dropping of hunger in the street; all the poor creatures
disinherited from the bounty of Heaven, all the *pariahs* who
spread like a leprous growth over this vast city where the
luxury is so scandalous and the poverty so frightful.

In London there are none of those sumptuous, monumental fountains which enliven the squares of Paris and
proclaim to all the language of art – but in many streets
you come across a plain upright drinking-fountain with a
pump. Fixed to the pillar is an iron chain from which there
hangs an iron spoon. This is the economical cup offered to
the pauper by his lord and master the rich man. 'You see,

here water costs the people nothing, they may drink their fill in comfort without having to draw it from the river.' So speak people of the affluent classes, who *never drink water* when they are in London.

In a country where untreated water is very harmful and where one has to take cordials to guard against the cold and damp, is it not the height of cruelty to put fermented liquors out of the reach of the people by piling enormous duties on them? Is it not an insult to offer the people of London drinking water which has been contaminated by every sewer in the city?

I appeal to you English aristocrats to allow free entry to barley and other cereals and to impose no higher duties on wine and beer than there are in France; then, and only then, shall we believe in your humanity and your love for the people; only then shall we acknowledge and even praise your generosity for giving the poor free of charge the water they cannot afford to buy from the company which supplies it to the city.

At ten paces from my lodgings there was one of these drinking-fountains; I was constantly hearing the noise of the chain and spoon as they struck against the pillar, and I knew that one of my fellow creatures was drinking the stale, nauseating London water. Not all the water supplied to the city comes from the Thames, it is true, but whatever its provenance it weakens the stomach and often causes dysentery and fever. That harsh clang of the iron spoon broke my heart and rang in my ears like the funeral knell. Poor people! Will God abandon you for ever to the mercy of your lords, those pitiless lords who watch you die that cruel and lingering death which every minute of every hour comes to claim the victim still vainly struggling in his agony? The thought is too horrible. The conqueror wreaks havoc with fire and sword; he comes openly as an enemy, not as a hypocrite who claims that he comes to *protect* the people even as he reduces them to slavery! But to destroy an entire people through poverty and famine, to impose upon them the heaviest yoke that any population of slaves has ever had to bear, to force them to be content with only rags for clothing, a few roots for food and water for drink, and to make them work sixteen hours out of twenty-four under pain of dying of hunger! Oh, you lords of England, this is the most vile and barbarous tyranny. God will not suffer it to endure!

Fifty years ago the people of France were burning down the châteaux, and twenty times over the armed might of Europe was powerless to prevent the triumph of their cause. Oh, lords! Repent, fear the vengeance of the people, appease their wrath, and be mindful of the saying, as old as the world; *'Vox populi, vox Dei!'*

A Complete List
of Flora Tristan's Works

Nécessité de faire un bon accueil aux femmes étrangères (Paris, 1835).

Pérégrinations d'une paria (1833–1834) (2 vols.; Paris, 1838).

Méphis (2 vols.; Paris, 1838).

Promenades dans Londres (Paris and London, 1840); 2nd ed. (Paris, 1840); 3rd ed. (published under the title *La Ville monstre*: Paris, 1842); 4th ed. (revised – the 'popular' edition: Paris, 1842).

L'Union ouvrière (Paris, 1843); 2nd ed. (Paris, 1844); 3rd ed. (Lyons, 1844).

Le Tour de France: journal inédit, 1843–1844 (Paris, 1973).

L'Émancipation de la femme, ou le Testament de la paria (rewritten with ref. to author's notes by Alphonse Constant: Paris, 1845).

ARTICLES, PETITIONS, CORRESPONDENCE

Lettres à un architecte anglais (published in *Revue de Paris*, 1837: vol. 37, pp. 134–139; vol. 38, pp. 280–290).

Pétition pour le rétablissement du divorce à Messieurs les députés (Paris, 1837).

Pétition pour l'abolition de la peine de mort à la Chambre des Députés (Paris, 1838).

Flora Tristan, sept lettres inédites (published by André Breton in *Le Surréalisme, même*: no. 3, Autumn 1957).

Flora Tristan, lettres inédites (annotated by Stephane Michaud, published in International Review of Social History: XXIV, 1979).

Flora Tristan also contributed articles on art and architecture to various journals and periodicals.

Select Bibliography

Baelen, Jean, *La Vie de Flora Tristan: Socialisme et féminisme au XIXe siècle* (Paris, 1972).

Desanti, Dominique, *Flora Tristan: la femme révoltée* (Paris, 1972).

Gammage, *History of the Chartist Movement, 1837–1854* (London, 1969).

Gattey, C N, *Gauguin's Astonishing Grandmother* (London, 1970).

Gorman, John, *Banner Bright* (London, 1973).

Hovell, Mark, *The Chartist Movement* (Manchester, 1918).

Marcus, Steven, *The Other Victorians* (London, 1966).

Mayhew, Henry, *London Labour and the London Poor* (London, 1851).

Owen, Robert, *A New View of Society* (1814; reprinted London, 1963).

Puech, J-L, *La Vie et l'Oeuvre de Flora Tristan* (Paris, 1925).

Rover, Constance, *Love, Morals and the Feminists* (London, 1970).

Sheppard, Francis, *The Infernal Wen: London 1808–1870* (London, 1971).

Stephens, Winifred, *Women of the French Revolution* (London, 1922).

Thompson, E P, *The Making of the English Working Class* (London, 1963).

Veitch, G S, *The Genesis of Parliamentary Reform* (London, 1913).

Ward, J T, *Chartism* (London, 1973).

Wollstonecraft, Mary, *A Vindication of the Rights of Woman* (1792).

Wright, Lawrence, *Clean and Decent* (London, 1960).

Young, G M, *Early Victorian England* (Oxford, 1934).

The London Diaries of Flora Tristan is the second in a new series of non-fiction Classics launched by Virago in 1981. The series will include reprints of diaries and journals, biographies and autobiographies, journalism and travellers' tales, essays, prose, some poetry and *belles lettres*.

For details of other books in the series, see following pages.

VIRAGO NON-FICTION CLASSICS

The Virago Non-Fiction Classics list will reprint diaries and journals, most particularly those of women travellers, biographies and autobiographies, journalism and essays, prose, some poetry and *belles lettres* – those delightful writings which defy exact categorisation but which, like all the titles on this new list, promise a multitude of literary pleasures. Here we announce some of the first titles.

Already Published

THE DIARY OF HELENA MORLEY
Translated and Introduced by Elizabeth Bishop

This is a true diary, kept by a young girl, half Brazilian, half English, in a provincial diamond-mining town called Diamantina, at the end of the nineteenth century. She was twelve when she began it, fifteen when it ends and through the sharp eye of this high-spirited, gifted child we enter another world. As Elizabeth Bishop says: 'Much of it could have happened in any small provincial town or village, and at almost any period of history – at least before the arrival of the automobile and the moving-picture theatre . . . this is an unwritten, Brazilian, feminine version of Tom Sawyer and Nigger Jim'. Though the scenes and events of *The Diary of Helena Morley* happened long ago, what it says, as with all works of art, is fresh, sad, funny, and eternally true.

Elizabeth Bishop (1911 – 1979), the celebrated American poet, awarded the Pulitzer Prize and a National Book Award for her work, spent many years of her life in Brazil, and translated this book in 1957. Helena Morley went on to marry and raise a large family and died in the 1960s.

Forthcoming Titles

Virago

If you would like to know more about Virago books, write to us at Ely House, 37 Dover Street, London W1X 4HS for a full catalogue.

Please send a stamped addressed envelope

Book Tokens

Give them the pleasure of choosing

Book Tokens can be bought and exchanged at most bookshops